FRE

AND BEYOND

Other books by John Holt

How Children Fail
How Children Learn
The Underachieving School
What Do I Do Monday?
Escape from Childhood
Instead of Education
Never Too Late
Teach Your Own
Learning All the Time
A Life Worth Living: Selected Letters

INNOVATORS IN EDUCATION

SERIES EDITOR: SUSANNAH SHEFFER

The *Innovators in Education* series brings back into print books that are both historically significant and that speak directly to to-day's concerns. We look for books that represent important developments in educational thought and have ongoing contemporary application. In this way, the series enables readers to connect newly published books with earlier works on similar subjects and enables current discussions to be informed and enriched by some of the best available writing on educational issues.

JOHN HOLT

FREEDOM AND BEYOND

Series Editor
SUSANNAH SHEFFER

Boynton/Cook Publishers
HEINEMANN
Portsmouth, NH

Boynton/Cook Publishers
A subsidiary of Reed Elsevier Inc.
361 Hanover Street
Portsmouth, NH 03801-3912
Offices and agents throughout the world

Credits continue on page 250.

Library of Congress Cataloging-in-Publication Data

Holt, John Caldwell, 1923–85
    Freedom and beyond / John Holt.
        p.   cm. -- (Innovators in education)
    Originally published: New York: E.P. Dutton, 1972.
    Includes bibliographical references.
    ISBN 0-86709-367-6
    1. Education--Philosophy.   2. Educational innovations--United States.
3. Child rearing.   I. Title.   II. Series.
LB885.H64F74 1995   95-31345
370'.1--dc20   CIP

Series Editor: Susannah Sheffer
Cover design: Barbara Werden
Cover photo: Tony King
The series editor wishes to thank Adrienne Reed Storey for her assistance.

Printed in the United States of America on acid-free paper
98 97 96 95   DA   1 2 3 4 5 6

*To the many people
whose questions, doubts, and objections
made this book,
my sincerest thanks.*

CONTENTS

FOREWORD TO THE NEW EDITION

Does freedom in education work?

The question comes from all sides. It comes from people who want to believe the answer is yes and from people who are convinced the answer is no. A mother asked me a version of it recently, as she remembered her own sons' very traditional education and admitted to curiosity about her neighbor's children, who had gone to a progressive school where, she said, "the kids never seemed to do much but lie around and stare at the walls." It comes up when people talk about getting more discipline into the schools, or when a teacher says ruefully, "I tried letting the kids choose what to do, but it didn't work—kids really need structure." It arises whether you think too much freedom is the problem in education or whether you think more freedom would be the solution.

Freedom and Beyond is a book for two groups: people who are trying to create a freer educational system and keep running into problems, and people who dismiss freedom as impossible or impractical or even dangerous. To both groups, John Holt is trying to say: Let's look more closely at what freedom really means and at what causes the problems that arise when we try to establish it. Let's not say, "Kids need more discipline," or "Teachers should have authority" without thinking carefully about the full possibilities of those words. Let's not say that giving kids choices doesn't work or that a particular classroom is a free classroom without looking much more closely at the situation.

Freedom and Beyond is a book very much of its time and, at the same time, one that resonates almost twenty-five years after its original publication. On the one hand, it is a book to be read for historical understanding, for the way it captures the central issues of the free school movement of the 1960s and 1970s and preserves them in all their complexity. Readers of this book cannot so easily dismiss the "failure" of this movement, for part of the meaning of the "beyond" in the title is about going beyond glib characterizations and explanations. On the other hand, this is a book to be read for its continued relevance. People who are trying to make changes in education are still wondering, "Why is it so difficult? Why do we so often feel frustrated when we try to make things more open, more flexible, better suited to the needs of each child?" Discussions of structure, authority, discipline, and choice are still going on, with new wrinkles, perhaps, or with new problems or issues as their impetus, but with the same basic roots. Bringing this book back into print is a way of bringing Holt's voice into today's discussions.

Freedom and Beyond represents a significant turning point in Holt's work. This is the first book in which he looked beyond schooling as the sole problem of education *or* as the sole solution. No longer would Holt argue that if we could only make schools better, the problems that he and other critics had outlined would be solved. "It no longer seems to me," he writes in the introduction, "that any imaginable sum of school reforms would be enough to provide good education for everyone or even for all children. People, even children, are educated much more by the whole society around them and the general quality of life in it than they are by what happens in schools." And because bad schools were no longer the only problem, better schools were no longer a sufficient solution, and for the first time Holt argued that "we must look beyond the question of reforming schools and at the larger question of schools and schooling itself. Can they do all the things we ask them to do? Are they the best means of doing it? What might be other or better ways?"

All of Holt's subsequent writing is rooted in the ideas in *Freedom and Beyond*. The vision described in the "Beyond Schooling" chapter became the axis around which his later work revolved, and his analysis in the "Schools Against Themselves" chapter of the true functions and purposes of schools foreshadows his book *Instead of Education,* which came out four years later and was a fuller treatment of this issue. The "Reading Without Schooling" chapter details how people *could* learn to read without traditional school instruction; five years later Holt founded a magazine called *Growing Without Schooling*, and began to publish stories about how children actually were learning to read outside of school. The whole notion of reading without schooling is no longer hypothetical, and in light of these stories, which could fill a book of their own, Holt's chapter seems very prescient.

Holt did not stop at the question, "Does freedom work?" but went on to ask the even more probing question, "Does schooling work?" and specifically, does it work to help poor kids, to lessen inequality? The chapters "Schooling and Poverty" and "Deschooling and the Poor" answer with a compelling and controversial *no*. As Holt wrote to a colleague in the free school movement six years after this book was first published, "*Freedom and Beyond* is an intensively political book. I tried to make clear in the latter half of it why schooling, and things done in schools, could not alleviate or change, much less do away with, poverty, and indeed only reinforced poverty in a country."* With some exceptions, people in the mid 1990s still cling to the notion that schooling and school's credentials are what will make a difference to poor kids. "Stay in school," proclaim the ads, the messages, the speeches to young people whose experiences and gut feelings are telling them something else. Holt offers another perspective, and it is a perspective we need to consider.

The purpose of the *Innovators in Education* series is to bring back books that need to be brought back, books whose ideas, whose perspectives, we cannot afford to forget. Having *Freedom and Beyond* in print is not just a luxury but a necessity. As we consider the current crop of school reform proposals or think about individual children in individual classrooms, we cannot afford *not* to learn from the people who thought and experimented and wrote years ago. For those trying to make things better for children, a book that originally came out in 1972 is not just a relic of another era. It is a badly needed reminder, a lens that enables us to see where we have been. May we then use it to get where we need to go.

—SUSANNAH SHEFFER

* In *A Life Worth Living: Selected Letters of John Holt*, Susannah Sheffer, ed., Ohio State University Press, 1990, p. 221.

Fear the man who feels himself a slave.
He'll want to make a slave of you.

Obedience is the great multiplier of evil.

1
Freedom and Beyond

"Maybe the time has come when we should stop talking about 'education,'" George Dennison said to me, about the time his book *The Lives of Children* was coming out. I was not quite sure what he meant. I thought he might mean that even to use the word "education" suggested wrongly that it was a process separate from the rest of life. As we often do when we think we ought to understand but are not sure we do, I kept still, hoping George would say something else to make his thought more clear. But for some reason our conversation turned to another subject, and I never did ask him what he meant.

At that moment, it certainly did not look as if the time had come for me to stop talking about "education." In the next two years I was to talk to and with hundreds of groups of people at meetings, large and small, almost all in schools or colleges and supposedly about "education." But more often than not, and particularly if we had time to get deeply into the subject, we found ourselves talking not about education but about such things as human nature, the meaning of life, the relations between children and adults, or American society. It has become hard to talk seriously about schools anymore, even with people who work on or in them, without finding soon that the subject of the talk has somehow moved outside the school building. In short, it has been a long time since anyone asked me a question like, "How are you going to teach children to spell (add, multiply, etc.) if you don't give them drill?" The national conversation about schools, like mine with George Dennison, has taken another turn.

In a way this book marks the end of an argument. For some time I and others have been saying—some before I was born—that children are by nature smart, energetic, curious, eager to learn, and good at learning; that they do not need to be bribed and bullied to learn; that they learn best when they are happy, active, involved, and interested in what they are doing; that they learn least, or not at all, when they are bored, threatened, humiliated, frightened.

1

Only a few years ago this was controversial, not to say radical talk. Not any more. Almost any body of educators, hearing such things, will yawn and say, "So what else is new?"

This is not to say that everyone has been won over. Some may never be. But on the whole these once radical and crazy ideas have become part of the conventional wisdom of education. Students in most colleges of education are regularly required to read, and I suppose take tests on, books by people who not long ago were being called "romantic" critics. The unthinkable has become respectable.

At any rate, what concerns me now is that so many people seem to be saying that our schools must stay the way they are, or at any rate are going to stay the way they are, *even if* it means that children will learn less in them. Or, to put it a bit differently, our schools are the way they are for many reasons that have nothing whatever to do with children's learning. If so, convincing people that most of our present schools are bad for learning is not going to do much to change them; learning is not principally what they are for.

Enough people now believe in learner-directed, non-coercive, interest-inspired learning so that we should be seeing in education far more widespread and profound change than we have. Only a very small number of those people who would truthfully say that *in theory* they accept these new ideas about learning, have made a strong effort to put them into action. Too many of those who have tried to make change have been ineffective, frustrated, disappointed, and even defeated. This book has grown out of many talks with such people, in which we have tried together to understand why the things we believe in so often appear not to work, or at any rate not to work very well.

In another sense the book has grown out of an article or chapter that Harold Hart asked me to write for his collection *Summerhill: For and Against*. After a while these ideas seemed to begin to collect around two centers, and the article to take shape in two separate parts. The first was about the way in which the school worked, and why it worked as well as it did, why it had been able to help so many young people that no one else had been able to help and who indeed had often seemed beyond helping. The other part was about some of the problems of Summerhill, questions or conflicts that had not completely been answered or resolved, either there or anywhere else. It seemed to me that we had to think about how to deal with these problems, how to carry Neill's work forward, in short how to go beyond Summerhill. I soon saw that I would have too much material for one article or chapter. I began to imagine a possible book. A natural title seemed to be *Summerhill and Beyond*. But this too soon changed.

More and more it appeared that a large part of our problem is that few of us really believe in freedom. As a slogan, it is fine. But we don't understand it as a process or mechanism with which or within which people can work and live. We have had in our own lives so little experience of freedom, except in the most trivial situations, that we can hardly imagine how it might work, how we might use it, or how it could possibly be of any use to us when any serious work was to be done. For our times the corporate-military model seems to be the only one we know, trust, and believe in. Most people, even in democracies, tend to see democracy as a complicated process for choosing bosses whom all must then obey, with this very small difference—that every so often we get a chance to pick a new set of bosses.

Not understanding freedom, we do not understand authority. We think in terms of organization charts, pecking orders, stars on the collar and stripes on the sleeve. If someone is above us on the chart, then by virtue of being there he has a right to tell us to do what he wants, and we have a duty to do whatever he tells us, however absurd, destructive, or cruel. Naturally enough, some people, seeing around them the dreadful works of this kind of authority, reject it altogether. But with it they too often reject, naturally but unwisely, all notions of competence, inspiration, leadership. They cannot imagine that of their own free will they might ask someone else what he thought, or agree to do what he asked, because he clearly knew or perhaps cared much more about what he was doing than they did. The only alternative they seem to see to coercive authority is none at all. I have therefore tried to explore a little further the nature of freedom, so that we may better understand how people of varying ages and skills may live together and be useful to each other without some of them always pushing the others around.

The title of the book has still another meaning. Not long ago I would have defined the problem of educational reform as the problem of somehow getting much more freedom into our schools. If we could find a way to do that, we would have good education for all children. Now the problem seems larger: if schools exist we naturally want them to be better rather than worse. But it no longer seems to me that any imaginable sum of school reforms would be enough to provide good education for everyone or even for all children. People, even children, are educated much more by the whole society around them and the general quality of life in it than they are by what happens in schools. The dream of many school people, that schools can be places where virtue is preserved and passed on in a world otherwise empty of it, now seems to me a sad and dangerous illusion. It might have worked in the Middle Ages; it can't work in a world of cars, jets, TV, and the mass media. Moreover, it seems clear from much experience that most adults will not tolerate too great a difference between the way they experience their own lives and the way their children live their lives in school. Even if the schools give up the idea that they should be preparing children for society as it is, and try instead to prepare them to live in or make a better society, they will not be allowed to go very far in that direction.

The "beyond" in the title of this book means, therefore, that we must look beyond the question of reforming schools and at the larger question of schools and schooling itself. Can they do all the things we ask them to do? Are they the best means of doing it? What might be other or better ways?

2
The Structure of Freedom

Two children, eight and five, sister and brother, are playing on the grass in the yard behind their house. I am watching and now and then, when asked, helping. Their main tool or toy is a long piece of clothesline, one end of which they have tied to a small tree. The eight-year-old is just learning, along with many of her friends in school, how to jump rope, so she wants to do things that have to do with jumping. The five-year-old is full of energy and enthusiasm, and wants to take part in whatever is going on. They play together a great deal, partly because, though they have other friends, none of them live close enough so that they can play with them whenever they feel like it, and partly just because they are fond of each other. As children often are, they are in a mood for striving and contests.

The eight-year-old, who is organizing the play—this doesn't always happen, often the younger one is the leader—knows exactly what she wants to do, and much of the time she does it. One game is high jumping. One end of the rope is tied to the tree, about two feet up from the ground. I am shown where to stand, given the other end of the rope, and asked to raise or lower it to certain heights. We start with the rope low, she jumps over it, tells me to raise it a little, jumps again, and so on, until we get it about as high as she can jump. In the other game we move the rope up the tree a little, I turn my end, and she practices "jumping in," which she is not very good at. She wants to be able to do this as well as the other girls in her class.

Her brother is there, and wants to be included. This creates difficulty and tension. The difficulty is that he can hardly high jump at all, and can certainly not jump a twirling rope. There is nothing in her games for him to do. After watching a few jumps he begins to clamor for a turn. The tension comes from two conflicting pulls or needs or desires. On the one hand, she wants to get on with her practice. On the other hand, if she leaves him out, he will get angry. He can get very angry, and since they live together, this will have to be dealt with, he will somehow have to be pacified and appeased and won over and made friends again. Besides, the rope game won't go on forever, and for other kinds of play she will need him. Also, she likes him. So without giving up her game and contest she has to find a way to include him in it.

All this calculating sounds very laborious and deliberate, but the fact is that she is thinking or intuiting these realities and these needs as she plays. There is no break in the play while she considers what to do with her brother. In the high jumping this is easy to manage. She takes a few jumps, and then we lower the rope, almost to the ground, and he jumps across it a few times. In the other rope jumping she introduces him—and me—to a game called Blue Bells, a wonderfully ingenious game that children must have invented as a first step in learning to jump a twirling rope. In Blue Bells the rope is simply swayed back and forth, and the child jumps as it comes toward him. He has to learn to time his run and jump with the swing of the rope. It turns out, as she hoped it would, that this was just hard enough to challenge and excite him, and just easy enough so that most of the time he could do it.

So the play goes on. Both children are active and having a good time. Yet there is still frustration and tension. Both children would like a real contest, but this is no contest and they both know it. The boy can hardly high jump at all, and he can just barely manage Blue Bells, which as he can see is a long way from being able to jump a twirling rope. She would like to have a rival with more nearly her own skill, to spur her on and give the game excitement. He would like to change the game into something in which the difference between her skill and his would not be so great or clear, in which he would feel himself not just a duffer, but a worthy rival or partner. So they must make a delicate adjustment to each other. If she works too much on things she can do much better than he can, he will get frustrated and angry and will quit. She must not rub his nose in the fact of her greater skill. At the same time he must accept in good part the fact that for the time being this is the game she wants to play, and that there is no way the game can be changed to hide the fact that she is much better at it than he is. If he gets too sore about being a loser she will stop trying to include him, tell him to go play by himself, and get on with her own business.

And so, with great subtlety and skill, as they play, they adjust to each other's needs and feelings, respond from one second to the next to what the other says and does. All of this is energetic and noisy. Indeed, the casual or careless observer might say that much of the time the children are quarreling or fighting. This is not true. They are simply doing what most of their elders have forgotten how to do or are afraid to do, which is to show their feelings as they feel them. It is because they show them so openly that they are able to adjust to them so quickly and adroitly. When they are not pleased with what the other is doing, they do not hide and nurse their displeasure or resentment until it becomes an anger they cannot cope with. They say or do something right away that gives the other a signal that things are not going right and that something must be done.

I have a reason for beginning with this story. This book is about freedom in learning, and among other things about some of the difficulties and tensions we meet when we try to create situations in which learners are free to learn. For most of us these situations are new, strange, awkward, perplexing, even threatening. We find it hard to learn even how to perceive them, how to see and hear what is going on. We find it harder yet to live in them, deal with them, make the best use of them. This task, difficult at best, will soon become impossible if we try to talk about these situations with words that do not fit, that do not describe what happens. We must watch our language. If we choose our words badly we will not be able to see or think about what we are doing.

One group of words, that twist and hide truth and understanding, is "structured—unstructured." Almost everyone who talks or writes about learning situations that are open, free, non-coercive, learner-directed, calls these situations "unstructured," and their traditional authoritarian, coercive, teacher-directed opposites "structured." People who support open learning use these words in this way as much as people who oppose it. It is a serious error. There are no such things as "unstructured" situations. They are not possible. Every human situation, however casual and unforced—and this is part of the point of my story about the children playing—has a structure.

If two men meet by chance on the street and for half a minute talk to each other, that meeting has a structure, perhaps even a very complicated one. Who are the two men? What is their relationship to each other? Are they more or less equals, or does one have some kind of power over the other? Is the encounter equally welcome to both of them? If not, why? If so, is it for the same reasons? Does one of them want the other to do something? Does he think the other wants to do it? Is he willing to do it?

We could ask dozens, scores, perhaps even hundreds of such questions. The answers to any one of them will have something to do with the structure of that meeting on the street. And the structure of this meeting exists within many other structures. For each man it is a small part of a life that has many other things in it. The meeting happens at a certain time and place, on a certain kind of street in a certain kind of town, in a culture in which these men, depending on their economic and social class, are expected and expect themselves to act in a certain way.

All of us live, all the time, within structures. These exist in their turn within other structures within still larger structures, like Chinese boxes. This is just as true of children. They live in the structure of a family; beyond that in a neighborhood, about which they feel in a certain way. This child also lives in the structure of his friends, of his school. His life is much influenced by the geography and climate of the land around him. If he grows up on the coast of southern California, his life will be very different than if he lived on a ranch in northern Wyoming. Children are not indifferent to these structures. They sense them, intuit them, want to know about them, how to fit into them, how to make use of them. We do not need to *put* structure into children's lives. It is already there. Indeed, we might well say of many children, including many poor city kids, that there is far too much structure in their lives, too many situations in which they must constantly worry about what is the right thing to do and whether they want or dare do it, or refuse to do it. What they often need, as Paul Goodman has so well pointed out, is a chance to get away from it all—more solitude, time, and space.

There are certainly great differences between the traditional classroom and the open or free classroom that I and many others are urging. But this difference is not made clear at all by calling these classes "structured" or "unstructured." Or even by pointing out that the open class has if anything *more* structure than the traditional, not less. Let us instead speak of two different kinds of structure, and to see how they differ. We might say that the structure of the traditional classroom is very simple. There are only two elements in it, only two moving parts, so to speak. One is the teacher and the other is the students. The children may be all different but in such a class their differences do not make any difference. They all have the same things to do, and they are all expected to do them in the same way. Like factory workers on the assembly line, or soldiers in the army, they are interchangeable—and quite often expendable. The second thing we can say of this structure is that it is inflexible, rigid, and static. It does not change from the first day of school to the last. On the last day as on the first, the teacher is giving out information and orders, and the children are passively receiving and obeying or refusing to obey. The third thing we can say of this structure is that it is arbitrary and external. It does not grow out of and has nothing to do with the life and needs of the class, what the children want, what the teacher has to give. It is dropped on them from above like a great glass box. The teacher is as much a prisoner and victim of this structure as the children. He has little more to say than they about what it should be, and can do little more than they to change it.

By contrast, the structure of the open class is complicated. It has as many elements as there are teachers *and* children in the classroom. No two of these elements are alike, and their differences make all the difference, since no two children will relate to the class and teacher, or make use of them, in quite the same way. Secondly, the structure is flexible and dynamic. The relationship of each child to the teacher and to the class changes from day to day, and may change enormously in the course of a year. Indeed the nature of the whole class may change. Finally the structure is organic, internal. It grows out of the needs and abilities of the children and teachers themselves. They create this order, in ways vividly described by James Herndon in *The Way It Spozed to Be,* or George Dennison in *The Lives of Children*—or like the children in my opening story. When and because they create it, the order works.

By that I don't mean that it looks neat and pretty; it often does not. I mean that it helps people to get things done, helps them to live, work, and grow. It does not squelch life. It enhances it.

The structure of a class can also be clear or unclear, straightforward or contradictory. This has not much to do with its being open or not, except that a very strict and traditional classroom is often both clear and straightforward—*anything* you do in there can get you into trouble. What the child wants to learn about the class is, are the rules easy or hard to find out? Once you have found them out, can you count on them? Some communities say, no problem about rules here, it's all out in the open, all down in black and white. Others say, we have no rules, don't believe in rules. Neither is true or possible. All communities have some rules, and all have more than they could write down. One of the things that makes a community is that it has more rules than it knows. People in the community do a lot of things the same way, and never even think about it—until an outsider comes in and does something completely different. A school I once knew used to boast that its only rule was No Roller Skating In the Halls. Nonsense. As the students well knew, there were plenty of things that you could get in trouble for doing.

In any classroom, traditional or open, rigid or flexible, kids want to know how to get along, how to become an insider instead of an outsider, how to get whatever good things are going. Most of all, to use the phrase everyone loves, they want to know where are the limits. If doing and saying something is going to get them in really bad trouble, they want to know beforehand what it is. Like the Constitution, which forbids it, they don't like *ex post facto* law—having the government (teachers) say that what you did was a crime, but not saying it until after you did it. Tyrants are on purpose vague about the law. Tearful child: "But what did I do?" Avenging adult: "You know very well what you did!"

It is not so important that the structure of the class, its rules and customs, be clear in the sense of explicit. Children are used to figuring out the rules in complicated human situations. What they don't like is a structure that is contradictory. In the early progressive schools, and, I suspect, in quite a few alternative schools right now, the adults have strong expectations about the way the chil-

dren will and should behave. They project onto children their the-
ories about right human behavior in general. They think, if the
children are healthy they will behave the way we think everybody
should behave. For that matter, this is probably true for all teachers, progressive or not. The difference is that the traditional teacher tells the children how he wants them to behave. The progressive
or so-called free teacher says, "Behave any way you like." So the
child has to look for clues, which the adults can't help giving, to
show whether he is doing the right thing or not. This can be exhausting. Sometimes the kid gets fed up with it, and like the famous (probably made-up) child in the progressive school, says,
"Teacher, do we have to do what we want today?", meaning do we
have to figure out what you want us to do today? Why don't you
just tell us?

When I first started visiting a lot of schools and classes, I saw,
by furtive glances darted toward me, by plaintive voices and
strained movements, that in some classes the children were very
anxious; in others, much less so. This didn't necessarily have anything to do with how strict the class was. From all I heard and saw
a notion that I call the Behavior Gap began to form itself in my
mind. Imagine a spectrum of behavior, from very Good to very
Bad. If we start at the Good end of the line and move toward the
Bad, for every teacher we come to a point on the line, call it point
A, which represents behavior that is bad enough to annoy her and
to make her wish that it would stop, but not bad enough so that
she thinks she can or needs to or ought to do anything to stop it. If
we keep moving toward the Bad end, after a while we get to another point, point B, which represents behavior so bad that she
feels she can, must, and will take some kind of action to stop it.
The distance between A and B is the Behavior Gap. When it is
wide, the class is going to be uneasy; when it is narrow, they are
probably going to be more at ease—unless point B is impossibly
close to the Good end of the behavior spectrum. For the most
part, how wide or narrow the gap is counts much more than where
it is on the spectrum. This is another possibly useful meaning for
the old saw about children and limits. Children certainly don't like
adults who are bugged by everything they do. But they equally
dislike being around an adult who lets them bug him. It is too

mysterious and threatening. What is he going to do when he does cut loose?

If a kid is doing something that annoys a teacher, better to say, "Hey, cut that out, it's driving me crazy." Or, "Please don't do that, I really don't like it." Then the structure is clear, and the kids get information about the teacher from which they can build up a fairly good picture of him and learn how to live with him.

3
The Uses of Freedom

"Freedom" is a word we use badly and strangely. We seem to be afraid of it. Not long ago a lady wrote a furious letter to one of the Toronto papers, complaining about all this talk about freedom for children. What would happen to me, she asked, if I yawned in my boss's face when he was expounding some pet theory, or if I decided to express my feelings by smashing my typewriter and throwing all my papers down on the floor? When she thinks of freedom, what she really would like to do *is* yawn in the boss's face, that old pompous windbag fool, throw his rotten typewriter on the floor and his stupid papers out the window. But she doesn't dare.

Why not find a boss in whose face she might not want to yawn, someone she might enjoy working for and with, might trust, respect, even like? She can't imagine such a person! Her life is poisoned by anger and hatred, which she dare not express—the consequences for her would be disastrous. Freedom, she says, along with millions of others, just means letting people do everything they want. If you let them do that, they'll do bad things. I know, because that's what I'd want to do. Freedom, for her and millions of others, means tearing the lash away from the overseer and using it to flog him to death. But a world without lashes and overseers? Impossible!

At one school I heard part of a lively argument between some antiwar students and the black custodian—unschooled but eloquent. What he said, over and over again, was that in any human organization you have to have a boss. Don't make no difference who it is, you have to do what he says. The president says we got to fight a war, no argument, we got to fight it. All this man asked or expected or even could imagine was that every so often he might be allowed to say whether he would like a different boss. But to anyone he sees as being above him on the ladder of power, and like most people he sees himself at the bottom, he can't imagine any way to act except total obedience. A poll taken not long ago showed

13

that a majority would give the name "violence" to any kind of group or mass protest against the government, however peaceful and legal. But they would not call it "violence" if, on the other hand, the government arrested, beat, gassed, or even shot and killed these people. People who feel they have no freedom hate the people who have it, or act as if they had it or ought to have it. What's all this about protest, they say. I got plenty of things I'd like to protest, but I keep my mouth shut, I can't afford to get in trouble. Such people don't want to be told that they might have protested all along, that it might have made a difference. The man in chains, seeing another man without them, thinks, is it possible I could have struck these chains off if I had only tried, that I didn't have to wear them all these years? The thought is unbearable. Better get some chains on the other guy.

Only a few slaves talk about getting free. The rest argue about who has the biggest house, the finest establishment, the richest and strongest master. My team can lick your team!

I once rode into New York from the airport with an angry cab driver. The mayor had just named a new chief of police, and he had *brought him in from outside.* What about all those guys who have been waiting in line? What did he have to go *outside* for? he kept saying furiously. Where is justice in the world if, after you've waited all those years for your turn, they move some joker from nowhere in ahead of you? What's the point of doing what you're told if at the end you don't get your reward?

Small wonder that for practical, everyday talk, real talk as opposed to political oratory, we have had to invent a substitute word for "freedom," a spiteful, mean-spirited word that lets us say right out what we really feel. The word is "permissiveness." "Permissive." One result is that when some of us urge freedom for children or for learners, we find ourselves arguing about whether children should be allowed to do *anything*—torture animals or set buildings on fire. If we say No we are then told that we don't really believe in freedom after all. Or people say, the idea of freedom for children is nonsense, children need limits. All such talk illustrates a great confusion about freedom, a confusion I have already touched in what I have said about structure. It implies that freedom means the absence of any limits or constraints, and that such a state is both desirable and possible; that the idea of freedom is opposed to the idea of limits, the idea of liberty opposed to the idea of law, so that you have to be for one or the other; that a free society or government and a tyranny are not different in kind but only in degree.

As there is no life without structure, so there is no life without constraints. We are all and always constrained, bound in, limited by a great many things, not least of all the fact that we are mortal. We are limited by our animal nature, by our model of reality, by our relations with other people, by our hopes and fears. It is useless to ask if life without constraints would be desirable. The question is too iffy even to think about—what is important is not whether there are limits but how much choice we have within those limits. A man in prison has some things he can do, and others he can't. So has a man outside. The man in the prison cell has *some* choice; he can stand, sit, or lie down; sleep, think, talk, or read; walk a few steps in this direction or that. But the two men are not equally free or equally limited. It is playing with words, and bad play, to say that we are all prisoners, or that the man in the cell is free.

There are two ways in which one person may limit the choices, the freedom of action, of another. He can say, You Must Do This. Or he can say, You Must Not Do This. They are not the same, and are not equally restricting. I did not really see, though it is plain enough, until Ivan Illich pointed it out in a small seminar at MIT, that telling people what they *may not* do, if you are clear and specific, allows them much more freedom of choice and action than telling them what they *must* do. Proscriptions are better than prescriptions. One mother says to a child, "Go out and play, if you want, but don't cross the street, don't play in the street, don't climb that little maple tree, don't play in that abandoned house, and stay out of Mrs. X's garden." Another mother says, "Time to go to your swimming lesson, or to Little League." No question about which child has the most choice.

Obviously—and I say it only to spare people the trouble of pointing it out—it is possible to say You Must Not in such a way that it destroys all freedom of action.

> *Mother may I go out to swim?*
> *Yes, my darling daughter.*

Hang your clothes on a hickory limb.
But don't go near the water.

The idea of limits is not of itself opposed to the idea of freedom. The difference between a free community or society and a tyranny—this is another way of saying what I tried to say about structure—is not that one has limits while the other does not. It is that in a free society you can find out where the limits are; in a tyranny you can never be sure. A society has moved well along toward tyranny when people begin to say (as many of our citizens do), "Better not do that, you might get into trouble." The free citizen says, "What do you mean, *might* get into trouble? If the law doesn't specifically tell me I *can't* do it, then I damn well *can* do it." The framers of our Constitution understood that an important part of what makes a tyranny is that its power is *vague*. It has no limits. You never can tell when it will move in on you. What is wrong with imaginary crimes like being unAmerican, counterrevolutionary, or uncooperative in school, is that you can't tell in advance what they mean. You only find out you've done wrong after you've done it.

In short, a free community differs from an unfree one, first, in that its rules are mostly of the Don't Do This rather than the Do This kind, and secondly, that it is clear and specific what you must not do. The second is as important as the first. People in our Congress often introduce and too often pass laws which would make it a crime to, let us say, undermine the morale of the armed forces, or threaten the American Way of Life, or conspire to create a riot and so on. Such laws are tyrannical, in effect *and intent*. They do not tell us what we must not do. What they tell us is that if we do any one of thousands of unspecified things, someone may *later* decide to call what we did a violation of the law. Such laws say, don't do anything that the government might not like. What we want of our laws instead is that they be as negative and as specific as possible. "Don't play where it's dangerous" is not as good as "Don't play in the abandoned house."

Finally, we don't want too many of these laws, because they will narrow too much our freedom of choice. Here the seeming conflict between the idea of freedom and that of limits or law sometimes becomes real. But it would be foolish and mistaken to say merely the fewer laws, the better. What really counts is the amount of choice they leave us.

Let me bring this closer to the world of children. The kind of influence or control or coercion that most adults exercise over children is wrong in all the respects mentioned. There is too much you *must* do this, you *must* do that, now it's bathroom time, now it's juice time, now put away your papers, now sit down, now stand up. When we say "Don't," we are too vague; too many of our rules are of the Be Careful, You-Might-Get-into-Trouble kind. And we have far too many Don'ts. As a result children have too little freedom of choice, or the choices they have are trivial. What I mean by freedom for children—and for all people—is More Choice, Less Fear. Why is this freedom important to children? How do they make use of it? How does it help them to move and to grow? No book answers these questions more fully, vividly, and powerfully than Dennison's *The Lives of Children*. Other books that I recommend elsewhere in this book (among my own principally *How Children Learn*) may also be helpful. So, perhaps, may be the following, from an essay I wrote for the book, *Summerhill: For and Against*:

How does Summerhill work? What does it do, and how? What is the secret of Neill's art? . . .

Over the years, many children have gone to Summerhill who were wholly defeated and demoralized by life, locked in their desperate protective strategies of self-defense and deliberate failings, filled with fear, suspicion, anger, and hatred. I knew one such child myself. Only a year before he went to Summerhill, he seemed not far from a complete breakdown. At Summerhill he got well. Most of the children there—not all, the school has had its failures—get well. They get back their strength, confidence, and courage, and turn to face life and to move out into it, as all healthy children really want to do, instead of running and hiding from it. In a school that does not care much about schoolwork many of these children, hopeless failures in school after school, begin to do competent and even excellent work, often progressing two, three, and even five times as fast as conventionally good students in conventionally good schools.

What else in the school helps children to get well? Children there do many things that most adults, in home or at school, will not let them do—swear, be dirty, wear raggedy clothes, break things. At the meeting I went to, a girl of about twelve contentedly sucked her thumb throughout the meeting, taking it out now and then to make some astute comment. Nobody teased her or seemed to take any notice. Is there something intrinsically therapeutic about being able to use four letter words, or go for days without a bath? I doubt it. What seems more important is that these children were freed from the enormous pressure under which they had been living. For many of them, life before Summerhill must have seemed one long battle, most of it against adults whose love or good will they needed and wanted. A hundred times a day they must have had to face the agonizing decision: shall I do what Mother or Father or Teacher or Authority tells me, or not? What do I stand to gain? What to lose? These are not light calculations. Having to make them day after day must be exhausting to children as it would be to many of us. They had to spend so much time and energy either doing or not-doing what others told them to do that they had no time and energy for doing things on their own. One way or another they were always reacting to others, giving in or resisting, but in neither case acting independently, autonomously, pursuing their own interests and needs.

Neill is so helpful and sustaining to these children, for this reason among others, they don't have to worry about him. They don't have to worry about what he thinks. They don't have to worry about disappointing him; he hasn't any great expectations for them, hasn't anything he wants them to become or do, so they can't disappoint him by not becoming or doing it. They don't have to worry about what he wants; he doesn't want anything, not from them. He likes them, more or less, as they are.

We all know of Neill's having given rewards to children who stole. This has excited much passionate, angry and, above all, confused talk. The reward does not say Neill approves of stealing, or even that he is indifferent to it. It simply and concretely expresses two rather old-fashioned notions, faith and forgiveness. I know you stole; I do not call you Thief or think of you as Thief because you stole; I know that one of these days in your own good time you will stop stealing; I can wait for it to happen. This seems to me the essence of Neill's love for children—he accepts them, forgives them, trusts that with any luck at all they will turn out okay. But he doesn't need them, and he doesn't need them to need him. At the root of his love—and though he might not approve of the word, I think it may be what gives his love purity and strength—is a benign indifference.

By contrast, I think of two children, two examples among many I might choose, that I met a few years ago. Their father loved them, was proud of them, was fiercely determined that they were going to be good—not just well-behaved, but upright, virtuous, strong, brave, and so on. In this sense and for these reasons he was strict and demanding. But although they were only four and six, and were fond of him, he had already begun to lose them. He had become less a person than a force to be dealt with—to be tricked or evaded whenever possible. The weight of his attention, hope, and concern was more than they could carry. They were already trying to get it off their backs. They were already learning to show him a different face from the one they showed the world. Many children have backs bowed and knees buckling beneath the weight of too much adult concern, even kindly concern, or perhaps especially kindly concern, too much worry, too much fear, too much hope. Everything the children say and do is a sign—are they going in the right direction? or the wrong? Are we doing the right thing? Everything becomes too big a deal.

From all sides we hear that what children need and lack is the careful and loving attention of people who have been specially trained to attend to them and have nothing to do *but* attend to them. One might think that growing up were a process that could not happen unless we made it happen. Not so. What children need and want are more chances to see us adults when we are about our adult business, whatever that may be, and more time in which we leave them strictly alone.

At Summerhill [the children] . . . do not have to decide all the time what to do about the people who are trying to force them to do things, because nobody is forcing them. As long as they don't interfere with other children's lives, they can do what they want, or as little as they want. At last, they have time. Time even to "do nothing"—though in fact this is impossible, nobody alive can "do nothing," awake or asleep our minds are working, usually on things important to us. What then are the children doing who seem to be "doing nothing," and how does it help them? Here I can only guess, drawing on what I can remember of the ways I have used thoughts or dreams or fantasies to overcome or digest or somehow get the better of experiences that had at first got the better of me. I suspect that much of the time they are thinking over their lives, their past, playing it over and over, reliving it, reworking it, until they have robbed it of some of its power to cripple and hurt.

Years ago I heard the psychoanalyst Theodore Reik give to young lovers, married or otherwise, what seemed a most astonishing piece of advice. *Don't,* he said, get into the business of talking over your happy memories of meeting, courtship, love, etc. Don't sit around saying fondly, "Remember that time we . . ." As long as that memory lives in your subconscious, the experience will keep its magic power and nourish your love for each other. But if you drag it up into the bright daylight of consciousness and talk, it will begin to fade like an old photograph in the sun, lose its freshness and intensity, become like something seen or read or that happened to someone else. It seemed to follow from this—whether he said it or not I no longer remember—that the way to rob a past experience of its power to hurt is not to try to forget it, but to try to remember it, over and over again.

Do this, and an odd thing happens. At first, remembering the experience, you literally relive it, are right in the middle of it. Then, gradually, you begin to draw away from it, get outside it. Whatever happened to you, you still see and hear, but increasingly as a spectator, as if watching a movie of yourself. At first the movie is painful, all close-ups, and that really is you in the middle of it. But as you play that movie over and over, it becomes less vivid and real, and that person there in the midst of it, having bad things happen to him or making some kind of dreadful fool of himself, is not the here-and-now living you, but a part you once played, a you that no longer exists.

And as you draw out of and away from that experience, you may begin to do something else, have that character in there play his role differently, avoid his mistake, say or do something other and better than what he did. You begin to reshape the past. We all do this. I think of an example, trivial but typical. Last winter, starting on a fairly complicated series of air trips, I put my ticket into my pocket. When near the airport, too far to turn back, I realized that my tickets were in two envelopes and that I had left behind the more important of them. I raged at myself for a while. Then in my fantasy world, I began to replay the scene in my room as I should have played it. I saw myself carefully looking in the file folder where the other ticket was, taking it out, putting it in my pocket. I saw myself doing a number of things that, had I really done them, would have reminded me to look for that second book of tickets. After a while I was no longer angry at myself, no longer distressed by the experience, able to see it as just another goof-up, ready to go on to whatever life brought me next.

What is the use of these mental tricks? I have suggested one: by replaying the experience we get away from it and outside it. Also, by adjusting the past we create as it were a new past or pasts, in which we were more sensible, prudent, closer to the kind of person we want to be. These made-up pasts can be a kind of preparation for the future. They are a way, perhaps the only way, to learn from our mistakes. Not only do we prepare ourselves to act better in the future, but to some extent we fool ourselves that we really did act a little better in the past. We see our real selves, the selves most real to us, not as that person who goofed back there, but as the person who thought—even if too late—of the sensible thing to do. So, imagining myself not forgetting instead of forgetting that airline ticket, or, as on another occasion, *not* locking my keys in my car, I am able to get the dunce cap off my head.

It seems very likely that children do some such things. It seems likely, too, that the fantasies by means of which they rework and get control of the past may be much wilder than my own humdrum efforts. Little children in their free dramatic play take all kinds of mythic and animal roles; perhaps they do the same in the privacy of their minds. At any rate, whatever the mechanism may be, the experience of Summerhill and like places has proved that in the human mind and spirit are healing powers comparable to those in the body. If the wounds in our souls are not rubbed raw and torn open each day, many of them will heal. This is what Summerhill makes possible.

It also gives children a chance, and this may too be a part of the healing process, to manage a great deal of their lives, to make decisions and to find out from their living which are better or worse than others, and from so doing begin to feel that they *can* make decisions, that not all of these will *necessarily* be bad, that if they are bad they can see this and make changes, that they are smart and capable enough to make some sense of their lives, and don't need indefinitely to depend on the guidance or commands of others. In short, more by what it does than says, Summerhill helps the children there to feel, and often for the first time, that they are human beings of some dignity, competence, and worth. Children get well and grow at Summerhill because of the freedom, support, and respect it gives them, and these conditions of freedom, support, and respect are the minimum conditions we must establish in other schools if we want health and growth for the children there. No educational reforms that do not begin here seem to me worthy of much attention, or likely to make any real or lasting improvements in the lives and learning of our children.

To what I have said in the above about play, and its healing uses and powers, let me add these words, from an introduction I wrote for *Open Education—The Informal Classroom* (see Appendix). I don't think I can say better what play is good for and why it is important.

In the second of two excerpts The Plowden Report discusses at length why play is important and useful for children, as their most natural and effective way of understanding the world around them and their own place and possibilities in it. All this is most well and truly said; it could not be improved upon. But I would like to add to it. One might feel, reading the Report, that play is fine for little children, and even the best thing for them, but that after a while they must outgrow it and learn more "serious" or "adult" ways of learning. This would be a great mistake. The fact is that in their play children are very often doing things very much like what adults do in their work. Like the economist, the traffic engineer, the social planner, or the computer expert, children at play often make models of life or certain parts of life, models they hope are a fair, if simpler, representation of the world, so that by working these models they may attain some idea of how the world works or might work or what they might do in it.

More important, what makes our truly inventive and creative thinkers, whether political, artistic, or scientific, what sets them apart from the great run of us, is, above all, that they can still play with their minds. They have not forgotten how to do it nor grown ashamed nor afraid of it. They like it, and they do it every chance they have; it is as natural to them as breathing. The ordinary, "serious," non-playful man cannot escape things as they are; though he is always talking about "facing reality," he is as trapped by his notion of reality as any rat in a cage. For him, whatever is, is all there can be. The playful man is always saying, and cannot help saying, "But suppose things weren't this way, didn't have to be this way. Let's just for the fun of it imagine what might happen if this were different, if we did that instead of this . . ." *Just for the fun of it.* Now we know from experience that out of such play may come, and often do come, ideas that may change the whole shape of human life and thought. But the playful man doesn't necessarily start with this in mind. He doesn't say to himself, like certain fanatics at their sports, "If I grind my teeth together and play hard enough, I will come up with a great idea." He plays for fun, ready to discard as useless and without regret, as he has many times in the past, most of the ideas that come to him. When a good one comes along, then a more directed thinking may begin, less like what the ordinary man calls "play," more like what he would call "work," though to the truly creative person there is no difference.

It is not hard to see why a stable society would find such men unsettling and dangerous and would try to silence or do away with them if possible. Indeed, they might be right to do so. But a society like ours, facing life-or-death crises and predicaments about which nobody knows what to do and about which most people think nothing at all can be done, needs for its very survival not just a few but hundreds of thousands, indeed a whole new generation of people who can play.

4
Some Tensions of Freedom

In my story about children playing I said that the older child felt a *tension*. I am using this word in a special way. "Tensions" many people might call by the more familiar name "problems." But by "tensions" I mean something quite different. When we call something a problem we suggest, first, that something is happening that we don't want to happen, and secondly, that if we can only find a "solution," we can make it stop happening. Tensions cannot be made to go away. They are built into the nature of things. A friend of mine speaks not of problems, but of predicaments, which is closer to what I mean. It implies, though, that we are in a bad place, forced to choose between evils. In what I call a tension we may be in a good place, forced to choose among things all of which we like and want. It is a little like a dilemma—I can't decide whether to go tonight to the play or the concert, whether to go for vacation to the ocean or the mountains. But we can resolve a dilemma by choosing. In a tension it is as if two hands were pulling us hard in opposite directions. Each is pulling us toward something good, one is as strong as the other, and *neither will tire or let go*.

Our language and habits of thought make it hard for us to deal with this idea of tensions. When we think of conflict, it is always between opposites, usually one Good and the other Bad. The founders of our system of logic, the Greeks, told us that a thing could not at the same time be something and its opposite, could not be A and not-A, and we have been painfully stuck with this notion ever since. We persist in thinking that in all conflicts, one side or the other must, after all, be Right, and that if we see clearly enough or think hard enough we can find out which it is. Also, we like to get things settled. It irritates us when a difficulty keeps coming up again and again. We think, "Why do we have to go through this, we've been through it before." If we could just find the right balance, the point of equilibrium, between those conflicting forces or demands, they would cancel out and leave us alone. But in a tension, this never happens, can't happen. The conflicting pulls are both legitimate, they keep on pulling, and so the tension is permanent.

When we attempt to put more freedom, autonomy, choice, into children's lives and learning, whether by making a conventional class more open or starting a new school, some of these tensions appear. One way to describe them is to let two people, A and B, state the case for each side, as if arguing or debating with each other. This is not altogether artificial. I have had many such arguments and am quoting as closely as I can remember.

Orderly Classrooms

A. One thing I'm not going to do for sure is spend all my time in the classroom telling kids to pick this up, put that away, and so on. I didn't come to a school like this so I could ride herd on kids, and they didn't come here to be rode herd on. Let them decide how much order they want.

B. Yeah, but the trouble with that is that an open classroom doesn't work unless there is a lot of stuff for the kids to use and work with, and they can't use it or work with it if they can't find it, or if when they do find it pieces are missing or it's all messed up. It's not a question of having order because things look nice when they're neat. It's a question of having a room where kids can find what they need and want.

A. I agree with that, but I still can't see spending half of my time saying to kids, "Why didn't you put that away, I told you three times to put it away, who is the last person to use this clay, he left it all over the floor, come over here and clean it up." That puts me right back in the bag I was in in a regular school. Let the kids work out a system for getting stuff away.

B. Sure, but they won't do it, and probably can't do it—they're little, they haven't had much experience working out complicated plans—unless you encourage them and help them. You've really only got four choices. One is that almost nothing gets put away, which means practically that there is less and less for kids to do—which will make other problems for you. Another is to put most of the stuff away yourself, in which case you'll be more custodian in the class than anything else—that can take you the whole day. Another is to cut down the amount of stuff in class to a point where you can handle it—but that too means less for kids to do. And the fourth is, with as much cooperation as you want or can get from the kids, work out a system of cleaning up and putting away that they will stick to most of the time and that will work.

One thing may help here. Children do tend to like to put things into places specially made and fitted for them. Woodworking shops where tools are stored on a pegboard with a silhouette for each tool, or according to some other plan in which the child can *see* where each tool goes, and that no other tool can go there, tend to be neater than those where storage is more haphazard. Maybe certain kinds of boxes, puzzles, games, tools could be stored in places where only they would fit. In that case, putting something away becomes a kind of puzzle in itself. Maybe we could work out a color coding scheme, particularly for little kids. All toys, games, or equipment of a certain kind would be in boxes of a certain color and would be stored in cabinets or closets of the same color. And, as in supermarkets, we might hang markers from the ceiling to show where the different colored boxes went. Or we could use other codes—different kinds of shapes, animals, etc. Giraffe for long box, elephant for big, mouse for little. In one of the environments made for preschool children by Paul Curtis and Roger Smith, all toys and equipment were stored in plastic buckets, which were suspended by ropes from pulleys attached to the ceiling and which the children could raise and lower. Kids find putting things in the buckets and hauling them up and down very exciting. They do a lot of discussing and deciding about what they want to put where.

I think it is possible to get blocks of styrofoam for not much money, and I have seen a kind of saw, in which the cutter is a fine wire heated by a flashlight battery, which cuts the styrofoam very easily. With this it might be possible to cut out of styrofoam a specially fitted box or niche for all the toys or equipment in the room.

In fact, some of the kids might be interested in designing storage boxes. For that matter, the entire problem of finding ways to store things so that all can find them could be made a problem for all or many children to work on. They might come up with more ingenious schemes than we could think of. Older kids might like elaborate number codes, or even secret codes—secret from anyone outside the room.

Public or Common Property

A.   Every free community, however it may feel about private property, has a ethic of public or common property. No one has the right to destroy or spoil what belongs to or is used or enjoyed by all. We see all over the world, and very much in our own country, the terrible things that happen when people forget or deny that. Free schools are confused about this. Many of them give kids the impression that it is OK to smash up stuff belonging to the school. Even if they don't positively say it is OK, they don't do much to discourage or prevent it. This seems to me a serious mistake. It is also a surprising one, since many of the people who start free schools, on a national or world scale believe passionately in conservation and environmental protection, in a loving regard for Mother Earth. But in their own schools they seem to think it is fine for kids to do anything they like with the environment.

B.   It's a question of what's most important. Everybody would rather not have kids smash things than smash them. But one of the things that we have learned from the experience of Summerhill and schools like Summerhill is that it is very important that children who may have a lot of frustration and resentment and anger bottled up inside them should have a way to let it out, get rid of it, instead of holding it in and making it worse. Better have them take it out on the walls or furniture than in being mean and cruel to other people, or carrying it with them into adult life as a love of power or a hatred of other races. That's exactly why Neill, instead of getting good furniture for his school, got old bus seats, so the kids would feel able to smash them up if they had no other way to let off steam.

A. Yes, but there seem to me two things wrong with that argument, at least. One is that if you fill a place with old junk, you're not just leaving them free to smash it up if they feel they have to, you're tempting them, *inviting* them to smash it up, you're making smashing up the furniture one of the OK things to do in a free school. The other is that you are then forced to have a very drab and ugly place for the kids. But kids are very sensitive to their environment—to space, form, light, color. They feel stimulated, as well as secure and happy, in an aesthetically satisfying environment. The experience of some of the best British public primary schools certainly proves this. Because they are well designed, and because the people who run them take the trouble to put beautiful things in them, the children themselves love and take pride in the school, and do beautiful work of their own in arts and crafts. In a civilization as ugly as ours, this is not something we should neglect.

B. I'm not sure the children care so much about whether their environment is beautiful or not. It's what they can *do* in it that counts. One of the things that makes children unhappy, that brings many of them to alternative schools in such poor health of mind and spirit, is that they have come from places where everyone acted as if things were more important than people. Our society is full of people who are ready to see someone killed for breaking a window. Sure, I'm all for a beautiful environment, but not if it means that we have to spend the whole day telling kids to be *careful,* be sure you don't *spill* anything, no you can't draw or paint on that wall, don't touch this, don't do that. They already get more than enough of it. Let *them* decide how they want to decorate a class.

A. You say, "Let them decide." The fact is, it never gets decided. One kid paints a peace sign, with the paint drooling down, and someone else paints a smiling face, ditto, and someone else writes something on the wall, and someone else writes The Awful Word, and before long you haven't got decoration, you've got a wall all smeared over with paint, a mess, no fun to look at, and no place to put anything more. I've seen kids painting that kind of stuff. They don't look particularly happy when they are doing it, and they don't show any signs of being proud of it when they've done it. They don't take you over to where they painted something on the wall and say, "Look, I did that." But kids in schools where there is a high standard of art and craft, such as Elwyn Richardson describes in *In the Early World*, take pride in what they do and what their friends do.

B.   Well, I don't think a kid paints on the wall, or should paint on a wall, so he can later tell an adult that he did it. Kids do too much of what they do to get adults' praise. I want to see less of it. And when I hear adults saying how kids like everything to be quiet, or neat, or orderly, or beautiful, I suspect that most of the time the adult is laying his tastes on the kids. The point about letting a kid paint on a wall is not that he may paint anything beautiful on it, but that in a world in which he feels that practically nothing and no place belongs to him, this wall, this room, this school do belong to him.

A.   I'm not saying they don't belong to him. I'm saying they also belong to everyone else. Free schools I know have a terrible time keeping tools, musical instruments, record players, tape recorders. Someone is always losing them or breaking them, smashing them up, either in carelessness or malice or to let off some of that steam. The result is that nobody else can use them. We talk about the rights of the kid who wants to break the guitar. But what about the rights of the kid who wants to play it? When that guitar is broken, he is out of luck. And I wonder about the kid who kicks a guitar instead of a wall or a fence post. I don't think he is putting people ahead of things. I think he is using things to get at people. I think he knows damn well that if he smashes the guitar, someone who might have wanted to play it is not going to be able to play it.

B.   . . . etc.

Perhaps a wider range of choices may ease this tension. In *This Magazine Is About Schools,* and later in *This Book Is About Schools,* Anthony Barton of Toronto described what he called Hard and Soft schools, schools in which there is a range of structures from a very tight, rigid, planned, antiseptic one at one end of the schools to a very loose, flexible, organic, improvised, messy order at the other. The British psychologist Margaret Lowenfeld years ago described a school she ran (and may still run) in London. It had a special room designed for people to make a mess in, as well as a soundproofed room to make noise in. Perhaps some of the spaces in a school could be more formally and deliberately planned, more elegantly decorated and furnished, designed to be aesthetically pleasing—though even there the students should have a chance from time to time to discuss and plan new ways of arranging and decorating the space. Other spaces in a school could be all-out smash-up, mess-up spaces. Still others could be somewhere in between decorating OK, smashing not. OTHERWAYS, a school in Berkeley, California, put up big sheets of brown paper for kids to draw, paint, and write grafitti on. When the paper was covered, they took it down and put up new paper. For children beyond a certain age, I would be inclined to say that if they wanted stuff they could feel free to smash, OK—but they would have to go and get it.

The whole question of order is difficult. How much do we need? Too little, and it is hard to get anything done, or find anything to do. Too much, and we spend more time keeping things orderly than in doing anything with them. Some people are by nature more tolerant of disorder than others. Some can't stand it. Some, like a lawyer I once knew whose desk was a mountain of papers, any one of which he could lay his hand on in a few seconds, can find order in what other people would call chaos.

How much should adults impose this order? How much should children make themselves? How long do we wait until they do? Herndon made the point in *The Way It Spozed to Be* that most adults, seeing what look like the hopelessly chaotic efforts of children to put some order into their own affairs, never wait long enough to give them a chance to do it. Then, not having given them enough time to do it, they assume that even with all the time in the world they never would have done it. We never find out what might have been possible. Every time we try to manage the lives of young people, we give up the chance to see how they might have managed their own lives, and to learn what we might have learned from their doing it.

Some time during the past year I took the following notes:

The other day I visited a free school, in a number of rooms in the large basement of a church, which had for some reason been deliberately made with the floor on a slant, no one could tell me why. There were about 45 children in the school, a few teenagers, most of them between the ages of 5 and 11 or 12. They were having lunch, or just finishing lunch and beginning recess when I came in. The noise was deafening. The ceilings were very low, and there was no sound deadening material of any kind, so nothing to keep the noise from bouncing around. Most of these children, poor and mostly black, had enormously powerful voices. They certainly were not nonverbal. They were talking to each other all the time, but at the top of their lungs.

The kids at the table were very friendly. That is, they didn't make a big fuss over me, but looked at me, when I was introduced, in a perfectly open manner, not hiding anything, not furtively, not pretending to feel what they did not feel, not putting on a show, not playing up to me. Just a very frank and open look.

After lunch, recess. There were a number of rooms that the kids could play in. Many of the boys were playing various kinds of war games, pretending to shoot each other with machine guns and falling over in imitation of people they had seen in movies and on TV. Their energy was tremendous. They leaped over and ran around furniture, shot, shouted, fell down, got up. I said something to one of the teachers about their energy, and she replied, "Oh yes, these kids can go like this all day."

By the criteria according to which many children these days are judged "hyperactive" these children would certainly be so judged. There seemed to be something quite frantic about their energy. I had been reading some Montessori stuff not long before. I felt sure many Montessorians would have said that these children were flying to pieces because there was no center, no focus, no purpose in their lives, they had never learned to collect and direct their energy. Then came The Trial.

I was invited after lunch to attend the school court. This is a regular part of the school's life. There were five student jurors, though they also acted as judges. That is, they directed the court and also decided whether people were guilty and what their punishment would be. The head of the school sat at a table at one end, not taking a very active part in the proceedings, there to maintain the presence of authority or perhaps prevent rebellion against the court.

Worth noting that all the children involved in this were a *good deal younger* than the youngest age at which Neill says children will take any responsible part in the government of a community.

The court was there to decide some of the kinds of things that are decided at Summerhill when one student "brings up" another at the General Meeting. The Summerhill General Meeting is both court and legislature. This was just court.

One boy was brought before the court because in some class he had hit and kicked another student.

Immense seriousness of the court. Boy playing a little bit to our gallery, (2 visitors), but less as time went on. Very careful to say exactly what he did and didn't do. Would be a real problem kid in most schools and was often at this one. But I had no sense of his being an outcast, or that he felt that the court was picking on him. He was not trying to cheat or lie to the court. Got very indignant when someone suggested that he had thrown a book at a boy. He had hit him and kicked him for "stickin' his nose into my business," but the idea that he would throw a book— ridiculous!

Punishment fairly severe—no dessert or gym for two weeks. I don't know whether these are rigorously enforced or whether there is parole or whether people forget.

Boy very hard to understand, very thick and careless speech, but as he heard that people were taking him seriously he concentrated hard on his words, trying to get them right and clear.

He was a tough kid, but I sensed no threat to any judges.

Other kid small white kid who hadn't moved over when his very nice teacher, retired lady, wonderful, had told him to. She was also called as a witness and said that the situation was partly her fault. There was nothing condescending about her way of saying this, and the child juror-judges took her testimony just as seriously, in just the same spirit and seriousness as that of the children. Small white kid was afraid that if he moved another kid, who had threatened to, would beat him up. Other kid kept saying he hadn't *done* it. Kid said that he knew the other kid was *going* to. Jury kept asking him if he could *prove* that, not knowing what is or is not proveable. Could such a court have legal adviser, bringing in some insights from the larger world of law? Would probably talk too much, I fear.

In case of white kid I think he genuinely was afraid of the other kid, but he couldn't think of right words to say. His sentence as severe as the other. Both boys told they could appeal. I don't know procedure. For that matter, I don't know how many people find themselves in court, who brings them in.

Singing later, just before they went home. So different from reedy, airy, pipy, unsteady self-conscious voices of little children singing in most schools I have seen. (Exception—kids singing folk songs with young man at Children's Community Workshop School, "Ya-*hoo*! Good old Mountain Dew!") Anyway, these kids sang with enormous gusto, very strong even when boys didn't know words and girls doing most singing, doubly so when all together. Better than almost any secondary school. Could we use their energy more in song and speech?

Children very unself-conscious about touching. Boys came over and leaned against me frequently, at lunch and in court. They didn't look at me, or say anything, or try to make anything of it. They weren't trying to get anything out of it. They just liked to lean against bigger people.

I assume, though I don't know, that adults had thought up the idea of the court, and had worked out much of the procedures. But if the adults had thought of it, the children ran it, a number of them the same children who a few minutes before had looked as if they were going right up through the roof. Who, seeing them play a few minutes before would have supposed them capable of such unfeigned seriousness, gravity, sustained attention, decorum? Nobody. Would any reasonable person have believed that the first accused, almost the wildest and noisiest of all the children there, would have defended himself with such dignity, or accepted in such good spirit the quite severe sentence of the court? Never. Would this same boy have allowed himself to be tried, judged, and sentenced by children most of them smaller and younger than he was, in a conventional school? Almost certainly not. Would most defenders of open as against free schools have approved of this school? I suspect many of them would not.

Decision Making

A. It is very important that we make as many as possible of the decisions about this school as democratically as possible, as at Summerhill, in a meeting where everyone can speak up, and everyone gets a vote.

B. I agree that's a good idea. But our kids are younger. Neill himself said that until the age of twelve or so children at Summerhill didn't take a very active part in, or even much interest in, the government of the community.

A. I think that's probably because the older kids dominated the school and the meetings so much that the younger ones thought there wasn't much point in saying anything. But in any school, however old the children are, even when they are all quite young, the oldest feel like leaders, feel responsible, and can take and like to take a lot of responsibility. Besides, if we don't give children a chance to make these kinds of decisions, how are they ever going to learn how to do it?

B. Yes, but we still have to decide which questions need a decision by the whole school, and which ones don't. Otherwise we'll be meeting all the time. I was in a school once where they tried to discuss and decide everything democratically. As a couple of third graders passed me in the hall, one of them said to the other, "Another school meeting today. I'm getting so tired of meetings. It seems like all we do is go to meetings." It reminds me of what Oscar Wilde said about socialism: "The trouble with socialism is that it would take too many evenings." We've got to make some decisions about what things *need* a meeting.

A. I suppose by "we" you mean the teachers. In that case we'll have exactly the kind of phony "student government" that they have in most schools. The adults decide everything they think is important, and things they think are unimportant they let the students "decide." Why not let the students, or the whole school, decide what things are important and what are not?

B. But then we'll be in the business of having meetings to decide what we'll have meetings about. That'll be even worse. I don't want the teachers to decide all the big questions, just the little ones. Should we go to the park Tuesday or Wednesday, stuff like that? Or decisions about buying things? Or what to have for lunch? We're surely not going to use meetings to decide the school menu, are we?

A. I suppose not, as long as anyone who wants to can get any particular question put before the whole meeting. Then the meeting can decide whether it wants to take it up again.

B. Well, but that makes problems too. These kids are young, and passionate, and they get into enough quarrels just in the business of living their daily lives. I can see someone saying, "I think we ought to talk about this at meeting," and someone else saying—they're always blunt—"Oh no, I think that's silly, it would be a waste of time," and the first kid would have his feelings hurt and be angry. I'm afraid we'd be manufacturing quarrels, constantly dividing up and tearing apart a group of kids that we want to help come together.

A. I think you worry too much about children's quarrels. Most adults do. We're so uptight about disagreeing, quarreling, about showing our feelings, we nurse our resentments and angers so long, that we forget how quickly kids get over their quarrels. We adults are always trying to keep everything looking nice on the surface, and never mind what's going on underneath. The kids can always decide. If they think they are spending too much of their time at meetings arguing with each other, they can always say, "Let's not talk about this at the meeting, we've been talking too much."

B. But then we run into this—some kids, like some adults, like meetings. They're politicians. They like to talk and argue. What's worse, they like to put other people down, show how much smarter they are than everyone else. Every school has some of these, and so do we. I've been to plenty of democratic school meetings where four or five people held the floor all the time, and all the rest sat around looking disgusted and watching them do their thing. If later on you ask these other kids why they never speak up, they say, "Yeah, and then some smart-ass will just say something that will make me look stupid. Besides, it doesn't do any good, these meeting freaks always get what they want anyway, they sit there and talk and talk and talk and everyone else gets so tired they just give up so they can get out of there." You run into this all the time.

A. We keep coming back to the main issue. Either we give the meeting a chance to discuss anything it wants, or we say that the adults have a *right* to decide what the children can decide about and what they cannot. What gives us that right? Why do I have the right to say to some kid, "I'm sorry but this is one of the things I have decided you can't decide about"? Just because I'm older?

B. You seem to be saying that we're all the same in here. In some ways maybe we are. In other ways, we're not. The kids have to pay to come here. We get paid. That surely means that they have some privileges we don't have, and that we have some duties or responsibilities that they don't. Our positions aren't exactly the same. Our responsibility for keeping this community running in a good way is greater than theirs. A kid can, if he likes, come here and do his private thing, pay no more attention to the other kids or the place as a whole than he wants. We can't do that. There are some kinds of decisions we ought not to lay on the kids—like whether one of them is making so much trouble that we can't keep him any more. Neill sent kids away from Summerhill, and he didn't let the general meeting decide whether to do it.

The point about this discussion is that it is never going to end. A and B are both right. They have to keep pulling. It would be a bad thing for their school or community if either of them gave up and let the other have his way. We must learn not to torment ourselves with the idea that arguments like this shouldn't go on all the time, that we ought to be able to find a way to get them settled. The tension is not a "problem," and there is no "solution" that will make it go away.

We might suggest—but there could be arguments about this, too—that meeting times should be limited or that it should take a two-thirds vote of the meeting to extend it past its regular closing time. We might also say that anyone, student or teacher, who could get enough signatures on a petition could call a special meeting. Or that anyone who could get enough signatures could get something put on the meeting agenda. But he would have to take his own time to go around and get the signatures; he wouldn't be able to take the time of the meeting to argue whether they ought to discuss his idea. As for students cutting down other students (or anyone cutting down anyone), I think adults would be making a proper use of their natural authority if they commented on this and protested against it. They could say, as I used to in a very argumentative English class, "Put forward your own ideas as strongly as you can, but don't try to argue by undercutting the other guy, trying to make him look or feel stupid or silly." In short, I think the adults could set and try to uphold in meetings a certain standard of dignity and courtesy as did the head of the school where I visited the court. If kids have to fight, let them do it in other places.

Individual vs. Community

The tension between the rights and needs of the individual and of the community can be painful. I once heard a number of students at a new and small free high school discuss it, more or less in these terms:

A.   We don't think that you guys ought to go off and just start a project all on your own, without asking us what we think or trying to get our support or giving us a chance to take part in it as a school.

B.   Look, I don't *want* to talk to everyone about it. It doesn't need everyone. It's just a small project that two or three people can do, and we want to do it. Why should I have to spend a lot of time talking about it with everyone else? One of the reasons I came to this school was so that I could do the things I wanted, without having to explain or justify them to a whole lot of other people. Now you guys are acting like a bunch of teachers, saying to me that if I can't convince you that this project is good, I don't have the right to do it. I'm not interested in trying to convince you. You find something you like to do, and that's fine. You don't have to tell me about it.

A. We're not saying you don't have a right to do it. We're just upset because you never told us that you wanted to do it or said anything about it. One of the things we all wanted to get away from were schools in which everyone was working against everyone else, nobody cared about or worked with anyone else or was interested in what they were doing or wanted to help. We want a school in which we can all feel together, in which we all know what the others are doing, and we're interested in it, and we'll help if they want us to and if we can. Sure, we want to live our own lives, but we want the school to have a life of its own, too, not just be a place we come to.

This tension can be very painful when one or a few students seem to be doing something that may hurt the entire community.

A. Listen, it's our business if we want to use pot, it doesn't concern you. If we get busted, we get busted. That's a risk we take. Don't you stick your nose in it.

B. But it does concern us. If you get busted, and it gets out that you are at this school, then everyone's going to get uptight about the school, and maybe they'll shut it down, and then we all get hurt. It's ours as much as yours, and you haven't got any right to risk it.

A. So what you're saying is that everything I do is everybody else's business, that every time I want to do something I have to think, "How will this affect the school?" That's just what they told me all the time at the last school I went to. "It'll give the school a bad name." Which is more important, the school or the people in it? I don't want to have to run my life for the sake of the school. I came here so I could live my life.

B.   So did we, and if the school gets busted we won't be able to
      live our lives, we'll have to go back to those places where
      everyone tells us what to do all the time, and we don't want
      that.

A.   Yeah, well, it feels to me like everyone is still trying to tell me
      what to do, and it doesn't make all that big a difference that
      they are kids my own age instead of adults, unless maybe kids
      are worse, because it's harder to get away from them.

This tension is part of what politics and government, at least
in a (more or less) free society are all about. When does the right of
one person to live his life cut into the rights of others to live theirs?
The point is that neither students nor teachers escape this tension
by setting up a school, calling it Free, and saying that they don't
have any rules. The tension still exists.

Sometimes it shows itself in what might be called the May-
flower Syndrome, thus:

A.   Just because you guys were here last year when the school
      started, you act as if you own the joint. So we did come in a
      year later. That doesn't make us second-class citizens. It's just
      as much our school as yours, and we have just as much right
      as you to say how it shall be run.

B.   We're not saying it isn't your school. But we've put more
      into it than you have. We thought of the idea, and we had to
      do a lot of work to get it started, and we had a lot of prob-
      lems that we had to solve. We didn't know whether we could
      get the school going, or whether it would be any good.
      We had to gamble. It's not quite the same when you come
      in a year later and things are running smoothly—fairly
      smoothly—and all the initial worry and struggle are over.
      This is just a place you came to, even if it is a place you like.
      For us it's a place we made. There's a difference.

A.   Yeah, and so now, every time we say, "How come this is this
      way instead of some other way?" or "How come we have to
      do this or can't do that?" you say, "That's what we decided
      last year." It seems like everything was decided before we got
      here. Why don't we get in on any of those decisions?

B.   But the reason we do things a certain way is that when we tried doing them another way we got all messed up, it didn't work, we weren't together. So we thought and thought and argued and argued, and finally we found something that worked. Now you want us to start all over again. How are we going to get any better if we never learn from experience?

A.   But that's just what they told us at the schools we used to go to. In fact, that's what the adults always tell us when we ask why things are done a certain way, or if we suggest a new way of doing them. "Well, we've learned by experience that this works best, so you just go along with it." Like they say we have to have corridor passes and all that stuff because experience told them that if they didn't kids would be running wild all over the building. Well, it wasn't *our* experience, and we don't want to be judged and treated according to someone else's experience. We may be different.

It is certainly foolish to learn nothing from experience. But we can learn too much from it. Indeed, one way of defining a bureaucracy might be that it is an organization that has learned so much from the past that it can't learn anything from the present. People say, why repeat past mistakes? Why indeed? But they might not be mistakes now. And if every time we make a mistake, we then make a rule to make it impossible ever again to make that same mistake, soon we have a nine-hundred-page book of rules that we have to look into before we can do anything. Mark Twain said that a cat that sat on a hot stove lid would never sit on one again, but it wouldn't sit on a cold stove lid either. Most human organizations get to be like Mark Twain's cat. How do we know that lid is still hot?

And when does the institution, which starts out as people, get to be more important than any or all of the people in it? Conventional, traditional schools, that do many children great damage by failing them and kicking them out, always justify this by saying that it is for the good of the school. We have everywhere situations in which instead of schools working for the children in them, the children are expected and urged to work for the good and glory of the school. Or where administrators and teachers say to students, "You can have nothing to say about this place, how it runs and what it does, because we've been here longer and have a greater stake in it, and hence the right to say how it shall run." This is another tension that will not go away.

Perhaps the most painful tension, particularly for high school students, is that on the one hand they want to get out from under all those adults who for years and more and more insistently, contemptuously, and angrily have been telling them what to do. On the other hand, they find that a world away from adults is no world at all. They want to get society, which they experienced as a great weight, off their backs. They do get it off, they stand up, and they find that the absence of society leaves them in a vacuum.

Let me make these words more concrete. One of the problems of many free schools, whether public or private—at least everyone (wrongly) experiences it as a problem—is that many of the students are surprisingly unhappy. They think, What's the matter? Here we've been saying, if we could only get away from the do this, do that, from the corridor passes, from the get-back-to-your-classroom, from the cutthroat competition with other students, from the constant endless struggle either to please teachers or to resist them—if we could only get away from that, we'd be happy. Then when a few lucky students do get away, they often find themselves no happier than they were before. They and their teachers worry about it. Is something wrong with us? Is something wrong with the school? Is there something we should be doing here that we're not doing?

Abraham Maslow's idea, what he called "preemptive needs," may help us here. There had been much futile argument among psychologists about which needs were more important or fundamental than others. Some said food, drink, sex, sleep, warmth, shelter, and so forth. Others said, no these needs are simply animal needs, having them satisfied does not make man happy, he has other and deeper needs. Maslow said that instead of arguing about which needs were more important, basic, fundamental, etc. we could arrange them in the order *in time* in which they make themselves felt. Thus, a person lost in a wilderness, without food or water for three days, thinks first of finding something to eat and drink. He is obsessed with this need; it occupies his whole mind; he dreams of banquets. If, somehow, he finds something to eat and drink, satisfies his hunger and thirst, he gets up and thinks, what next? If he is cold and wet, he thinks about getting warm and dry. If bad weather seems to be coming on, he thinks about shelter. If he has been wandering a long time and is tired, he thinks of rest and sleep. If and when he finds a shelter, makes a fire, dries off his clothes, gets warm, makes himself a resting place and gets some good sleep, other needs appear. How do I get out of here? How do I make a signal? How do I get help? That becomes his first need. If he manages this, and help comes, he thinks, how can I get word to family and friends? How soon can I get home? What's been going on while I have been away? Vanity begins to appear. What am I going to say when everyone starts to kid me about getting lost in the woods? I'd better cook up a good story. The human desire to make use of experience also appears. What did I do wrong? How can I be sure I don't get lost that way again? He begins to feel his connections with other people, to want to be useful, to help them. What can I tell others that will prevent them from making my mistake? What could we do to improve our rescue services? And so on. As each need is satisfied, another surfaces and appears in its place. There may never be an end to the list, a final need which, if satisfied, would leave us content and at peace.

Back to the students: Their very powerful and preemptive need was to be free of the constant pressure of adults, rules, regulations, to be left alone, to not be harassed all the time about hair, clothes, homework, exams, college. Now this need is satisfied. But people, particularly young people in their teens, at the peak of their energies, need things to do. In many free schools, small and broke, there's not much to do. Some people try to excuse this by making a theory or ideology or way of life out of it. They put up picture of Buddha saying, "Don't just do something; sit there." It doesn't work, not for most of them, not for long. Beyond something to do right now, they need something even more important. Paul Goodman put it very well in *Growing Up Absurd,* and no one has said it better since. They need a society to grow in and into, a society that makes some sense, has reasonable purposes, that they can trust and respect. What if no such society exists? What if the society, the very world they live in, is not just dishonest, unjust, corrupt, and murderous, but suicidal? Next best thing might be to find whatever people are working to make a decent and just and viable society and world, and join them in their work. But what if they can't find them? Or if, having found them, they are prevented, by the laws and customs that declare them to be children, from working with them in any serious way? What sense will their present freedom make if beyond it they can see only a life that looks like a kind of slavery? What if this pleasant present world they live in seems to have no connections with any larger reality? We might put it this way. The more freedom a student has in his life in school, the more he is likely to see how pointless and wasteful it is, in times like these, that he should be in school at all.

In short, free schools, at least free high schools, by satisfying one very important need allow others to surface that they cannot satisfy, that no school *could* satisfy, and that perhaps in these times nothing can satisfy. To the extent that a free school really works, the student who before was saying "If only I could get in" may now begin to say "If only I could get out." It is a little like the tension of the parent—the better he brings up his kid, the sooner that kid will want to take his energy, enthusiasm, and confidence out of the house and into the world. And if the world will not let him out—then there is a misery that even the best parent and home cannot cure. Perhaps the most we can do is understand that this tension, like the others, is one that we cannot make go away.

5
Authority

Some people who write and talk about school reform make much of the distinction between what they call open schools and free schools. Open schools (which they say are good) are schools like the new British primary schools, in which, supposedly, teachers do not "abdicate authority." Free schools (which they say are not good) are schools like Summerhill or any one of a large number of American schools, in which, supposedly, teachers do "abdicate authority." Many people in free schools make the same distinction, only in the other direction. Describing themselves, they say, often with defiance and contempt, "We are not an open school, but a free school." From all this one might think that there was a nice sharp line between open schools and free schools, clear and easy to see. There is not. Among the new British primary schools, called open by those who admire them, no two are alike. In some I have seen teachers do things, or allow things to be done, that teachers in other open schools not far away would think terrible. Within a given school teachers may differ sharply about what they should or should not do. Any one teacher may be very relaxed, easy, accepting about some things, and very tight and strict about others. We all have our own ideas about what is important or unimportant, allowable or not. There is no simple way to arrange these differences under such headings as open or free, and so say which is right.

So much depends on the children themselves and their actual needs. In *The Lives of Children* Dennison describes vividly the interactions, quarrels, and outright fights that took place among the children of the First Street School. The instinct and policy of the adults in the school were not to intervene in these unless it looked as if someone might get seriously hurt. These conflicts are amusing, exciting, and often moving to read about. But if I had been on the spot they might often have made me very anxious. I know from experience that the anger of children upsets me, probably more than it should. I might have felt some need to step in and calm things down. It is almost certain that very few of the new British primary schools, and very few of the educators who advocate open as against free schools, would have allowed these incidents to take place, or go as far as they did. But it is exactly because they did take place and went as far as they did, not once but many times, that this school was a place in which these children, through their free interactions with the others, could begin to find out who they were and get a strong sense of their own being and place in the world. It is only because they were free to quarrel and even to fight that in time they became free to learn. And yet, in other circumstances and about many other things, the adults in the school intervened very positively in the lives of the children. As Dennison says, they made demands, which the children were free to refuse if they seemed unreasonable or excessive. The school was very far from a place where the children could do anything they wanted, and no one is or could be more scornful than Dennison of many such schools and the people who run them.

The question of what are the right relations between adults and children is a difficult one, not settled merely by invoking something called "adult authority." In a conversation not long ago I said, as I often do, that we ought not to correct the speech of children. Someone asked why not, and then offered an answer to his own question: because the children are young, sensitive, easily embarrassed and shamed, and might by too much correction be discouraged from further talking. True enough. But there is a much more important reason for not correcting the speech of children. It is the grossest kind of discourtesy, unless asked, to correct the speech of *anyone*. We cannot imagine doing it to anyone of our own age, and we would not put up for long with anyone who did it to us.

Not long ago I spent four days in France, much of it with friends who are trying to free French education. Though I once spoke French fluently and quite correctly, and even taught it, I had had few occasions to speak the language in the sixteen years since I had been in France. It was a great pleasure and excitement for me to find myself again hearing, speaking, and thinking in the language, and to feel myself to some degree becoming at home in it again. But I was sure that I was making many mistakes as I spoke. Often, not certain whether something I had just said was true French, or just a word-for-word translation from English, I would ask my friends and hosts if it was French. *Then* they told me, very tactfully, whether I was correct or not, and if not, what would be a good French expression. But unless I asked, and I seldom did, they said nothing, partly because they were courteous, and partly because they were wise enough to know that as I spoke French and heard them speaking it my speech would get better.

To live well with other human beings, adults or children, is a subtle art. Rules for doing it are not much help. But if I had to make a general rule for living and working with children, it might be this: be very wary of saying or doing anything to a child that you would not do to another adult, whose good opinion and affection you valued. "Mind your own business" is not a bad minor rule in human affairs. Of course, if we saw someone walking toward an open manhole or some other grave danger, we would shout, "Look out!" In this spirit we often and rightly intervene in the lives of children. But this has almost nothing to do with anything that should be called "adult authority," some kind of general and permanent right and duty to tell children what to do. It would be equally right and natural if a child, in some kind of lab where he was working, seeing me reach toward something acid or hot or electrical or otherwise dangerous, should say, "Don't touch that!" Or if an eight-year-old I know, already an expert skier, should tell some adult that a certain trail was probably too hard and dangerous for him, and that he should stay off it. What is speaking here is not the authority of age, but the authority of greater experience and understanding, which does not necessarily have anything to do with age.

Children feel safer, freer to live and to explore, if they feel that people are protecting them from situations in which they might get badly hurt. To put it another way, they don't like unpleasant surprises. The crying of a small child who has unexpectedly slipped or pulled something down on top of him has more outrage in it than grief or pain. Also, if by doing certain things they are going to get into trouble with people who have the power to hurt them, they want to know what those things are. If there are rules, let them be plain, not hidden. But this is by no means to say that they always want rules. To have always to wonder or ask, before doing anything, "Is this OK? Is this going to get me in trouble with some grownup?" is in the most literal sense, a drag. It slows down life.

For years, visiting classrooms, I have taken in tape recorders, to let children talk into them and later hear their own voices. Not long ago I went with my recorder to visit a small free school. The children there were mixed middle class and poor, white and black. As always, seeing me talk into the recorder, they came up to ask what it was. As always I answered by recording some of their questions and then letting them hear their own voices. Soon they were crowding around to get a turn to say something into the machine. One older child was particularly insistent. Every time I gave him the mike, he would mumble into it a song or verse, full of forbidden words. The first time, he did not even stay around to hear it played back, but fled. Next time, seeing that nothing bad had happened to those who had heard the song, he stayed around to hear it. But his face and tense laughter showed he was still anxious. Each time he looked at me, silently asking the old question, "Is this going to get me in trouble?" Perhaps he was looking for limits, or to see if there were any. It slowly became clear to him that in this situation there were none. Nothing he said, whatever he said, would offend me. I was only interested in what he wanted to say. A great change came over him as he saw this. He stopped straining to get at the mike. His pace became calm and thoughtful. Since he could say anything he wanted, the question became, what did he want to say? When his turn came he began to talk, slowly, tentatively, and in an altogether different voice, about something to do with his own life. Nothing very profound, no great revelation, but at least something true and real. It was as if this question, "What do I really want to say?" was a question he had never asked himself before. It was as if his talk had always been a reaction to what was going on around him, to what other people were saying or doing, to what others wanted or expected of him, or to what he expected or wanted of them. Now all this was out of the picture, and he was, as it were, speaking for himself alone. It is not a thing children, or adults for that matter, often get a chance to do. And it will never happen in a situation in which they have to wonder and worry about limits. My authority, for indeed I had some, lay elsewhere. It lay in the fact that I had a tape recorder, knew how to work it, and was for whatever reason strong enough so that I could not be frightened or hurt by anything he might say.

Of course if I had been in a conventional school, public or private, the situation would have been very different. I would to some extent have been worried about what his teacher might be thinking, whether I might be getting in trouble with her, or getting him in trouble with her, or getting her in trouble with some parent or higher authority. I would have had to get into the limit game, in which case this child would probably have amused himself for some time with making me set the limits exactly—children, when at such work, are great natural lawyers—and in testing me to see what I would do when he went over them. This might have been fun, even exciting; but it would never have led him to the important question of what he really wanted to say.

As a rule we greatly exaggerate children's interest in power struggles with us. We are so concerned about maintaining our power over them that we think they are equally concerned about taking it away from us. They are very much aware that they are powerless, that we have great power over them. They don't like this, and in a vague way look forward to a time when it may not be true. But they are realistic enough to know that at the moment they are not going to be able to do much to change this. In any case, if they are to any degree healthy and happy, they have other things to do, they are busy living. They don't want to quarrel with us all the time. As long as we don't abuse our power intolerably, or weary the children with our constant struggles to assert it, most of them, most of the time, are willing, perhaps even too willing, to accept it. Most of the quarrels between adults and children that I see are needlessly provoked by the adults for no other reason than to prove what the child never for a minute doubts, that they are Boss. How many times, in airports and other places public and private, have I heard this old refrain, to children as young as three or two years old, "When I tell you to come here, you *come here,* do you understand?" And so, struggling frantically to maintain an authority which was never really in question, we may erode it, bit by bit, until suddenly it is gone, and we wonder in surprise and agony where it went. The child no longer cares. He has felt the sting or weight of our displeasure for so long that he can no longer feel it. We have argued with him so many times about trivia, and when no argument was necessary, that he decides that everything we argue about is trivial, and that we argue only because we like to argue. And then, when there is perhaps something serious to argue about, when we really want—perhaps even then mistakenly—to try to save him from what looks like a disastrous misstep, the lines are down, he cannot hear, he is not listening.

Writing about adult authority is full of such phrases as "We mustn't get down to their level," or "It's wrong to try to be a buddy or a pal to a kid," or "We mustn't confuse our roles," (Is being an adult a *role*?) or, "We shouldn't pretend that we're not an adult." It is hard to tell what any of this means. Is "buddy" the same as "friend"? If so, does the statement about buddy mean that people older than twenty-one (or wherever else we may want to draw that line) should not be friends with people younger? If it does not mean that, is there some magic age gap beyond which friendship is impossible and improper? Is it OK for a twenty-three-year-old to be friends with a seventeen-year-old, but not with a twelve-year-old?

How could I pretend not to be an adult? The implication here is that there are a certain number of things that "children" do but that "adults" never do, and that if I do them, I am "pretending not to be an adult." There is a further implication that children might somehow be taken in by this pretense, might really think that I really wasn't an adult.

If all these cautionary statements mean anything, it is this. Anyone defined as "adult" has *ex officio,* simply by virtue of being over twenty-one years old, the unlimited right to tell anyone defined as being "nonadult" or "child" what to do, and to punish them or cause them to be punished if they don't do it. Indeed, this view is backed up by both law and custom. Neither the police nor the courts could be expected most of the time to uphold a child's right to disobey an adult, any adult, unless the child should show that he was in effect obeying some *other* adult. Not many parents, if another adult complained to them that their child had disobeyed them, would defend the child, saying, "What right do you have to order my child around?" A child without an adult defender is largely defenseless before other adults. Now, accepting for the moment the fact that this is true (without agreeing that it is right), I admit that I should not pretend to children that I have given up this unlimited right to correct and chastise them if in my mind I have not given it up. Kids have a right to ask, in effect, "Are you, or are you not, someone who can get us into trouble? Are you officer, or are you enlisted man? We don't want to have to keep guessing about this all the time." Fair enough.

Once, while visiting some friends during the winter, their quite young children asked me to come and have a snowball fight. I agreed. Soon they were coming at me from all sides, I dodging and ducking as best I could, occasionally hitting them with a very loose snowball, or charging at them and tumbling them in the snow. As this went on I became aware of something. One of the older children was really trying to hurt me. He was taking time to pack snowballs as large and hard as he could, and when he got one ready he was watching for a moment when I was busy with another child, when he could sneak in close and throw it with all his might right at my face. After a couple of near misses I began to pay attention. It was soon clear that he was aiming to hurt. When there was no more doubt in my mind, I said, "OK, that's all, the fight's over, I quit." They all said, "How come?" I looked right at him and said, "You're trying to hurt me, trying to hit me in the face from close up. You think you can get away with it, because you know that I'm not going to hurt you. Well, I'm not going to play by that kind of rules." He didn't argue; he knew I was right. The others protested a little, not really understanding, but I meant what I said, and went inside. I didn't want to hurt him or be hurt. Neither did I want to get him into the kind of serious trouble with his parents that he would have been in if he had hurt me. It would have been cowardly to play on his terms, to fight as seriously as if I had been his age, because I was so much bigger. It would have been equally cowardly to let him think I was doing that—he would not have got in trouble for blacking another kid's eye—when all the while I was ready to fall back on my privileged position as adult if things went wrong. None of us said a word about this inside; we just said we were tired out.

Here is quite a different play story, which may make clear in another way some of what I am trying to say. With two friends and their five-year-old daughter, whom I know well, I am visiting the house of some friends of theirs. We are in the living room, talking and listening to music. The child and I are sitting on the couch. Very gradually, step by step, over a period of about a

half-hour, and along with the music and conversation, a game
evolves between us. Nobody else in the room (I found later) no-
tices it. At its fully developed stage, it goes like this.

The child, J, is on my right on the couch. I am apparently
paying no attention to her. My right hand is curled into a fist. She
takes my hand and very carefully opens it up, one finger at a time.
Into the open hand she puts a bottle top, one of the kind that you
put into an already opened soda bottle to keep it from losing all its
fizz. Then she just as carefully closes the hand into a fist. All this
time I seem to be paying no attention, to be unconscious of my
hand and what is happening to it. When the hand is made back
into a fist, she says to me, "Look at it." I bring my hand in front of
me and look at it, as if becoming aware of it for the first time. I
slowly open the fingers. On seeing the bottle top, I start in surprise, as if I had not known there was anything in my hand. I look
at it in amazement. "What could it be?" I say in a voice of wonder.
"It's a bottle top," she says. "A bottle top," I say. I continue to
gaze at it. After a while I say, "Where could it have come from?"
J waits. "Where could it have come from?" I say again, this time
looking searchingly at the ceiling. This is J's cue. "It came from
the sky," she says solemnly. "From the sky," I repeat in amazement. Then, after a while, and still gazing at the ceiling, I say,
"Who could have made it?" Again very solemnly J intones, "The
clouds made it." Again I repeat in wonder, "The clouds made it.
The clouds made it." Then very slowly and as if reverently, shaking
my head at all these miracles, I put the bottle top down on the
table in front of us. The game is over. I sit back, again listening to
or even for a while taking part in the conversation. After what
seems to J like a reasonable wait, she says, "Make your hand into a
fist." Then we go through the cycle again, always with the same
deliberateness, seriousness, and sense of wonder. How many times?
It took quite a number of repetitions, each one adding a little to·
what had gone before, to develop the game to its final form. In
that form, we must have played it at least six or eight times. At
some point, without anything being said, J stops the game, simply
by not starting it up again. We go on to something else—I now
forget what. Perhaps J is tired, and wants to snooze or dream for a
while. Perhaps she, like me, is interested in the music or conversation. Perhaps it is time to go home. At any rate, the game is over.

On another occasion, she may remember it and try to resurrect it, in which case we will probably add some new variations as we go along. Or we may never play this particular game again.

What has happened here? In playing this game, did I abdicate my adult authority? Get down on her level? Try to be a buddy? Pretend not to be an adult? Confuse my roles? And so on and so on? Clearly I did none of these things. I was in one sense an equal partner and companion in our game. At the same time, I was very much an adult. Can you imagine J developing such a game with another five-year-old? Not that they might not and do not invent many other good kinds of games, including many I would never think of. But it was because I was playing this game as a serious adult that I was able to give it, or help give it, a certain special quality. To put this another way, the game could not have developed as it did if I had been *pretending* to be five years old. The only thing I was pretending to be was an otherwise normal and serious adult suddenly and utterly mystified by the appearance of this strange object in my hand. That is what made the game a good game. If J wants to play, and I say, "I'm sorry, J, not now, I'm busy" (or I don't feel like it), she doesn't press me, not because she fears that I will get angry at her or get her in trouble, but because she knows that feeling that way I wouldn't be any fun to play with and the game would be no good. As the old song goes, it takes two to tango.

Dennison speaks of the "natural authority of adults," as opposed to bureaucratic or official authority, which has no source or expression except in the power to punish. Our natural authority as adults does not come from the fact that we are over twenty-one—to a five-year-old someone eighteen, or even fifteen or twelve, seems grown-up—but from the fact that we are bigger, have been in the world longer and seen more of it, and have more words, more skill, more knowledge, and more experience. To the extent that our authority is natural, true, and authentic, we *cannot* abdicate it. When J and I play, which we do often, my natural authority comes from the fact that I am fun to play with—I think up good and funny games, and I play them as an equal, entering fully into the spirit of the game, and enjoy them as much as she does. I would have no natural authority at all if I were thinking up or playing the game *only* to amuse her, or if I played in a fake or condescending way.

Herndon makes this point very clear in *How to Survive in Your Native Land*. For a while he and his colleague, like many other gifted teachers of open classrooms, were very busy thinking up interesting things for the kids to do. It was only later that he saw clearly, not just that these things were not really interesting for the kids, but that in urging them to do things that he would never have done himself he was being fake and dishonest. He was not using but undermining his natural authority by pretending to be interested when he really was not, by not revealing his true interests or being his true self. In *What Do I Do Monday?* I suggest a great many projects for teachers and students to do, but with a warning that I fear too few teachers will take seriously—if this project doesn't interest you, *leave it alone,* don't imagine that you can make exciting for children what to you is only a bore. Find instead something to do that you can throw yourself into. Let the students see *you* genuinely interested. Let them see *your* intelligence, imagination, and energy at work. Then and only then will you be exercising true adult authority.

A very good and widely read book on education is Charles Silberman's *Crisis in the Classroom*. It is a report of a three-year study of American public schools that he made for the Carnegie Foundation. In the book he says, quite rightly, that most public schools are mindless, joyless, rigid, petty and that they destroy the minds and hearts of most of the children in them. He urges that instead we make our schools and classrooms more open and flexible, allow students to work independently or in groupings of their own choosing, and give them a much more wide and interesting range of choices of ways to pursue their learning. With all this I could not agree more. But at the same time, in many places in the book, and like many others who generally urge more freedom and choice in learning, he says that teachers must not give up or abdicate their responsibility and authority. This sounds very reasonable, hard-headed, feet-on-the-ground—but the problem is more complex than that.

In *How to Survive in Your Native Land,* Herndon shows us very clearly that this matter of authority puts us in a most difficult and painful tension. Authority, in the sense of coercive authority, the right to give orders, carries a price tag on it. If we lose something when we give up such authority, we also lose something when we keep it. In the book he describes a most successful class that he taught in a San Francisco junior high school, the very model of a gifted teacher's open classroom. He had suggested all kinds of fascinating projects—they really were good—to his students, who had done them with energy and enthusiasm. Everyone was pleased, students, parents, administration, and above all Herndon himself. So he and a colleague decided next year to teach a class called Creative Arts, which students would take only if they wanted, in which there would be no grades, no coercion, no threats, no required attendance, none of the usual school carrots and sticks. In this class they felt sure the kids would do all the things they had done in their regular classes, and since the class would attract all the eager, creative kids in the school, many more besides. So they hoped. But as he tells us, it didn't work. The kids didn't do anything.

> . . . After a while, Frank and I, on the edge of complete despair, began to figure out what was wrong with the ideas that had worked so well in our regular classes. Why did the kids in regular class like to do all that inventive stuff? Why, only because it was better than the regular stuff. If you wrote a fake journal pretending to be Tutankhamen's favorite embalmer, it was better than reading the dull Text. . . . But that only applied to a regular class where it was clear you had to 1) stay there all period and 2) you had to be doing something there or you might get an F. Take away these two items, as Frank and I had done in all innocence, and you got a *brief vision of the truth.* [Italics mine.]

After a while, Herndon and his partner Frank decided to reassert their authority as teachers, and gave the children a speech. Since nobody was doing anything, there would be assignments. There was instant rebellion. Most of the students said they would leave the class. Worst of all the few students who had been doing things on their own now said that if they were made to do things, they would do nothing. Three girls had been putting out a literary magazine, complaining a good deal because none of the others ever wrote anything for it. Herndon asked them if it wouldn't be better if everyone wrote and drew things for it. No, said the chief editor; if they weren't doing it because they wanted to, the magazine would be no good. He could have a good magazine, or he could have a magazine with everyone contributing, but he couldn't have both. Which did he want? He and Frank decided they'd rather have a good magazine.

The class continued as it was. Most of the students, most of the time, did not seem to do much. But they had a very good magazine, and each time it was ready to come out, there were always plenty of kids in the class eager to help put it together and distribute it. It was their magazine. But very few people working anywhere in adult society feel that what they are working on is "theirs." Don't ask me, the saying goes, I only work here—that is, I get paid to do what someone tells me, I don't worry what it's for, or how it comes out, or even whether it is any good or not. A complicated technical society can only stand so much of this, and we seem to be getting close to that limit. Much has been written about the rapidly declining quality of work and workmanship in almost all parts of our society. More and more, the things we buy and use don't work, and when they stop working it is harder and harder to find anyone who can fix them. Some say this is not important; what men can't and won't do well, we can make machines to do. Wrong, for many reasons. Having machines do work is no guarantee of better quality or service. Our automobiles are made less by men and more by machines than they used to be, but this does not mean that their quality is better. The growing use of computers in many fields has not done away with errors, just made them almost impossible to correct. In many places, telephone service, though more expensive and far more automated than it used to be, is of far poorer quality. Such a society grows terribly inefficient; things once done directly and simply now have to be done in elaborate, expensive, and roundabout ways. The machines we built to take the place of men themselves break down in turn, and are harder to fix. As Paul Goodman has long pointed out, we grow more and more independent on what we cannot reach, see, or understand. Also, as society grows more complicated it becomes more vulnerable; little breakdowns lead to big ones—a flat tire on a crowded freeway ties up traffic for miles; one short circuit makes a power blackout over an entire region of the country. In any case, people must put their lives into something, whether they think of it as work or play, get paid for it or not. They must have something to do that they really want to do, and do as well as they can. And the point Herndon is making, and that I join him in making, is that no one can find his work, what he really wants to put all of himself into, when everything he does he is made to do by others. This kind of searching must be done freely or not at all. When are we going to give young people a chance to do it?

Much later in this very profound, very realistic, and very funny book, Herndon underlines the point more strongly. If children don't go to school, they can be put in jail. Talk about motivation or innovative courses or inspiring kids to learn is simply dishonest nonsense. When you threaten people with jail if they don't do what you want, the only thing you can find out is whether they like doing what you want better than going to jail. This is why, when people say that the teacher must not abdicate his authority, they must be clearer about what kind of authority they mean. They may mean that the teacher should not try to *pretend* that he does not have more experience than his students, or that his experience does not count, or that there are not things that he is interested in and thinks are important. If so, no argument. But if by the authority of the teacher they mean something else, his power to bribe, to coerce, to threaten, to punish, to hurt, then they ignore a serious difficulty. Teachers with that power cannot get any feedback. They may want to do what is best for the student, but they cannot really find out whether what they are doing is any good or not, or if good, how, and if not, why not. They are in the position of a man who, after becoming president of one of the largest corporations in the country, told a friend that his hardest job was simply to find out what was going on. No one would tell him. Everyone wanted to tell him what they wanted him to think, or thought he wanted to think. This is the age-old and insoluble problem of the boss. No one wants to take bad news to the king.

In one elementary school where I worked years ago, I had a small office-classroom-workshop next to a regular classroom. The teacher of that class, a bright, demanding, and fairly hot-tempered person, had a "favorite subject." He thought children liked that subject better than any other, and he thought he could teach it better than most others. He taught it first period every day. I soon learned through the wall something that the children in that class must have also learned. When the teacher's first period class went smoothly, when the kids did what was expected, the rest of the day

was very likely to go smoothly as well. But, if that first class didn't
go well, if the children didn't perform as expected, if they made
any fuss, then the teacher would get in a "bad mood" and they
would probably be in trouble all day long. At the end of the year
the teacher was as convinced as ever that his favorite subject was
also the children's favorite. He may have been right. I don't think
so; I think the children were afraid enough of his anger to go to
some pains to deflect it. The point is that in a situation like that he
could not know, could not learn about his own work, could not get
any better at it. There was no way for him to find out what he most
needed to learn. For the same reason, we have not learned much
and are not likely to learn much about our work of teaching and
education—because our students are held in our classes either by
the fear of going to jail or the fear of not getting a piece of paper
that they think they will later be able to cash in on a good job.

When I first visited the schools in Leicestershire County in
Great Britain, I was enormously excited and impressed by them—
so much variety and richness of material, so little tension and fear,
the children working so independently and behaving so sensibly. In
later visits I remained impressed, but as we all do, I began to see
other things—what Bill Hull calls the seamy side. There was none
of the shouting, the threats, the anger held back or let out that we
hear in so many of our own schools. The classrooms were full of
the most interesting materials. What they lacked was leisure. The
teachers seemed constantly to be saying, in the most pleasant of
voices, "Get on with it," meaning keep busy. It became clear after a
while that this was the great unwritten rule of these classrooms—
you had to keep busy, you had to be working *on* something, *with*
something. You could work on it with other children, and while
you were working you could talk. But you could not spend much
time *just* talking, and least of all pondering, reflecting, musing,
dreaming. If you did, after a while a kindly teacher would appear
with suggestions. They might be very interesting, like the projects
in Herndon's regular class. You could choose any one you wanted.
But you could not choose none, say "No, thank you." Children
adjust to the ground rules of wherever they happen to be, and to
these kindly and flexible ground rules they adjusted very happily.
Yet important things may still have been lost. Children absorbed in
their work may talk about the work, but not about other parts of

their lives. The scientist or artist or artisan or workman in the child may be satisfied, but the philosopher, dreamer, and poet neglected. The children, unlike children in conventional schools, were surely learning to take their work seriously, which is good. But they may also have been learning not to take their ideas, their thoughts, their wishes, fears, or dreams very seriously, which is not so good. Also, many of them, inarticulate children from families where little talking was done, or where they were not allowed to do it, needed more practice talking than they were getting.

This is not to say, either, that all the materials and activities in the classrooms had been proposed or brought in or begun by the teachers. The children also brought in stuff and invented projects on their own. They were not prevented from thinking or deciding about what they wanted to do. They just were not given much time to think about it. Always that kindly, "Get on with it" hung in the air. The trouble with this is that we don't know what the children might have thought of if they had had more time to think. There may not have been time for really important ideas to work their way up from deeper consciousness or for them to perfect these ideas. Deny children—or anyone else—the chance to do "nothing," and we *may* be denying them the chance to do "something"—to find and do any work that is truly important, to themselves or to someone else. There is a tension here. A child who appears to be doing nothing is not *necessarily* doing something more important. Perhaps much of the time he is not doing anything important. Perhaps any one of a number of things that we might suggest to him might be better, even in *his* terms, than what he is doing. But when we act as if this were always so, the child never finds his true work, and worst of all, never thinks of himself as capable of finding it.

Part of the tension here is that the more we intervene in children's lives, however intelligently, kindly, or imaginatively, the less time we leave them to find and develop their own ways to meet their true needs. The more we try to teach them, the less they can teach us. But we have a great deal to learn from them, not about some quality of "goodness," which may or may not exist, but simply about their great powers of learning, powers that most of us have lost or forgotten how to use. We do not know how great these powers are or how to help children make fuller use of them.

Defenders of the open classroom say that in them children learn to read at least as quickly and well as in traditional schools, with all their rigid instruction. But this is nothing to boast about. Reading is not hard. If we knew how to make a learning environment for children that was truly effective, the children would gain what we have come to think of as five or six years worth of ability in reading in a matter of months. They might not all do this when they were six years old, but what difference would that make?

This point cannot be made too often or stressed too much. Learning to read involves learning three related ideas of pieces of information. The first is that writing, in general, is speech, and that written letters represent spoken sounds. The second is that the order of the letters in space, from left to right (or sometimes top to bottom), corresponds to the order in time of the spoken sounds. The third is the set of relationships between the 45 or 50 sounds of our speech and the 380 or so letters and combinations of letters that represent these sounds in writing. That is all. There is much less information here, and vastly simpler ideas than those that children must grasp in learning speech. We have seen many times that children or adults, of whatever age, race, background, economic condition, or whatever, *under the proper conditions,* i.e. that they are learning to read for their own reasons, that they are not afraid of the task or of their own ability to master it, and that what they have to learn is not made needlessly obscure or difficult, can learn to read and write at a level probably higher than that of at least half of our own population in a matter of months. It follows therefore, that when children do not learn to read with this ease, rapidity, and power, it is because the conditions are *not* right, because they are not learning for their own reasons, to meet their own felt needs, or because we have made the task needlessly difficult, obscured what was already clear and that we might have made more clear, or because the children have somehow been blocked, cut off from the full use of their powers.

What sort of things may block them? This is one of the things we must learn from them, and may be able to learn if we give them a chance to teach us. What very often blocks them is that they have a problem or condition or tension in their own lives that they have not yet been able to understand or accept or master. But one thing we have learned by now is that children, indeed people of any age, may have much more power than we think to grasp and master such problems. If, that is, we give them time and space to do it. If we don't pile new problems on the old. If we don't make the fact that they have a problem into a bigger problem. To be specific, a child, like one I once tried to teach, who is not learning to read because he is in some kind of struggle with his brothers/sisters/parents, may find a way to resolve that struggle (and then very easily learn to read) if we do not (as we almost always do) make his not reading into a still bigger problem, and a further cause for anxiety and struggle. In short, as is shown in rather different ways by the work of A. S. Neill and Ronald Laing, people, and above all children, may not only have much greater learning powers than we suspect, but also greater self-curing powers. Our task is to learn more about these powers, and how we may create conditions in which they may have a chance to work. This is one of the things that children may be able to teach us, if we are not always busy teaching them.

Some people I know, impressed by the primary schools they have seen in England, and depressed by the early primary schools in their own area, started a very small nursery-kindergarten-primary school of their own, using a couple of converted rooms in the basement of a house and some space in the yard. They began with one teacher and a group of about a dozen or so children, most of them four and five years old. With the British schools in mind, they filled their classrooms with a variety of interesting things to look at, experiment with, work with. Then they waited eagerly for the children, like the ones in England, to get busy being miniature scientists, artists, and craftsmen. It did not happen. The children had quite different ideas. For most of the first year, and on into the next, they spent many hours every day on a kind of free-flowing dramatic play. None of the wise, experienced, and sympathetic adults connected with the school had expected such play or seen anything like it, and indeed at first they felt they understood very little about it. In much of the play the children took the parts of animals, large and fierce, small and gentle, mixing the parts around, so that a child might be a lion or bear one day and a rabbit the next. One day a boy, not wanting much action, said, "Today I think I'll just be the sky." This was perhaps the most popular form of their drama. Another popular game was War, which on the day I saw it did not look at all like what I expected. The children were not, as older ones often do, shooting at each other with imaginary machine guns and imitating movie or TV people falling over dead. Some of the children were bombers, flying around the classroom and dropping bombs, and others under the tables were people hiding in the basements of houses. Whether the war game took this form every day I do not know.

If only we had a detailed journal of this play, covering a period of months. There is none; the teacher, and others in the school, were too involved with the children to make it; and indeed, if they had tried to make it, the children might have become self-conscious, or artful, or anxious, or even unwilling or unable to play at all. Perhaps the play went on so freely only *because* no one was paying very close attention to it. But from such a journal, if we could ever get one, we might learn far more about children than we now know, above all about the use and importance of such play in their lives. One example shows what it may have meant in the life of one child. She was four, living with her father, the parents separated, whether by death or divorce I don't know. Father and child loved each other and were happy together. But in all the animal games, day after day for a period of many months, when the parts were being given out or claimed, this child would announce that she was an animal with a hurt leg. The other children accepted this as a part of the given, the *structure* of the play. It meant that in their play, whenever the animals had to move somewhere or do something, they had to find a way to take care of this hurt-leg animal. They always did. This went on for months. Then, one day, she stopped, and never asked for that particular part again. We cannot be sure how that child was using her play, what she was getting from it, but we can make the obvious guess that she was reenacting the loss or departure of her mother, expressing her own sense of need, and reassuring herself that other people would take care of her and that eventually she would be all right—for after all, the animal she played always had a *hurt* leg, never a missing one, so there was always the hope of getting better.

In most open schools or classrooms, even kindly ones, she would have been very unlikely to be allowed to play this game and so to express, reveal, and meet her deep needs. The game was too energetic and noisy, took up too much time and space, would probably have seemed to most teachers what they like to call "chaotic" (meaning they can't figure out what is going on), and would not have resulted in any visible learning. Nor would any other activity have served her as well. Some schools have a period every so often in which the children are encouraged to talk about their feelings. Would she have been able to put into words what she felt about her mother's not being with her? Would she have been willing to? Would she have had from the other children the kind of understanding and support that she got from the fact that day after day in the animal game the other animals were willing to take care of her? It seems hardly possible.

Such are the kinds of things we have yet to learn, and can only learn, as Herndon tells us, when we give up our power of coercion. But it is not always easy to give it up even when we want to. It is not even easy to know how much and in what way we use it. The teacher I spoke of earlier, whose students were afraid not to seem to want to learn what he wanted most to teach, would indignantly have denied that he was trying to coerce his students. Yet they were nonetheless coerced. Many of us may coerce without meaning to. The question is, what kind of influence do we exercise over other people, what kind of open or hidden pressure do we put on them, what chance do we give them to say No, what do they risk if they do say it? Many years ago I rode in a car with two eleven-year-olds. They were in the front seat with me, talking—not including me in their conversation, but not excluding me either. At one point one asked the other, "Do you believe in God?" After thinking a bit, she said, "Yes, I suppose so," and then, after a pause, "After all, what choice do we have?" They lived in a culture in which no one would have threatened or punished them for not believing in God. In that sense they were not coerced. But they were surrounded by people who believed or *talked as if* they believed in God, and as if it was important that the children too should believe, and who would have been most hurt and disappointed if they did not. In effect, they had no choice. There is no use in our offering a choice to someone unless we can make him feel that it is a real choice, that he has an equal right to choose either way, that he can do so without having to worry about disappointing us or losing our friendship. We all know the kind of person of whom others say, "Oh, we could never do or tell him that—he would be so disappointed." Such people wield terrible power. They also never know what the people around them, busily protecting them from disappointment, really think.

People say, "Don't we have a duty to expose children to whatever seems to us best, most enjoyable, most significant, etc. in human life?" (Or, to use a popular cliché, The Best That Man Has Thought and Done.) Why think of it as a *duty*? It is a pleasure, one of the most natural things in human life. We constantly tell our friends about the things we like, urge them to read books, see movies, hear music, or do this or that. The problem is that if we urge too strongly, our friend may think that he must do what we urge lest he hurt our feelings. So with the gifted teacher in the open classroom, filling it full of all kinds of wonderful things to look at, work with, do. He must still leave the children a chance to say No. Otherwise exposure, or call it temptation, crosses some kind of boundary and becomes seduction, hidden coercion, do it to make me happy, do it because otherwise I'll be unhappy and maybe even won't like you.

People in open classrooms proudly show me children doing this or that free, creative, interesting thing. Do they do any of these things out of school? Hardly ever. But, say the open classroom teachers, they can't, they don't have the materials, the facilities, to do these things. Would they do them if they could? Would a child finger paint (How we adults love to see children finger painting! All the teachers in a little kids' school are happy when finger painting time comes around.) at home, if he could? Do many children go home from finger painting at school and say, "Mommy, how come I never get to finger paint at home, please can I have some finger paints?" Perhaps a few, but not many.

This boundary between temptation and seduction is not sharp or easy to see. How do we keep from slipping across it? For a couple of years I taught at a school that got out at noon on Friday, making it possible for me to stand in line for inexpensive "rush seats" to the Friday afternoon concerts of the Boston Symphony, then and now one of my greatest pleasures. After a while I thought that some of the children, first in my own fifth-grade class, later in other classes, might like to go with me. I made an offer. I would escort them to the symphony, no more than three at a time, and get them on the right trolley or subway to go home, or bring them back to Harvard Square. They had to pay the sixty cents for their own ticket, and twenty cents for their subway fare, and bring their own lunch or money to buy food at the cafeteria. The rules of the game were that while the music was playing everyone had to sit still and quiet, lest they bother other people, or lest the fear of their bothering other people bother me. Anyone who could not follow this rule would not be asked again, on the sole grounds that he spoiled my pleasure. Those who liked the music could come again when their turn came up; those who did not did not have to. Take it or leave it. Most of the children in the class tried it once. About half did not try again; the rest did, some several times. One boy, without much previous experience of music, became a fanatic, like me—in two years he went to eighteen concerts. (His favorite piece of all the music we heard was Bruchner's Eighth Symphony. He liked all that brass.)

One day I arranged to meet a friend, the mother of a child in the school, at Harvard Square, and to go to the concert together. We rode in, sat on the floor in the ticket line, ate our lunch, talked. The children busied themselves with comic books or whatever. When the doors opened the children, as was our custom, explored the building, joining us just before the music began. The concert over, we took the subway back to Harvard Square. The children disappeared, as usual without saying thank you, which always seemed to me a good sign—perhaps that they were still in the grip of the music, and at least that they weren't worried about me. When they had gone my companion looked sternly at me and said, "I think you're horrid!" I reeled back, and asked what I had done. She said, "You were so mean to those kids." I said, "How was I mean?" She said, "You weren't a bit nice to them—all afternoon long you hardly paid any attention to them." I said, "Look, you've got things all mixed up. This isn't supposed to be an afternoon of fun with kindly old Uncle John. It's the Boston Symphony. I'm not trying to beguile them into liking music. I just want to put it before them." And, from all that happened, I think they felt genuinely free to choose.

What is crucial here is that I was not going to the symphony for their sake but for mine. I had not planned the Friday expeditions as something nice for them to do. I was going for my own reasons. I was glad to have them along, but I had been perfectly happy going alone, and I would have been perfectly happy if none of them had wanted to go, or to go a second time. This is what made it possible for them to take the music or leave it alone. But it is hard for a teacher in a classroom to feel this much detachment, because for the most part, he is not doing anything in there he would be doing if it were not for the children. Indeed, but for them, he wouldn't even *be* there. If he gives up being a boss, he must find himself to some degree being an entertainer. He has no business in the classroom except to think up things for children to do. If they don't want to do any of them, he can hardly help feeling something of a failure. This is almost sure to make him anxious about his offerings, his anxiety will make the children anxious, and in will come an element of subtle coercion.

My friend, Mosse Jørgensen, the Norwegian teacher and writer, was talking to me not long ago about the Forsøkgymnaset (experimental school) in Oslo. This was an open, alternative high school, as far as I know the first in Norway, started by students who were fed up with the rigid conventional schools. They had organized this school, got a building from somewhere and money from the city government, and asked some of the teachers they had liked in their regular schools to teach them at the new school. One of these was Mosse. Since the school needed someone to represent it, be its spokesman, sign the letters, and so forth, they elected a school leader every couple of years, and Mosse had been the first. Anyway, she was telling me about some of the teachers who had been in the school when I first visited it. So-and-so has left; he was just exhausted. What about So-and-so? She is leaving too; she has to have a rest. And So-and-so? Oh, he has been there three years; he is completely exhausted. After a while I said, "Mosse, there is something very strange going on here. Here are all these teachers, who have taught for years in conventional schools without getting exhausted, saying all the time how they hated the narrowness, the rigidity, the petty discipline, and how they wished they could teach in a very different kind of place. So one day they get a chance to teach in this very different kind of place that they have always wanted and after a couple of years teaching they are all exhausted. What's the trouble? Why should this be so exhausting?"

We thought and talked about this for a while. After a while I said, "Mosse, a picture is beginning to come clear in my mind. I see a restaurant, a man sitting at a table, an anxious waiter serving him. The man is very rich, very influential; if he wants, he can close down the restaurant. The trouble is, he doesn't want anything the waiter is serving him. It has too much salt, not enough wine, it is overcooked, too tough, take it back! The waiter rushes to the kitchen and the equally anxious chef and they try to whip together something for the angry customer. But this is no better than the other. Too much garlic, not enough wine, too sour, too sweet. Away with it! What can they do? What can they offer him? What is wrong with their cooking? Is the whole restaurant going to be shut down? And this chef and waiter—of course—are the teachers in this free school, trying to cook up something that the customers will eat."

"Or I have another picture, of a baby, a year, year and a half, two years old. He is sitting in a highchair, and his anxious mother is trying to get him to eat some dinner. None of it pleases him, he will have none of it. In desperation she tries one thing after another. 'How about a little cereal? Try some of this nice cereal.' The baby turns away, twists his head from side to side, spits the cereal out. 'Here's some yummy vegetables, your favorite. Look at these nice peas, take a bite, come on, for Mommy.' He knocks the spoon out of her hand. 'Here is some delicious applesauce, you know you like that, come, eat some of it. You have to eat, otherwise you won't grow up to be big and strong. And it's good—see Mommy likes it. Now you try some.' The dish lands on the floor." At this Mosse began to laugh, saying, "Yes, I can see that baby, I know what that is like. And yes, that is exactly the position we are in, I hadn't thought of it that way, but we are just like that anxious mother, and it wears us out." It does indeed wear us out, for the same reason that being a cop in the classroom (except for people who like being cops) wears teachers out. It is not a proper task or a right relationship. It is not a fit position for an adult to be in. We have no more business being entertainers than being cops. Both positions are ignoble. In both we lose our rightful adult authority.

For this reason and others, it seems most important that a teacher in a classroom should some of the time be doing things that he would do even if no children were there. One good fifth-grade class project began this way, out of something that I was doing just to amuse myself. I had never done any art in school, and had thought of myself as being no good at it. But I liked to doodle, make certain kinds of (to me) interesting shapes. At that time I had just discovered Magic Markers—felt-tipped pens, a perfect medium for the unskilled. At first, I only had red and black, but with them made some shapes that pleased me. Then the Magic Marker company put out a whole line of colors. I bought a box, brought them eagerly to class, and one day, during a read or work period, in between talks with the students, I began making a colored design on the 6-by-9-inch yellow manila paper that was our chief staple. While I was doing this one of the boys came up, watched a bit, and then said, "What are you making?" I said, "I don't know, I suppose you could call it a design." He watched a bit longer, then looked at the box of Magic Markers and said, "Can I use some of those?" I said OK, and off he went. Within a few days the whole class was making colored designs. At first, they were variations on the sort of design I had been making, but later, variations on variations, and so to original work. Many of the children's designs were interesting and lovely. We covered the walls of the classroom with them. The first passion for design making wore off after a while, as such things do; but from time to time during the year people would come back to it. It was an important part of our year's work together. But if I had presented it as an art project, something Fun for Children to Do, it would never have gotten off the ground.

What we really need are schools or learning resource centers that are not just for kids, but where adults come of their own free will to learn what they are interested in, and in which children are free to learn with and among them. How can children be expected to take school learning seriously when no one except children has to do it or does it? It seems a sound beginning. In Boston we have the Beacon Hill Free School, which in its first year has attracted three hundred or more pupils, and on a budget of practically nothing—a good example of the kind of open educational network that Ivan Illich has written about. Since its classes meet in the evening most of its pupils so far are adults; but younger people are welcome and I hope will soon be attracted in. If so, I think they will find the school a good place, precisely because it is not just their place, was not started for them, has other purposes than to keep them happy and busy. Only such a school can be said to be truly open.

6
The Problem of Choice

Teachers very often say to me, "Suppose we tell kids that they now have the freedom to choose what they are going to study, and how and when they are going to study it, and they don't choose anything, don't do anything? Then what do we do?" A good many teachers who have tried to open up their classrooms, usually in a junior high school or high school, have said that this has in fact happened.

First, we should try to see this situation through the eyes of the student. For years he has been playing a school game which looks to him about like this. The teacher holds up a hoop and says "Jump!" He jumps, and if he makes it, he gets a doggy biscuit. Then the teacher raises the hoop a little higher and again says "Jump!" Another jump, another biscuit. Or, perhaps the student makes a feeble pretense of jumping, saying, "I'm jumping as high as I can, this is the best I can do." Or, he may lie on the floor and refuse to jump. But in any case the rules of the game are simple and clear—hoop, jump, biscuit. Now along comes a teacher who says, "We aren't going to play that game anymore, you're going to decide for yourselves what you're going to do." What is the student going to think about this? Almost certainly, he is going to think, "They're hiding the hoop! It was bad enough having to jump through it before, but now I have to find it." Then after a while he is likely to think, "On second thought, maybe I don't have to find it. If I just wait long enough, pretty soon that hoop is going to slip out of its hiding place, and then we'll be back to the old game where at least I know the rules and am comfortable."

In short, if we make this offer of freedom, choice, self-direction to students who have spent much time in traditional schools, most of them will not trust us or believe us. Given their experience, they are quite right not to. A student in a traditional school learns before long in a hundred different ways that the school is not on his side; that it is working, not for him, but for the community and the state; that it is not interested in him except as

he serves its purposes; and that among all the reasons for which the
adults in the school do things, his happiness, health, and growth
are by far the least important. He has probably also learned that
most of the adults in the school do not tell him the truth and indeed are not allowed to—unless they are willing to run the risk of
being fired, which most of them are not. They are not independent
and responsible persons, free to say what they think, feel, believe,
or to do what seems reasonable and right. They are employees and
spokesmen, telling the children whatever the school administration, the school board, the community, or the legislature want the
children to be told. Their job is by whatever means they can to
"motivate" the students to do whatever the school wants. So,
when a school or teacher says that the students don't have to play
the old school game anymore, most of them, certainly those who
have not been "good students," will not believe it. They would be
very foolish if they did.

We must try to understand and accept this, without getting
hurt feelings, or taking it as some very personal kind of rejection.
This may be far from easy. A school, or teachers, or teacher, that
offers students very much choice has probably gone to some trouble to be able to do so, and even risk—risk of misunderstanding or
hostility from parents or community or fellow-teachers. If after we
have run this risk to give students some freedom, choice, and control in their learning, they show us that they do not believe or trust
us, we may be tempted to think "Well, you weren't worth going to
this trouble for in the first place, the hell with you, we'll go on doing things in here the old way if that is what you want." But we
must resist this temptation, and keep our offer of freedom and
choice out on the table even though at first it is not believed or
trusted. It might be helpful, if we feel comfortable doing it, to say
to the students that we understand their skepticism and suspicion,
and the reasons for it, and are sympathetic rather than hurt or angry. We might even invite them to talk about their reactions to our
offer. On the other hand, if students do not believe our offer they
may not trust us enough to talk candidly about their reasons for
not believing it. Also, they may not really know, well enough to
put it into words, why they don't believe it or are afraid to make
use of it.

Some may think that in all this talk of trusting and not trusting I am too cynical, making complications where none exist. In some cases, they may be right. There are many schools and classes in which the students, given this chance to plan and direct their own learning and growth, have seen it right away for a good thing and have wasted no time in making good use of it. If only it could be this way everywhere. But from experience we know that it often has not been and is often not going to be. For one thing, in offering freedom and choice to students, we may be trusting them less than we think. Many parents, and more than a few educators, have seized on the idea of the open classroom, freedom, and choice, not as a way of having students direct their own learning, explore the world in the way that seems best to them, but only as a way of getting them to do conventional schoolwork more willingly and hence more rapidly than before. In short, they believe in freedom only as a "motivating" device. This is a cruel deception, bound to lead us to disappointment. If we have such an idea anywhere in our minds, students will be aware of it, even if we are not. They will see the offer as not being real. They will know that the old hoop is still there, but hidden.

Not long ago I saw a vivid example of this. I was invited to a conference, held in a new high school, built only a few years before at great expense, and already quite famous. The school, like most, was too big, too elaborate, too inflexible, and too ponderous. Handsome enough in its way, but without color, humor, warmth, or grace. Why do we think that humane learning can go on in buildings that look as if they were designed to hold atomic secrets? Inside, the usual bare walls, unrelieved by any decoration or human touch. The big talking point of the school was that it had been designed for a program in which the students would do a great deal of independent learning. Instead of the usual classrooms, there were a number of resource areas and centers— in Mathematics, Physical Sciences, History, and so forth. The idea was that students would have a great deal of unscheduled time that they would be free to use as they wished, going to this or that center. Though the program was only in its second year, we were told it was "not working." The students were not making good use of their time, it was said, just loafing around talking to each other. The school had to cut back on the unscheduled time and schedule more regular classes—for which the building was not well designed.

One student spoke mournfully to me about this. He had two or three very strong interests—photography, writing, and something else. He said, "Last year I had a lot of time, I could really get into these things. This year they have taken more than half of it away, and they'll probably take more away next year. But already my day is so chopped up with classes that I can't really do any serious projects in the darkroom. I might as well forget it." I asked him why the school had changed. He said, "Of course, a lot of the kids weren't doing much of anything. But they didn't give us time to find out what we might want to do. I already knew what I wanted. Most of them didn't. But at least you'd think that they'd let the students who were making good use of the program go on doing what they were interested in. But I can't get out of classes even to do projects. I have to go like everyone else. In another year or two this will just be like any other school."

If the school was sincere in its offer to the students, it was unwise to have lost heart so quickly. What would probably have happened, if they had let it, if they had had the patience to wait for it, is that more and more students, like the one I talked to, would have found things to do that they could put their whole energy into, and that gradually more and more students would have learned about this, followed their example, or been drawn into their activities. Young people naturally like to share what gives them real pleasure and satisfaction. My student friend's interest in photography would certainly in time have touched and enriched the lives of other students. But the school did not allow this to happen.

At another time during the day I was being shown around the school by someone who knew it. We went by one of the biology resource centers. It was lavishly equipped, but with few of the signs—human junk, stuff brought in, bones, skulls, skins, nests, shells—of a place where people really care about what they are doing. Five or six boys and girls were sitting in a group in the middle of the room, talking. My guide looked at them for a while through the door. Then, as we moved away, he said to me sourly, "Doesn't look to me as if they're doing much biology." In his voice there was a world of suspicion and contempt. Worse yet, satisfaction—I knew those kids were no good, and they're proving I'm right. I said mildly that for all we knew they might be talking about biology. He made no comment. I let the matter drop. What seems clear to me even now is that students must from the very first have read and understood the secret feelings of this man and perhaps many others like him. Perhaps they knew that in this school, resource centers or no, they were never really going to be allowed to learn and talk about what really mattered to them. Small wonder most of them decided to escape from the usual grind for whatever time they could.

But lack of trust in us is not the only reason why students may be slow to use the freedom and choice we offer them. Suppose we get over this first hump, and the students believe our offer is genuine. The next problem is that they may not trust themselves enough to be willing to choose. We must not be surprised at this either. They have been taught in school to distrust themselves, and they have learned. It is one of the few things that schools teach well. Everything the traditional school does says clearly to the student that he cannot be trusted to do anything, not even to make the simplest choices about what he will learn or do next or how he will do it. Nothing is left to chance or the student's own design.

To choose is to risk. Faced with a choice, the student may well think, if I have to decide what I'm going to do, how do I know that I will like it or get anything out of it. The choice may be no good. But then I'll have no one else to blame. I can't say, as at least I can if I mess up regular schoolwork, that it was the teacher's fault for asking an unfair question, or not telling me what she really wanted, or not teaching me what I was supposed to know. There is nobody to blame but me. If I fail, it will be my fault. This is too much for most children. They learn in school—another one of the few things they really do learn—that since to fail is the worst thing of all, it is best to take no chances. We must realize that when we ask or invite them to make choices we are asking them to take a risk much larger than the risks we have spent years teaching them never to take. No wonder many of them hang back. This too may be something it would be helpful to talk about.

It is not just the people we call children who find choosing difficult. A few years ago I taught at the Harvard Graduate School of Education a one-semester course called Student-Directed Learning—which came to be called T-52, its number in the catalog. Many of the students were in their early twenties, still on the schooling ladder, but many others were experienced teachers and school administrators, some as old as I was or older. At our first meeting I talked a while about how I saw the course, what I planned to do in it. I had a certain amount of resources and experiences, all having to do with student-directed or open learning, that I was going to put before them. I would talk and lead some class discussions; I had some other people coming in; the class was welcome to find and bring in people of their own. I had some films to show them of alternative schools already at work. I had a list of books and articles about open learning that had seemed to me useful, that I liked, and that I strongly recommended. If they were interested in and wanted to find out more about anything on the list, I would be glad to tell them. I also had a list of places in the area where, in different ways, student-directed learning was going on, and I encouraged them to visit such places, spend as much time there as they wanted and could arrange, and get involved in any way that might seem useful. I also said that the course was Pass-Fail, that everyone enrolled would get a Pass, that there would be no exams or compulsory written work, that attendance at class sessions was optional.

I urged them to keep a private journal or notes, in whatever form they liked, of thoughts or reactions or observations that came up in the course of their work, inside class or out. I said that I would be very glad to read any such writing that they wanted to share with me. I said that if anyone has some ideas that he wanted to give to everyone, I would give him a ditto stencil, he could write his piece on this, and I would make copies for the whole class. I suggested that we might make up a kind of open journal, rather like the correspondence columns of some British newspapers, and magazines, in which they could write whatever thoughts they wanted others to hear, or respond in various ways to what other people had written. I said that as I found new articles, newspaper stories, or interesting material, I would post them on the walls of the classroom, and invited others to do the same—to use the walls as a kind of open bulletin board. I was full of bright ideas and suggestions.

But having proposed all this, I said that none of this was required. Here were these resources on Student-Directed Learning. They could use all of it, or any parts of it they wished, or substitute something else of their own choosing, or do nothing whatever. The class seemed satisfied with this; indeed, they shouted down one young angry who said that I was dominating the class, and why did they have to sit around and listen to what this guy Holt said, why couldn't they just get themselves together? Why did they have to sit in the chairs in this lecture hall? I said they didn't; sit on the floor or the lecturer's platform, if you like. They all came and sat on the platform. Next class they were back in the chairs—and why not, they were more comfortable.

Anyway, the class seemed to think my offer and plan were reasonable. We went along smoothly enough for six weeks or so. Nobody did any writing, nobody put anything in the journal, nobody took up most of those bright ideas. But the class sessions seemed interesting, and I knew some things were happening outside. Then at one class meeting there was an explosion. Many people in the class began to attack me about the course. They were very angry. You don't care what we think! You never tell us to write anything! You're not interested in our ideas! I repeated the suggestions and offers I had made at the beginning of the course. They said, You'd don't care about us, *otherwise you'd tell us what to do*. I said I did care about them, that was why I didn't want to tell them what to do. If it was true, and it seemed to be, that many of them had never had the chance to decide for themselves whether to read a book or not, write a paper or not, go to a meeting or not, then I thought it was time they decided.

Later, one of the students sympathetic to me told me about the book problem. He said, "You've no idea what a bind you put us in. Here are all these books on your list. You say they are good, and on the whole we believe you. We'd like to read them. But they are not required, we're not going to be tested on them, and meanwhile here is all this other stuff we have to do at the Ed School, more reading than we can ever get finished, a lot of it probably not as good as the stuff on your list. But those other courses are graded, and we need those grades. So we'd better read those required books and let these books go. Then we think, 'But Holt says they are good books, and I'll bet they are. I'd like to read them.' 'But I haven't got the time!' 'But it's not fair to Holt not to read any of his reading stuff just because he said we didn't have to!' 'Not fair, hell! He *said* we didn't have to.' 'Yes, but . . . but . . .' The more we think about it, the more guilty we feel for not reading those books, and the madder we get at you for making us feel so guilty." He said all this in a good-natured way, and I laughed, and said I was sorry to make life so difficult, and I hoped someday he might read some of those books.

Part of the point here may be that it doesn't take much sense to talk of "giving freedom" to people. The most we can do is put within reach certain choices, and remove certain coercions and constraints. Whether doing this creates for other people something they sense as release, liberation, opportunity, freedom, or whether it just puts them in a more painful spot than ever, is very much up to them and how they see things. There isn't much we can do to control it. We have to assume, or at least I choose to, that in the long run more choices and fewer constraints, less coercion, less fear, is good for most people—if only because it gives them a chance to look for and maybe find something that they really want.

Well, we went round and round about this in class. I don't think I converted everyone. Some of the people who were mad stayed mad. Some people just left the class without saying anything. Some of them, perhaps, needed the time to work for those grades in those other courses, or simply to think about things, or amuse themselves, or sleep. More power to them. Some people were glad to grab the easy credit. Enough of the class stayed with me, and took an increasingly active part in it, including running it, to make me feel—as I wanted to feel—that my effort was worth making. Except that I might do more to prepare people for the anxiety of choosing, in the same circumstances I would probably do things very much the same way again.

Another problem for these nonchoosers may be that they do not know what there is to choose from, what choices are possible. Perhaps none of the choices available may appeal to them. All too often teachers or schools say to children, "Now you can do anything you want," when in fact there is nothing to do. Once I visited an elementary school class run by a very nice young man. He had heard about the British style open classrooms and the integrated day and was trying to introduce them in his room. He couldn't figure out why the children didn't seem to want to do anything but run around and bother each other. I looked around the room. Nothing there but the traditional classroom junk—basal readers, workbooks, texts. No games, puzzles, tools, equipment; no typewriter, camera, tape recorder, music stuff, science stuff; no art supplies, not even good magazines or books. As tactfully as I could I tried to suggest that it wasn't much help to tell the children they could do what they wanted if there was in fact almost nothing for them *to* do. He saw my point, and we began to talk about some of the kinds of things that he might bring into the class, or projects he might get going.

If it is frustrating to be told to choose when there is nothing to choose from, it may be frightening, confusing, and paralyzing to have too much to choose from, like a child in a huge toy store. Even in well-established open classrooms, comfortable in the integrated day, it may be wiser not to have all the available equipment and material in the room at the same time. It clutters up the room and makes a major problem of putting things away and keeping some kind of order. Also, if something is under their noses too long, children may no longer notice it. What is too familiar becomes invisible. It would be sensible, if a given piece of equipment has not been used in some time, to take it out of the class without saying anything, store it, and then, after a while, bring it back. Perhaps seeing it after an absence, the children will notice it and be interested in it.

When we first try to open up our classrooms it may make the change easier for everyone if instead of offering a wide choice from the start, we widen the range of choice very gradually. If we say to a student used to traditional classes, "Now you may choose to do anything you want," he may do nothing. If instead we say, "You can choose between these two or three possibilities," he may be more able to choose. Next time we can offer four or five choices. When students seem comfortable with this we can say, "Choose between any of these, or if none of them suits you, substitute a choice of your own." Thus we may change so smoothly from formal class and teacher-directed learning to open class and learner-directed learning that the students will not be threatened by it.

When I taught my last fifth-grade class, I began the year with a fairly traditional class structure, the day divided into periods, schedule written on the board. The schedule wasn't very tight and we didn't stick to it to the minute, but it was there. Soon I introduced what I called a read or work period. In this students could read whatever they wanted, or do any other kind of schoolwork they wanted. Very gradually we began to push out the boundaries of this period. It was the students' idea as much as my own. Someone would say, "Can I draw a picture, or do a puzzle, or write a letter?" I would say Yes. So these became OK activities. Later, someone might ask such things as, "Can I play checkers, or chess, with so-and-so? Or, Can I talk with so-and-so into the tape recorder? Or, Can I listen to some music over the phones? Or, Can so-and-so and I have a conversation?" I would say, fine, if you can do it quietly enough not to bother other people. Most of the time, they could. And so we developed the free period. It was less useful than it might have been; I had not yet visited the British primary schools, and had far less in the way of materials and projects than I would have had a few years later. But it was still the best part of the school day. More and more, the children themselves would ask for a free period, not just to have a chance to do nothing, but because there was something they wanted to do. Sometimes they would ask for a straight read or work period, or a quiet free period.

I see now, though I didn't then, that I might have used the same gradual method to open up the physical arrangement of the class. I was still stuck with the idea that the desks had to be in rows. Every so often I would say that the children could swap places with someone else, or make any new arrangement that was agreeable to all parties, and several times I moved my own desk to a new part of the room to give the whole class a fresh outlook. Even such minor changes as these seemed stimulating to the class, as if with the desks in a new place many new things might be possible.

Often, when I describe to teachers or would-be teachers this fifth-grade class and the way I gradually made it more open, someone will say that since I still controlled the class and the choices, and since the students still could not do anything that I did not approve, the class was really no different from conventional classes, and its seeming openness was a fake. There is some truth in this. It never occurred to me that it might be a good idea to give up my control of the class, and I would not have been allowed to even had I wanted. The students and I knew that their range of choices was limited by what I or the school would approve, and we did not pretend otherwise. One day when I announced a free period and said they could do what they wanted, one boy asked, "Can I go home?" The children all laughed. I apologized for careless speech and said, No he could not, when I said they could do anything they wanted I meant provided it was within the classroom and did not disturb the rest of the building. But he knew that before he asked. As a matter of fact, I suspect that he was at least as happy in that class as he was at home, and that given a real choice of going home he would not have gone. I don't think the children felt that the class was basically like the ones they had been used to, or that their choices were not real because not unlimited.

Finding interesting things for children to do is not too difficult, if they have not been in school too long, or have not been made to feel, by being tracked and labeled, that they are unusually stupid or worthless. We can easily buy, borrow, or salvage many kinds of materials that will be interesting in many ways to young children. We can invent many projects that many of them will find interesting, and they can invent many more themselves. For older children the task may be harder, for many reasons. If they have interests or hobbies, they may need more specialized or expensive equipment than the school has or can afford. They may be more bored, more distrustful, more ashamed of their own curiosity and ignorance, more unwilling to expose themselves and their interests to adults or even their peers.

In this connection I think of a question I am often asked by teachers, sometimes in a tone of bafflement and concern, all too often in a tone of anger and contempt—"What do you do with the student who isn't interested in anything?" First of all, there is no such person. Everyone alive is interested in something, if only himself—and usually much more than that. We might say of a student that he doesn't *appear* to be interested in anything, or at least any of the things we try to interest him in. But this only means that he has chosen not to let us see his interests, perhaps because he has learned from experience that the less the adults, teachers above all, know about what he cares about, the safer he is from mockery, contempt, put-downs. He has learned to put barriers between himself and us, and to wear a mask of elaborate indifference, unconcern, and disdain. But this mask is not the person. Behind the mask and the barriers is the true person, full of fear, shame, self-hatred, self-contempt. Afraid of the world, he uses all his energy to protect himself against it. But this protection comes at terrible cost to himself, for all these strategies of deliberate failure, incompetence, withdrawal, and resistance only add to his sense of shame and worthlessness.

We cannot leap over those barriers, or break through them, or force them down. They can be raised as high and made as strong as they need to be, and they can only be lowered from inside. The question becomes, how do we help that person inside to become less afraid? Sometimes it may help to talk about his fear, or anxiety, though it is probably true that at least some of the barriers will have to be lowered even before such a talk could take place. But many fearful people, particularly boys from low-income cultures, would rather die than admit that they were afraid. Perhaps with such boys it might be more helpful not to talk at all of fear or being afraid, but instead talk as concretely as possible about things they expect to happen that they don't want to happen—for if we are afraid, we are almost always afraid *of something,* and the more clearly we can see what it is we are afraid of, the more likely we are to be able to cope with that fear.

It is no help at all to tell people who are afraid that their fears are groundless, that there is nothing to be afraid of, or that what they're afraid of won't hurt them. It is a little like telling someone who fears that a dog may bite him, "Don't be silly, that dog won't bite, unless he thinks you're afraid of him." When we dismiss someone's fears as foolish and groundless, we only make him more afraid. "They don't understand," he thinks. "They don't even *see* the danger. Because they don't see it, they may try to 'help' me by pushing me into it." We have to accept people's fears as real, as being caused not by their imaginations but by their experience. In R. D. Laing's phrase, we must not "invalidate their experience." What we can do is to try in every way not to add to their fears, not to give them new reasons for being fearful. It is like the old fable of the Sun and the Wind, trying to see who could make the traveler take off his cloak. The Wind tried to blow it off by main force, but the harder he blew, the tighter the man wrapped the cloak around him. The Sun in his turn beamed his rays down on the man until he was so warm that he took off his cloak. The way to get people to lower their barriers is to create as much as we can a situation in which they feel no need for them.

One way to get the student to come out from hiding, is to do all we can to legitimize his interests. In other words, to make him feel that whatever he is interested in is OK, a perfectly good place from which to look at and begin to explore the world, as good as any other, indeed better than any other. We will not make him feel this unless we understand ourselves that it is true. This will be hard for people who have for years been misschooled into thinking that life, the world, human experience, are divided up into disciplines or subjects or bodies of knowledge, some of them serious, noble, important, others ignoble and trivial. It is not so. The world and human experience are one whole. There are no dotted lines in it separating History from Geography or Mathematics from Science or Chemistry from Physics. In fact, *out there,* there are no such things as History or Geography or Chemistry or Physics. Out there is—out there. But the world, the universe, human experience, are vast. We can't take them in all at once. So we choose, sensibly enough, to look at this part of reality, or that; to ask this kind of question about it, or that. If we look at one part, in one way, and ask one kind of question, we may be thinking like a historian; if we look at another part, ask another question, we may be thinking like a physicist, or a chemist, or a psychologist, or a philosopher. But these different ways of looking at reality should not make us forget that it is all one piece, and that from any one place in it we can get to all the other places.

Teachers have often asked me, and always with contempt, "What do we do with a kid who is only interested in hot rods?" Nobody is *only* interested in hot rods. But let's agree that he is mainly interested in them. What's wrong with that? A hot rod is an automobile, and in all of man's history few inventions have done so much to change the whole shape of human life, and indeed the face of the earth itself. It has greatly changed, and in many ways se-riously damaged, our cities. It has created the suburb, and so doing destroyed much of the country. Some people (including me) think that it is one of the most destructive of all man's inventions. It has enormously changed the ways in which we live, work, spend money, and amuse ourselves. Also, it is a machine, and so embodies Physics, Chemistry, Thermodynamics, Metallurgy, and so on.

It takes a great many men and enormously complicated machines to make it. Indeed, it probably did more than any other single product to advance the techniques of modern mass production. Both as an invention, and as an economic product, it has a history. How did men come to invent it? By what steps did they perfect it? How was it first manufactured and marketed? How did today's enormous automobile companies grow into being?

One teacher said, after I had posed some of the questions above, "But how is all this going to help him make a living?" Strictly from the point of view of money, everything that a kid, especially a poor kid, learns messing around with hot rods will probably be worth more than most of what he is told to study in high school. And any young person who out of curiosity begins to find out all he can about the automobile and the many ways in which it affects other aspects of our life and society will have enough to keep him busy for a long time. Someday he may be better able than most conventionally schooled experts to think of ways to tame the automobile, to make it less destructive and more humane and useful—itself one of the urgent problems of our time.

At another time someone asked—not angrily, because pottery is more respectable than hot rods, less lower class—what to do about some kid who was "only" interested in pottery. But look at what is in pottery. Geology—how clay is made, in what sorts of places we look for it. The Physics and Chemistry and Mathematics of firing, kilns, cones, glazes. There are endless connections with History, Art, Anthropology, Archaeology.

This doesn't mean that if we find out that a student is interested in hot rods or anything else, we ought to try to make him think about all the questions I have suggested. He might be interested in hearing about them, but he should not feel that he has to do anything about them. If he wants to explore them further, good. Nor am I trying to suggest that, whatever a student may be interested in, we can always find clever ways to lure him into thinking about things that we think are more important, because they are closer to conventional school subjects. It's a great mistake to think that a young person with a strong interest in something like hot rods or football is somehow cut off from the mainstream of life, that if he thinks seriously about them he will be some sort of narrow specialist, that for the sake of breadth of learning we have to pull him away from what he cares most about. Any interest, any aspect of life, is connected to many other aspects of it and to life as a whole. Our task is to find ways in which we might help a student, who may already have been made to feel by ignorant, prejudiced, contemptuous adults that his interests were trivial, realize instead that they are not trivial, but as good a place as any other from which to look at and explore the world.

People who object to giving students in school a chance to talk to each other like to say that their talk is trivial. If it is, we have made it so by never taking them seriously, by teaching them through our indifference or active contempt not to take themselves seriously. Gail Ashby shows us this in an essay called "The Child I Was," which appears in the book, *This Book Is About Schools* (a collection of pieces, many of them excellent, from the magazine, *This Magazine Is About Schools*). In this story, and perhaps more indirectly in the film, *High School,* we see how young people are cut off from and learn to fear and despise what is most real, important, and serious in themselves. We hear very clearly the effect of this in the speech of a lot of poor kids, which when not hostile, challenging, quarrelsome, is offhand, mocking, uncommitted, cynical, and full of an elaborate indifference.

I took part once in a writing class in a small, open high school, part of a larger, more conventional system. Most of the students in the class were typical of the school, upper middle class, excellent students, bound for college and probably graduate school. One boy was an exception. I might have thought him a fish out of water, except that he seemed a welcome and respected member of the group. Also, since attendance at class was not compulsory, I assume that he would not have gone had he not enjoyed it. He was of lower middle- or working-class background. When I arrived, the class had just started to read and discuss a short piece he had written. It described an almost serious accident he had had while driving too fast in a souped-up car. His story was well-written, but what struck me about it was its tone. He would not let the reader *into* the incident. He had seemed for a second close to death, and described his feelings very vividly; but every few sentences, just as his story began to take hold, he would throw in some mocking, sardonic observation altogether out of keeping with the rest of the story. They seemed to have no purpose except to say, "You know, I don't take any of this seriously, and you're a fool if you do."

We were all interested in what had happened, and encouraged the boy to talk more about it. The setting was informal; teacher, six students, and I were all jammed into a small office. His talk took us into a strange world, a world of souped-up Detroit cars—we were all foreign car snobs, Porsches and BMW's we could relate to, not 450-cubic-inch Chevys and Pontiacs—a world in which it was perfectly a commonplace amusement to get in a car, often by yourself, and just drive around, not going anywhere, at suicidal speeds. He talked freely and well and had a gift for the right word and phrase; obviously a very bright and perceptive young man. But in all his talk as in his writing there was this same mocking, stand-offish tone, the same refusal to commit or invest himself in what he was saying, to put himself into his words. Even when he seemed most involved in his story, with voice, expression, and gesture he was constantly saying, "This isn't real or important; don't take it seriously, I don't; believe it or don't believe it, I don't care either way."

Lower-income children are not the only ones who learn to feel this way. An eighth-grade private school teacher once invited me to talk to her class. On a warm spring day we sat outside on the grass and discussed what it might mean to be able to direct one's own learning, explore the world in one's own way instead of someone else's. The students were very excited, involved, and serious. They began to talk about the many ways in which adults seemed never to take their ideas and wants seriously, but always to find reasons for preventing them from doing what they most wanted. Thus, in this particular school they wanted very much to have a lounge or common room for the older students, a room of their own where they could go, meet, and talk without teachers hovering around. But the school kept putting them off, talking about not enough money, maybe in a few years, we'll think about it—all the delaying tactics that children and students everywhere know so well. (If we stall them off, they'll soon forget about it.) I suggested to them that they consider and take up with the school the possibility of building this lounge themselves. They were very excited by this, and discussed with great animation possible ways of doing this. The hour went very quickly, and they all urged me to come back a week later to talk about these things further, which I gladly agreed to do.

When I came to the classroom a week later the students were at another class. Their teacher told me that they had all discussed our first meeting with their parents—upper middle class, successful, business, professional, and academic people—and had had some interesting reactions that they might be willing to talk about. Soon the students came into the room, and sat at their desks in a circle. From the first I sensed something strange and wrong about the situation. There seemed a barrier between us. A week before they had been friendly and open; now most of them would hardly look at me. I felt a stranger and outsider. The teacher suggested that they might talk about their discussions with their parents, but though nobody refused, argued, or commented, it was clear after a minute or two that they did not want to and were not going to do that. So I tried to change the subject in a more general direction, toward the things we had talked about the week before. These the students were willing to talk about, but so differently from the way they had in our first meeting that I scarcely knew them for the same people. Before, their talk had been open, vigorous, natural, easy. Now it was full of the awkward, nervous, embarrassed, self-deprecatory phrases and gestures and giggles that we so often associate with teen-agers. I waited hopefully for this to change; it never did. One by one, in different ways, they told me the same story. They were no good. If they were not made to do things by older people, they would never do anything. The only things they really cared about were silly, trivial, and worthless, if not actually harmful. They were incompetent; they couldn't do anything; it was ridiculous to think of their being able to build a common room by themselves. Their only chance of doing anything or getting on in the world was to spend a great many more years doing exactly what the adults told them. Then, maybe, someday, they might amount to something. Maybe. They didn't even sound very sure about that. The hour crawled to its end. When the time was up, the students looked relieved. The teacher said that they all thanked me for coming to talk with them, but it was clear she spoke for herself.

No student thanked me. None suggested in any way that they might want to talk about these things further, or indeed see me again. I wished them all good luck and left, with a heart of lead.

In many schools the problem is not that the students seem not to be interested in anything, or in only one thing, or that we can't find out what they're interested in. They are interested in many things, and once they trust us, and believe that we respect their interests, they will tell us, or show us what they are. The problem is that because of pressure from anxious or angry adults in the community, or our own worries about what is important, we are afraid to let the students think, talk, read, and write about what we know very well they are interested in. There have been and will be many conflicts over this. In many schools, all over the country, students have asked for and have been given, sometimes gladly, sometimes grudgingly, a day or several days, during which they can make their own program, have classes or seminars in what interests them, invite outside speakers and resource people and so on. In one school I know of, Shortridge High School in Indianapolis, the program lasted for an entire week—called Soul Week. The students put a great deal of work into it. They polled the entire student body to find out what subjects and seminars and activities people wanted to take part in, collated these, listed the activities for which there was the greatest demand, found resource people, made up a schedule, and went ahead. The program seemed a great success and involved many students. Some of the most popular courses and activities the school continued as part of the regular school curriculum. But in many communities in which the students have planned school programs, these have aroused a good deal of opposition in the community. Radical ideas! Frills! Why are they fooling around with this stuff instead of studying their school subjects?

One teacher, hearing this, said to me, "But I asked my students what they were interested in, and they wouldn't tell me, they just said, 'Nothing.'" I asked her if she had friends. Yes, she had. I asked if she knew something about their interests. Yes, she did. I said, "Did you find out by asking them, 'What are your interests?'" She laughed. I said, "No, of course not. That's not how we find out. We find out by living with people, talking to them, getting to know them, seeing what they get excited about. It takes time and trust." In one of my fifth-grade classes, I discovered that one of the girls was not only crazy about horses, like almost all fifth-grade girls, but that she was an expert rider and jumper. From this I got the idea that she might like to read *National Velvet*, as in fact she did. From another boy I learned, a little bit from his conversation with other kids, a little from what he told me, mostly from what he was willing to write on his free papers, when he could stop worrying about spelling, punctuation, etc., that he was passionately interested in the woods, wild country, climbing, skiing, camping. All his writing was about travelers in a rugged country with night coming on, no shelter around, snow beginning to fall. From such clues I got the idea that he might like some of the books of Jack London (of whom he had never heard), and he did. And so for the others in the class. But I never would have learned these things in a conventional class, no matter what sort of questions I might have asked. I had to try to create an atmosphere in which the children, free to be themselves, would show their interests, let them come out. Then and only then was I able to help them go further with what they already liked.

It is easy to talk about legitimizing the interests of students and getting into honest communication with them. But there are still more than a few schools in which a teacher who tries to do this may meet increasing opposition, may be ordered to stop, and if he persists may be fired. How much this is so has much to do with the social and economic class of the students. In a school where most of the students go to college, there is a general feeling that words and ideas are important, even if they are only the words and ideas that belong to the school. The school knows that it will be judged by how its students do in the word and idea oriented worlds of college, graduate school, and professional life. Any one in such a school who tries to get the students talking and thinking has at least a chance of getting a sympathetic hearing—though as many teachers have already found out, this is by no means certain. In a lower-income school, the situation may be tougher. Nobody there expects most of the children to go to college. When they get out of school, they are going to have to start doing dull and pointless work, and they will be doing it for the rest of their lives. To the parents and teachers of such students, words, thoughts, ideas are dangerous. They say, "Don't give these kids (my kids) ideas; they'll just get them in trouble. Teach them to keep their mouths shut, their noses clean, and to do what they're told. That way they'll get along fine."

A teacher in such a school who tries to legitimize the interests of his students, take them seriously, talk to them honestly, and give them some sense or worth and self-respect may well be seen, by fellow teachers, administration, and parents as an intolerable threat. This is not a guess; it has happened many times. Word of what he is doing will seep out. The students will look, feel, and talk differently. They may begin to stand up for their rights, against the kind of official bullies and petty tyrants shown in the film *High School*. Or they may just begin to stand up. One of the things that saddens me most in many high schools is the hangdog look on the faces of so many of the students. This look is not an accident. The schools, and often the parents, have worked hard to put it there, and they will be alarmed and angry if they begin not to see it. Many schools expect their students to look servile, and if they start looking otherwise, will look for the cause and will trace it to the teacher. The teacher himself will begin to have a relationship with the students quite different from that of the other adults in the school. This too will be noticed and opposed. Finally, as the teacher knows the students better and begins to make human connections with them, he may not be able, even if he wants to, to avoid being drawn more and more into their struggles with the arbitrariness and injustice of the school. He will begin to take their side. This may well be the last straw.

There is no easy remedy for this. Teachers who want to work in an open and humane way with lower-income high school students would do well to find a school in which they are already treated fairly and humanely, or at least a school in which the administration would like to move in this direction. Some radical student teachers seem to feel that their duty is to find an authoritarian and rigid school and, by teaching in it and struggling with it, to try to make it more humane. I think the task may well be impossible, and that they will just get themselves fired. This may be a very useful experience for them, but the school will go on much as it is. In short, an oppressive high school in a low-income community may not be a very promising place for a teacher to work in to bring about educational change.

7
On Discipline

"If we give children freedom how will they ever learn discipline?" This is a common question—really a statement. When people talk about their child "learning discipline," what is it that they really want him to learn? Probably, most or all of the following:

1. Do what you're told without questioning or resisting, whenever I or any other authority tell you to do something.

2. Go on doing what you're told for as long as you're told. Never mind how dull, disagreeable, or pointless the task may seem. It's not for you to decide.

3. Do whatever we want you to do, *willingly*. Do it without even having to be told. Do what you're *expected* to do.

4. If you don't do these things you will be punished and you will deserve to be.

5. Accept your life without complaining even if you get very little if any of what you think you want, even if your life has not much joy, meaning, or satisfaction. That's what life is.

6. Take your medicine, your punishment, whatever the people above you do to you, without complaining or resisting.

7. Living this way is good for your soul and character.

Rather like the sermon the rich used to preach to the poor in the early days of the Industrial Revolution: accept the station in life, however humble, to which God has called you, and there meekly and gratefully do your duty. This preaching still goes on, of course; the rich and powerful, for obvious reasons, always like to tell the poor and lowly about the virtues of duty, obedience, and hard work. Not long ago, after an evening meeting in a town of about 15,000 people, a man came up to me and said, "I run a bank here, and what I want to know is, if kids get the kind of education you're talking about, what are they going to do when I tell them that if they want to work in my bank they are going to have to get their hair cut and wear a suit and show up promptly at eight thirty in the morning?" I said, "Well, I suppose if a young person really wants to work in your bank, he will accept those conditions as part of the deal." He walked away looking dissatisfied. What I might have said to him, but didn't, was that if willingness to obey his orders was all he was looking for in his employees, he would probably not be in the banking business for long. Also, that perhaps the way he and many like him felt and behaved toward young people might have something to do with a problem others had told me about that day—that all the young people in the town were leaving as soon as they finished high school.

Some people who worry about discipline may not necessarily want their children to believe *all* the ideas listed above. But most of the Americans who said in a recent nationwide poll that what they wanted above all else in schools was more discipline probably had all these ideas in mind. *The Boston Globe* reports that Vice-President Agnew recently said to a convention of farmers in Chicago, "I would think restoration of discipline and order ought to be a first priority—even ahead of curriculum—in the schools of this country." They add that this statement won Agnew louder applause than anything else he said to the farmers. What those farmers want is more coercion, more threats, more punishment, more fear. Above all, more fear. Make them afraid! They experience their own life as a kind of slavery, and this is what they want for their (and everyone else's) child, perhaps on the theory that if it's good enough for them it's good enough for him, if they can put up with it then by God he will, perhaps on the theory that nothing else is possible.

The word "discipline" has more and more important meanings than just this. A child, in growing up, may meet and learn from three different kinds of disciplines. The first and most important is what we might call the Discipline of Nature or of Reality. When he is trying to do something real, if he does the wrong thing or doesn't do the right one, he doesn't get the result he wants. If he doesn't pile one block right on top of another, or tries to build on a slanting surface, his tower falls down. If he hits the wrong key, he hears the wrong note. If he doesn't hit the nail squarely on the head, it bends, and he has to pull it out and start with another. If he doesn't measure properly what he is trying to build, it won't open, close, fit, stand up, fly, float, whistle, or do whatever he wants it to do. If he closes his eyes when he swings, he doesn't hit the ball. A child meets this kind of discipline every time he tries to *do* something, which is why it is so important in school to give children more chances to do things, instead of just reading or listening to someone talk (or pretending to). This discipline is a great teacher. The learner never has to wait long for his answer; it usually comes quickly, often instantly. Also it is clear, and very often points toward the needed correction; from what happened he can not only see that what he did was wrong, but also why, and what he needs to do instead. Finally, and most important, the giver of the answer, call it Nature, is impersonal, impartial, and indifferent. She does not give opinions, or make judgments; she cannot be wheedled, bullied, or fooled; she does not get angry or disappointed; she does not praise or blame; she does not remember past failures or hold grudges; with her one always gets a fresh start, this time is the one that counts.

The next discipline we might call the Discipline of Culture, of Society, of What People Really Do. Man is a social, a cultural animal. Children sense around them this culture, this network of agreements, customs, habits, and rules binding the adults together. They want to understand it and be a part of it. They watch very carefully what people around them are doing and want to do the same. They want to do right, unless they become convinced they can't do right. Thus children rarely misbehave seriously in church, but sit as quietly as they can. The example of all those grownups is contagious. Some mysterious ritual is going on, and children, who like rituals, want to be part of it. In the same way, the little children that I see at concerts or operas, though they may fidget a little, or perhaps take a nap now and then, rarely make any disturbance. With all those grownups sitting there, neither moving nor talking, it is the most natural thing in the world to imitate them. Children who live among adults who are habitually courteous to each other, and to them, will soon learn to be courteous. Children who live surrounded by people who speak a certain way will speak that way, however much we may try to tell them that speaking that way is bad or wrong.

The third discipline is the one most people mean when they speak of discipline—the Discipline of Superior Force, of sergeant to private, of "you do what I tell you or I'll make you wish you had." There is bound to be some of this in a child's life. Living as we do surrounded by things that can hurt children, or that children can hurt, we cannot avoid it. We can't afford to let a small child find out from experience the danger of playing in a busy street, or of fooling with the pots on the top of a stove, or of eating up the pills in the medicine cabinet. So, along with other precautions, we say to him, "Don't play in the street, or touch things on the stove, or go into the medicine cabinet, or I'll punish you." Between him and the danger too great for him to imagine we put a lesser danger, but one he can imagine and maybe therefore want to avoid. He can have no idea of what it would be like to be hit by a car, but he can imagine being shouted at, or spanked, or sent to his room. He avoids these substitutes for the greater danger until he can understand it and avoid it for its own sake. But we ought to use this discipline only when it is necessary to protect the life, health, safety, or well-being of people or other living creatures, or to prevent destruction of things that people care about. We ought not to assume too long, as we usually do, that a child cannot understand the real nature of the danger from which we want to protect him. The sooner he avoids the danger, not to escape our punishment, but as a matter of good sense, the better. He can learn that faster than we think. In Mexico, for example, where people drive their cars with a good deal of spirit, I saw many children no older than five or four walking unattended on the streets. They understood about cars, they knew what to do. A child whose life is full of the threat and fear of punishment is locked into babyhood. There is no way for him to grow up, to learn to take responsibility for his life and acts. Most important of all, we should not assume that having to yield to the threat of our superior force is good for the child's character. It is never good for *anyone's* character. To bow to superior force makes us feel impotent and cowardly for not having had the strength or courage to resist. Worse, it makes us resentful and vengeful. We can hardly wait to make someone pay for our humiliation, yield to us as we were once made to yield. No, if we cannot always avoid using the Discipline of Superior Force, we should at least use it as seldom as we can.

There are places where all three disciplines overlap. Any very demanding human activity combines in it the disciplines of Superior Force, of Culture, and of Nature. The novice will be told, "Do it this way, never mind asking why, just do it that way, that is the way we always do it." But it probably *is* just the way they always do it, and usually for the very good reason that it is a way that has been found to work. Think, for example, of ballet training. The student in a class is told to do this exercise, or that; to stand so; to do this or that with his head, arms, shoulders, abdomen, hips, legs, feet. He is constantly corrected. There is no argument. But behind these seemingly autocratic demands by the teacher lie many decades of custom and tradition, and behind that, the necessities of dancing itself. You cannot make the moves of classical ballet unless over many years you have acquired, and renewed every day, the needed strength and suppleness in scores of muscles and joints. Nor can you do the difficult motions, making them look easy, unless you have learned hundreds of easier ones first. Dance teachers may not always agree on all the details of teaching these strengths and skills. But no novice could learn them all by himself. You could not go for a night or two to watch the ballet and then, without any other knowledge at all, teach yourself how to do it. In the same way, you would be unlikely to learn any complicated and difficult human activity without drawing heavily on the experience of those who know it better. But the point is that the authority of these experts or teachers stems from, grows out of their greater competence and experience, the fact that what they do *works,* not the fact that they happen to be the teacher and as such have the power to kick a student out of the class. And the further point is that children are always and everywhere attracted to that competence, and ready and eager to submit themselves to a discipline that grows out of it. We hear constantly that children will never do anything unless compelled to by bribes or threats. But in their private lives, or in extracurricular activities in school, in sports, music, drama, art, running a newspaper, and so on, they often submit themselves willingly and wholeheartedly to very intense disciplines, simply because they want to learn to do a given thing well. Our Little-Napoleon football coaches, of whom we have too many and hear far too much, blind us to the fact that millions of children work hard every year getting better at sports and games without coaches barking and yelling at them.

Some experts, in writing about discipline, try to equate and lump together what I have called the Discipline of Nature and the Discipline of Superior Force. They say that when we tell a child to do something, and punish him if he does not, we are teaching him to understand the natural consequences of his acts. In a widely praised book one expert gave this typical advice. If your child comes home late to dinner, tell him that he can't have any dinner, and he will soon learn the natural consequences of being late and come home on time. The example is confused, foolish, and wrong. Being denied any dinner can be called a "natural" consequence of coming home late only in the sense that anything and everything that happens is a part of reality and hence can be called "natural." One might as easily say that being flogged was also a "natural" consequence of being late. In fact, getting no dinner is not a natural consequence of being late at all, but a purely arbitrary one imposed by the parents. The *natural* consequence of coming home late to dinner might be that your dinner would be cold, or that you would have to eat much or all of it alone, or that you would have to clear your place when you had finished and wash your dishes yourself. Not getting any dinner might be a natural consequence of coming home *unexpectedly,* so that nothing was prepared for you. But it is not a natural consequence of being late. It is punishment pure and simple. As such, it might be effective, and it might not. The child might learn the lesson. Or he might think bitterly, "Boy, some family, you come home late and even though they've got your dinner all cooked, just sitting out there in the kitchen, they won't let you eat it, they'd rather throw the food away, waste it, like they're always telling you not to do, just to make you go to bed hungry and teach you a lesson. I'll show them. I'll get my food somewhere else and come home late every night. I won't come home at all." Punishers always tell the punished that their punishments are the natural consequences of their acts. Not so. They are the result of a choice which the punishers, or the authority they represent, have forced on the punished. The choice may be a wise and just one, or it may not; in either case, it is imposed, not natural.

Some people say, "I agree with all you have said so far. I don't want to make my child servile and docile, I want him to have an interesting and exciting life. But to do anything interesting and worthwhile he is going to have to do a lot of plain, old disagreeable hard work. If he's never been made to do anything he didn't like, how is he going to be able to do the hard work, stick to it until it is done?" Now I don't deny for a second that much of the work done in the world is disagreeable and hard. But that is not what these people are saying. They say that to do anything takes Disagreeable Hard Work, that all work is Disagreeable Hard Work.

In those three words is a whole way of life and of looking at life, very widespread, very deeply rooted, and very wrong. First, the old Puritan split and opposition between work and play. Work is what you don't like, but you do it because you have to, or someone makes you, and so it is good for you. Play is what you do like, but it is bad for you, because you like it. Beneath that there is a still deeper and more destructive splitting, a splitting up, in the name of logic or reason or analysis, of our whole lives and indeed the whole of human experience into tiny and disconnected fragments. Alan Watts, in *The Book,* said that Western thinkers like to divide into parts an experience that is all one whole, and then get into endless tangles and arguments trying to decide which parts are cause and which effect. Whether other cultures do this or not, I don't know. We certainly do, and it does a great deal to kill the joy and meaning in our lives.

In Honolulu I had a vivid illustration of this. After a meeting with students at the university, I stood outside the building for a while in the warm and wet night air talking with a few of them. At one point a girl said that one of the things she did was to make candles, but that the only part of this that she really liked was taking the finished product out of the mold—everything else leading up to this final step seemed only time-wasting dull drudgery. In other words, Disagreeable Hard Work. I said, "But why do you divide up in your mind, in this strange way, your experience of making candles? I should think it would be more natural to see the experience as one whole, and that if you like making candles, everything that you have to do to make them is also part of the experience, and therefore entitled to share in the pleasure of it." It was hard for her to understand me, trained as she was, not only by her upbringing and schooling, full of Disagreeable Hard Work, but also by the habits of Western language and thought. She has spent too many of her not very many years learning to believe that all life is divided into pleasures and pains, that all pleasures must be paid for in pain, and that in general the pain must far outweigh the pleasure.

Trying to make my point clearer, I talked about my own experiences learning to play the cello. A few years ago, when I was only teaching part time, I worked very hard on the cello for two years or so, practicing or playing as much as six hours a day. I could not practice at home, so I worked out a deal with the Commonwealth School—I would coach their soccer team, and they would let me practice in the building, in the morning before classes and in the evening after the end of school. So, during those two years, it was my regular custom to get up at about four or four-thirty in the morning, get dressed, pack up cello, music, and music stand, walk to the school, open the building, find an empty room, set up stand and music, and start to practice. When the building began to fill up, around eight o'clock, I would pack up, returning again in the evening, if I was not playing with a group. My friends were baffled by this regime. They didn't know whether to call it work or play. It didn't seem to be work, because nobody was making me do it or paying me for it, and there was no other kind of reward or benefit I would get from it. At the same time, they couldn't think of it as play—how can anyone call "play" getting up at four and walking through dark winter streets just to practice for three hours. They explained everything with awed remarks about my will power. This missed the point. I suppose one might give the name "will power" to whatever it was that got me up at that hour on those winter mornings to do what nobody was compelling me to do. But this suggests that inside of me somewhere there were two people, one of them a lazy, good-for-nothing lying in the bed, enjoying the warmth and wanting to stay there, and the other a stern taskmaster saying, "Get up, you no-good bum, get out of bed and go practice that cello," and finally winning the argument because he was stronger. But there are not two people inside me, only one. The fact was that I loved to play the cello. I don't just mean that I wanted very much someday to play it well, though I wanted that too. I mean I loved playing it as I played it, a struggling beginner. I loved the scales, the exercises, the feeling of strength, skill, accuracy, quickness gradually coming into my hands and fingers, the sounds I could get from the instrument. Many other things in my life have given great pleasure, but nothing more than those hours of early morning practice. I wanted to play the cello and since the only time I could play it was early in the morning, that was when I had to get up in order to play it.

On some pitch black mornings, hearing what I knew was a cold wind howling outside, I might think, "Well, it is certainly comfortable in this bed, and maybe it wouldn't hurt if I just skipped practicing today." But my response to this was not to draw on something called will power, to insult or threaten myself, but to take a longer look at my life, to extend my vision, to think about the whole of my experience, to reconnect present and future, and quite specifically, to ask myself, "Do you like playing the cello or not? Would you like to play it better or not?" When I put the matter this way I could see that I enjoyed playing the cello more than I enjoyed staying in bed. So I got up. If, as sometimes happened or happens, I do stay in bed, not sleeping, not really thinking, but just not getting up, it is not because will power is weak but because I have temporarily become disconnected, so to speak, from the wholeness of my life. I am living in that Now that some people pursue so frantically, that gets harder to find the harder we look for it.

Splitting, splitting. Not long ago I heard another worried parent say, "But if you won't do the Disagreeable Hard Work of playing scales, you can't play Mozart." I hear this all the time—

mostly, I would add, from people who were made to play the scales but never got to the Mozart. The answer—aside from the important question of how much scale playing students should do in their work with music—is that for someone who really loves playing an instrument, scales are part of that playing. Like melting and mixing the wax to make candles. On those winter mornings I did not feel so much that I was getting out of bed and getting dressed and walking to school *so that* I could play the cello, as that they were all *part of* playing the cello. When I start to play, I take the cello out of its case and tune it—always a slow job for me. When the cello is tuned, I very often do what are called percussive exercises with the left hand, banging my fingers down on the fingerboard as hard as I can. And so from there into various other warm-ups, scales, position exercises, left-hand stretching exercises, bowing exercises, trills, and some of the music I may be working on, with a good deal of improvising thrown in. But all this *is* playing the cello. I don't divide my practice into pleasant and unpleasant parts, and then use "will power" to make myself do the unpleasant ones so that I may later have the fun of doing the pleasant. It is all one.

Music teachers, but perhaps not more than others, tend to be very much under the spell of Disagreeable Hard Work—perhaps because that is the way they were taught. When I was playing in an amateur string orchestra, a lady came in for a few evenings to join our small cello section. It was soon clear that she was even less skillful than I was. There was something very stiff, tight, and anxious about her playing. She didn't seem to like her cello. In a moment between pieces, as music students often do, we asked each other about our teachers. She had been studying for five years with a player in the Boston Symphony. This was surprising; she was so far from being at home with her instrument. I asked, "What music does he have you working on, what pieces are you playing?" She said, "Oh, he doesn't let me play any music, just various scales and exercises. Every now and then he says, 'Perhaps I will let you play a little Vivaldi,' but he always changes his mind." Her playing showed it. Such teachers spoil music for too many students. Fortunately, not all are like that, and probably less all the time, under the influence of such spectacularly successful teachers as the Japanese violinist Suzuki, who from the beginning has his young pupils, three and four years old, working on real music, which in only a year or two they learn to play with astonishing skill. My own cello teacher, Harold Sproul, had the same understanding; long before I was "ready" to play them, he started me playing movements from the Bach Suites. In trying to play this lovely music I found there were other things I needed to learn, scales in different keys, position exercises, and so forth. But these exercises, instead of being *a getting ready* to play the Bach Suites, were part of playing them— all the difference in the world. A very talented friend of mine, soon after he began studying the cello with one of the best teachers in New York, asked him what exercises he should play. "Why play exercises?" said the teacher, "Play music! When you meet a passage that is hard, practice till you can play it beautifully, make that your exercise." Wise advice. I know right now a child of eleven who has been playing the piano with a very fine teacher. I have never heard the child play a scale. She has a lot of real piano music, and plays that. She does very little of what most people would call "practicing." She plays as the spirit moves her, for perhaps ten or fifteen minutes at a time, and entirely for her own pleasure. Certainly during the first year of her playing, she spent less time at the piano than most children who are compelled to practice. But as she has become more skillful, and able to play better music, she has enjoyed playing more and more, and so spends more and more time on it, and this in the midst of a life that is by no means dedicated to music, but has a great many other things in it. The progress she has made in a short time is astonishing, all the more so in a family in which she is the only playing musician. She is not practicing to get ready someday to play the piano. She is playing it.

Anyone who has known many children growing up knows that many of them, even though they may not have much time of their own after school and schoolwork, throw themselves with great energy and discipline into very demanding kinds of work, often much harder than the work they can't or don't do in school, often involving the very "skills" that the school says they don't have and can't learn. Several come to mind. There was a boy who, when in the third or fourth grade, became interested in baking, and came home from school, where he was failing Arithmetic, to bake very complicated recipes from an advanced and difficult cookbook, recipes which he had to divide, since he was baking only for himself and his mother, and not for the six or eight persons specified. There was a girl, a very unsuccessful student, who in her own time took up printing, which requires much mathematical calculation, and became so good at it that before long, out of her bedroom, she was running a commercial printing business from which she earned enough to pay for new equipment, with money left over. There was another girl, a phenomenally unsuccessful student, who became an expert photographer, developing, enlarging, printing her own work, all of which requires much measurement and calculation.

I wrote once about a boy declared by school to be a second-grade-level reader who was reading *Why We Can't Wait,* by Martin Luther King, Jr. Some of my students at Berkeley, teaching ghetto kids in the Oakland schools, told me that there was an epidemic of out-of-school reading among all the high school nonreaders, set off by a sudden supply of really far-out pornographic paperbound books. Within the last year, a man who has spent most of his working life teaching in the low-income high schools of New York City told me that though he had known hundreds of kids who had been officially tested and certified by the school as being unable to read, he doubted if he had ever known even as many as a dozen who really couldn't read. The only way to know with any certainty anything about what a kid knows or likes or does is to know something about his real life outside the school.

One more word on will power. Perhaps an exaggerated and ridiculous example will show what's wrong with always dividing experience into Cause and Effect, Ends and Means, Skills and Acts, Getting Ready and Doing It. Suppose I am thirsty. Do I tell myself that I must take the trouble, use will power to force myself to go to the cupboard, then open the door, then take out a glass, then go to the sink, then turn on the faucet, then fill the glass, then raise the glass to my lips—go through all this Disagreeable Hard Work so that I may *then* have the pleasure of feeling the cool water in my mouth and going down my throat? It's ridiculous. If I am thirsty, and if there is anything to drink, I take a drink, which means I *do all the things I need to do to get the drink*. I don't have to use will power to do them; they are part of the act of getting the drink. Does it take will power to get in bed when we're sleepy? Babies have more sense than we do about this. No one could explain to a baby, even if he had the words, what we mean by will power. Babies live their lives all of a piece. Imagine a baby on the floor, playing or exploring. He sees a toy or ball or bear on the floor at the other side of the room, and the feeling or thought comes to him that he wants to play with it. Does there then arise a little conflict inside the baby over whether it is worth the trouble to crawl all the way across the room just so he may then seize the toy? No. To want the toy is to want to do whatever must be done to get it. Instantly the baby sets out across the floor, probably already feeling some of the excitement and pleasure of playing with the toy. In his mind, he is playing with it. His play with it *begins* when he thinks of playing with it and begins to move toward it.

No one has said this any better than Robert Frost, in the poem, "Two Tramps in Mud Time." The story of the poem is this. Frost is outside on one of the first days of spring, before there are leaves on trees, but when the snow and frozen ground are first starting to thaw and turn to mud. He is splitting wood and enjoying it, liking the feel of his muscles working, the action of the ax, the clean falling apart of the wood itself, and all the while letting off a little steam.

> *The blows that a life of central-control*
> *Spares to strike for the common good,*
> *That day, giving a loose to my soul,*
> *I spent on the unresisting wood.*

In the midst of his work he sees two tramps watching. They say nothing, but he knows what they want. They want to split his wood for pay. This creates a tension. Frost is enjoying splitting the wood, doesn't want to give it up. At the same time, he knows that the men need the work, and asks himself what right he has to do for pleasure what other men need to do for gain. How he resolves this we never find out. Instead, he brings the story, his thoughts, and his lesson—if only we could learn it!—together in the last verse:

> But yield who will to their separation,
> My object in living is to unite
> My avocation and my vocation,
> As my two eyes are one in sight.
> Only when love and need are one,
> And the work is play for mortal stakes,
> Is the deed ever truly done,
> For Heaven and the future's sakes.

8
Beyond Schooling

The summer after my first year of teaching at The Colorado Rocky Mountain School, we ran a work camp. One of our tasks was to build a small classroom building for the coming year. The building had been designed by a teacher who was an experienced carpenter, but much of the work on it was done by me and another faculty member, equally unskilled. By the end of the session the building was finished. It had two classrooms, well lighted by windows just under the ceiling. Each room was large enough for teacher, tables and chairs, and about a dozen students. It was designed so that it could be split easily into its two halves, which could then be towed or skidded to wherever on the campus it might be needed. During the winter months, which in the mountains were sometimes very cold, it was heated, and adequately, by a small wooden stove, which it was the morning job of some student to feed and light. The building worked very well for a number of years; I taught one of my own classes in it.

The materials cost of the building was less than $2,000, the labor cost less than half of that. Not many years later, when I first heard that on the whole it costs the public schools over $50,000 to build each new classroom (the figure is surely much higher now), I began to wonder about the cost of conventional school buildings. Indeed one of the things that the founders of this school, John and Anne Holden, hoped to show was that if people would design their school buildings more modestly and make it possible for students, teachers, and citizens to do much of the building work themselves, we might get a lot of needed school facilities at much less cost. For many reasons this lesson has not taken hold. But in some back corner of my mind it must have started me questioning the whole institution of schooling.

A few years later a very close friend of mine, then teaching at Harvard, asked me as he often did to join him for dinner with some young Africans who were studying in universities in Boston and Cambridge. I was then teaching fifth grade and among my friends had already begun to talk and write critically about schools and schooling. At some point in the evening—I forgot what led up to it—one of the Africans asked me a most surprising question: "If I were to take back to my country a message about education, what do you think it should be?" I reeled back. All of my thinking had been about what to do within the four walls of a classroom. I had never thought about education for a whole nation, least of all an African nation about which I knew nothing. I said I had no answer. We went on to talk about many other things.

But his question must have started a thought working, for many hours later, when we were driving our guests to where they lived, some words came up into consciousness. I said, "Remember that question you asked earlier about the message on education? Well, I think perhaps I have an answer for it." He said, "Oh, what is it?" I said, "My message to your countrymen might be that you don't have to have school buildings in order to have schools and you don't have to have schools in order to have education." I had a faint vision of people talking and learning under roofs of palm leaves, or under trees—anywhere, everywhere. He thanked me for the message. If he did take it home, certainly no one paid any attention to it.

Some years later, after my first book had come out and I was beginning to talk to meetings about education, people asked me now and then what I thought an ideal system of schooling might be. In the long run, I said, an ideal system would probably be to have no schools at all. Explaining further, I used to say:

> Imagine that I am traveling into the future in a time capsule, and that I come to rest, five hundred years from now, in an intelligent, humane, and life-enhancing civilization. One of the people who lives there comes to meet me, to guide me, and to explain his society. At some point, after he has shown me where people live, work, play, I ask him,
> "But where are your schools?"
> "Schools? What are schools?" he replies.
> "Schools are places where people go to learn things."
> "I do not understand," he says, "People learn things everywhere, in all places."

"I know that," I say, "But a school is a special place where there are special people who teach you things, help you learn things."

"I am sorry, but I still do not understand. Everyone helps other people learn things. Anyone who knows something or can do something can help someone else who wants to learn more about it. Why should there be special people to do this?"

And try as I will, I cannot make clear to him why we think that education should be, must be, separate from the rest of life.

This was my first vision of a society without schooling. Since then I have come to feel that the deschooled society, a society in which learning is not separated from but joined to, part of the rest of life, is not a luxury for which we can wait hundreds of years, but something toward which we must move and work as quickly as possible.

Within the last century and mostly the last half-century, almost all people, in almost all parts of the world, have come to believe that education, planned and purposeful learning (as opposed to the learning I do when I stub my toe or accidentally touch something hot) is, ought to be, and must be separate from the rest of life; that it should take place in a special place, where on the whole nothing else takes place; that it should happen at special times, special hours of the day or evening, when nothing else happens; and that it should require the work of two special classes of people, the one students, the other teachers, who for the most part have no other work. Almost all societies and people now *define* education or learning as schooling, and measure people's intelligence, competence, job-worthiness, and capacity for further learning almost entirely in terms of the length in years and the expense of the schooling they have already received. This is a most serious mistake. When we do this, we put ourselves into an impossible position, face contradictions that we cannot resolve, create problems that we cannot solve or even live with.

For one thing, we make education so expensive that no country, not even the richest, can provide or even come close to providing for its citizens as much education as they want and think they ought to have. In 1969 the United States spent about 36 billion dollars on elementary and secondary schooling; in 1971, over 40 billion. The resources bought with this money were, as we know, very unequally distributed among all children. What would it cost to provide for all children the kinds of school resources—buildings, grounds, classrooms, books, equipment, laboratories, teachers, special people, athletic and recreational facilities—now available to the most favored 20 percent. Two independent sources quoted by Illich estimated that to do this in 1969 we would have had to spend about 80 billion dollars. The projections for 1975 were that we would spend about 45 billion dollars (which already looks low), but that to provide for all children the resources available to some (and that more and more are beginning to demand as a matter of right) we would have to spend roughly 105 billion dollars. These figures are guesses, of course. If anything, they seem to me quite conservative. Much of the facilities of rich suburban schools could hardly be provided to the many children who go to school in cities, at any price. For one thing, there is simply not the space. But space is one of the most important assets of the suburban schools. It gives the students room to get away from each other, if they have to; room for at least some occasional quiet or privacy; room, when that is needed, to burn off steam—all things that city kids desperately need and never get.

These figures are for elementary and secondary schooling only. They leave out so-called higher education (which we might better call longer), which is much more expensive per pupil and for which the demand is rising much more rapidly. What might it cost to provide for all young people, not only at the elementary and secondary but also at the college level the school resources now available to some? What must we do to the estimates we already have to take college into account? For a first rough guess, we would have to double them—the total schooling bill for 1969 is about double the elementary and secondary bill. But this is obviously much too low. The cost of college, now equal to the cost of elementary and secondary schooling, is only for those students now in college, only a small part of those who would go if they could. If we tried to provide for all what only a few now get, our college bill might very well double or triple our elementary and secondary bill. Even in the most factorylike state universities the cost of schooling per pupil seems to be three or more times what it

is in most elementary or secondary schools. The disproportion between what the most favored and the least favored students get is
far greater at the college age level than at earlier levels. To provide
for all young people at all levels through college the kind of schooling resources that 20 percent now get we might well have to spend
as much as 250–300 billion dollars per year. That is about what
true equality of educational opportunity for all young people, a
phrase we all like, would probably cost us.

Clearly, we are not going to spend on schooling between a
quarter and almost a third of our gross national product. We now
spend about 8 percent, and there are many signs that this is about
the limit of what people are willing to pay. Yet this has in no way
cut down the demand for schooling, which every day becomes
more insistent. We have in short created about 250 billion dollars
worth or so of the most urgent demand for a product of which we
are not likely to supply more than a third that much. This puts
school people in the position of the architect who, on asking his
client what sort of house he wanted, was told that he wanted a nice
little house with lots of nice big rooms in it. All over the country
voters are refusing to meet school budgets. Meanwhile, they criti-
cize the schools for "lowering standards," or for cutting out the
programs they refused to pay for.

At the same time, we have set off an intense struggle between
classes and social groups for these scarce educational resources.
People's concern with what they call "quality education," meaning
"I want my kid to stay ahead of your kid," has probably made more
difficult the already painful problem of racial tension, prejudice,
segregation, and hatred. At least some people might have been
willing and might still be willing to have minority or low-income
people live near them if they did not feel that this would somehow
hurt the life chances of their own children. This struggle among
social groups for their fair share of these scarce educational resources is today one of our most bitter and divisive social problems. And within our present definition of schooling there is no
way to solve it.

Furthermore, nobody concerned with "education" believes
even now that the resources available to even the most favored students is anywhere near high enough. The people who direct, teach
in, and work for our "quality schools" are deeply dissatisfied with

what they have. Our best, most prestigious and expensive schools, colleges, and universities all sing the same tale of woe. Faculty salaries are too low; classrooms, lecture halls, and dormitories are too crowded; parking space is short; new laboratories and equipment are badly needed; there are not enough social amenities; and so forth. At the high school level we hear again and again that classes are too big, and should be cut down by a third, or more; that teachers are not paid nearly enough. One "expert" commission recently recommended that all elementary school classes be limited to 20 and high school classes to 16. If we were to ask people at the "quality" level of education, in the "best" schools or colleges, how much they would have to increase their present budgets in order for them to be fully satisfied with what they were offering, we might well hear talk of 20, 30, or even 50 percent. What it would cost to provide schooling of *that* quality for all children? And in all of this, we have talked only of schooling for the young. What about all the people who are grown up, have had all their schooling? What would it cost us to make the words "lifelong learning" a reality? And we must indeed make it so; our country and the world are changing very rapidly, and are beset with serious problems, and we simply cannot survive if our citizens remain as ignorant of these changes and problems as most of them now are. What would it cost to provide continuous, lifelong (if part-time) schooling for all adults? Twice again the estimate we have? The mind reels.

As if costs were not high enough, everything that is done or suggested or urged to "raise educational standards" requires spending more money. Indeed, all the criteria by which one institution is judged to be better than another come down in the long run to a matter of money. It has more books in its library, or better facilities, or bigger more up-to-date laboratories, or a better faculty, which means that by paying them more it is able to hire them away from other places. When a new president takes over a university with a strong mandate to improve its quality and reputation, one of his first tasks is to try to hire prominent faculty away from other universities. *Life* magazine some years ago ran an article about the new head of a state university who said quite frankly that his first and most important job was to get out into the professor markets and hire away from other universities what he called "stars." Shades of pro-football and show biz! Though schooling is already our most expensive and least productive industry, everything in our present understanding and definition of education tends to bid the price of it higher and higher. Nobody talks about how we may have more learning for *less* money, and most of those who do talk about spending less are roundly attacked from all sides for wanting to lower "quality."

Even if by some miracle we were to spend the 250 or 300 billion dollars a year needed to give all young people the schooling now available to some—even then it would not be enough. Most young people (and their parents) believe that their life possibilities, their chances of getting interesting work, power, prestige, money, success however measured, depend more than anything else on the length and quality, i.e. expensiveness of their schooling. This has set off what can only be called the competitive consumption of schooling. My being able to get ahead of you in the world depends on my having been able to consume more schooling than you, or if we consumed the same amount, a schooling more expensive than yours. This has strange consequences.

The competitive consumption of automobiles has produced absurdities enough, masses of expensive, fragile, short-lived, swollen, overstyled and dangerously overpowered dream machines. But there is at least some limit to this particular foolishness. If a man owns a car, and a neighbor down the street gets a new car, longer, shinier, more powerful and more expensive than his, his own car does not die of jealousy in the driveway. Whatever transportation he had before, he still has—at least until the car wears out. But this is not true of schooling. If someone buys a certain amount of schooling, spends so many years of life and so much money to get a certain kind of school ticket to put him ahead of everyone with a lesser ticket, every time somebody is able to buy more or fancier schooling than he, get a better school ticket than his, or even one just like his, the value of his school ticket goes down. If everyone gets a school ticket like his, his will become worthless.

Signs are posted in major cities, where poor kids can see them. They say, "Finish high school—get a good job." As the kids very well know, there are not good jobs around right now for all the people who have already finished high school—and even college and graduate school. Also, the cash-in value, the job value, of any given school ticket is much less for a poor kid than for a rich one. Still, even for a poor kid, a high school diploma today has some cash value. Anyone with a diploma is slightly better off in the job market than anyone without it. Or so we have always been told. A report in the November 6, 1971 *New York Times* now suggests strongly that even that may not be so. Under the heading, "Study Finds School Dropouts Do Not Appear to Suffer," the story reads, in part:

> A four year study of what happens to high school dropouts has led a University of Michigan social scientist to a conclusion . . . that dropouts do not appear to suffer financially or emotionally by quitting high school before graduation. . . .
>
> Dr. Jerald G. Bachman of the University of Michigan's Institute for Social Research . . . and his colleagues selected a sample of 2,213 10th grade boys in high schools across the country . . . chosen to be representative of all 10th grade boys in the United States.
>
> The students were given tests to measure their personal family and social situations. . . . Similar tests were given at yearly intervals to assess any changes. The last test was given one year after graduation for the class of 1969, by which time some had quit and sought jobs and others had stayed to get diplomas and then look for work. Those who went on to college were not included in the comparisons, Dr. Bachman said. There is no question that college graduates have greater earning potential than high school graduates. . . . The stay in school campaign does not urge students to go on to college. . . . Rather it argues that simply staying in long enough to get a high school diploma will improve the young person's life.

Yes, but someone arguing against this study might make the point that the school-leaver, even if he gets as good a job as the one who graduates, by leaving school gives up a shot at an even better job that a college diploma might have given him.

"Our findings simply do not support this campaign," Dr. Bachman said. . . . "The difficulties experienced by the dropouts we studied . . . were already present or predictable by the start of the 10th grade and there is little evidence that dropping out made matters worse."

In one area, dropping out even appears to have had a good effect. Once they were out of school, the dropouts' self-esteem increased, coming closer to the higher self-esteem of the graduate than when both groups were still in school.

At the end of the study, 71% of the dropouts had full-time jobs as compared with 87% of the graduates. Dr. Bachman said that the difference could be accounted for by the dropouts' preexisting problems more than by the fact of having dropped out. [My note: I suspect this is true, but I doubt that it can be proved, by this or any other study.]

Comparing the employed members of each group, the study found the weekly income levels to be nearly identical . . . the average weekly income of the dropouts was $118 while for the graduates, it was $112.

I don't think that this study *proves,* though it strongly suggests, that having a high school diploma brings no advantage in the job market. Let's just say that *if* it is true that someone with a diploma has an advantage, however slight, over someone without it, it is true only because some are still without it. Suppose all kids who read the "Finish high school" sign believe it. Suppose we persuade all young people to get that diploma. What will it be worth then? It will be worth just the same as the elementary school diploma that everybody now has—nothing. We will then have to paste up new signs over the old—"Go to College—Get a Good Job." And if by spending 250 or 300 billion dollars a year we should make it possible for all young people to get a four-year college degree, that in turn would be worth no more than the earlier diplomas, and we would have to start again, piling new degrees on top of the old. More than once I have heard or read talk among academic people to the effect that we need a degree beyond the Ph.D. since so many people now have the Ph.D. that it no longer "means anything."

Clearly there is no end to this. Everything now works to push up the price of education, for learners as well as institutions of learning, because the advantage always goes to the person who has learned whatever it is he knows in the most expensive way possible. Suppose three people are in the market for a certain job. All have about equal knowledge and skill. One has learned what he knows without school, by himself, in libraries, from friends. The next has learned what he knows in school, but a cheap school—night school, or community college, or low ranked state university. The third has learned what he knows in an expensive and prestigious private or state university. Which one will employers hire? Other things being equal, they will pick the third. Many holders of cheap college degrees are not finding jobs right now. Students understand this very well. When they apply for college their first choice is always the fanciest they think they have a chance of getting into. It is time to wind down this spiral, to find ways to give the advantage or at least an even break to institutions that can make knowledge available, and learners who can learn it, as cheaply instead of as expensively as possible.

When we define education as schooling, and put public educational resources into schools, the children who benefit most are the children who can stay in school the longest. These are, necessarily and in all but a few cases, the children of the well-to-do. (See *Deschooling Society* and *School Is Dead* in Appendix). Tax-supported schools, and even more so tax-exempted colleges and universities, simply create a situation in which the poor have to pay a large share of the cost of schooling the children of the rich. In poor countries, the children of the well-to-do have hundreds of times as much public money, tax money, invested in their schooling as the average child. In the United States the disproportion is not so great; holders of college and graduate degrees, almost all of them from the middle class, have had roughly ten times as much public money invested in their schooling as the average low-income child. Now the richer child will naturally have more of Daddy's money invested in his schooling than the poor child. But that he should also have much more tax money invested in it, money raised in considerable part from poor people, is most unjust. It is also an injustice that we cannot remedy unless and until we give educational resources to learners instead of to schools, and beyond that let these learners decide whether they want to do their learning in school or in some other place and way. For the rich, for obvious reasons, will always be able to outlast the poor in school. And schools, even if their intentions are good, and in spite of anything poor people may do to get control of them, are by their very nature, structure, style, and purpose bound to be middle-class institutions favoring middle-class kids. It is interesting, but not at all surprising, to read that even in Russia, in spite of laws that give university preference to the children of farmers and workers, most students in the universities are the children of university graduates. This has nothing to do with intelligence or ability. School is a very special world, and the school game a very special game, not like anything else, and people who like that world and play that game well will probably have children who do the same, just as the children of musicians are likely to be musicians, or the children of circus people are likely to work in circuses. Only in China, in Tanzania, and (I was told in Norway by a newspaperwoman who had been there) in Albania do the leaders of the state seem determined to prevent the schools from producing a self-perpetuating elite. Even they may not be able to prevent it.

There are three other consequences of our defining education as schooling that I must discuss together, since they are related, reinforce each other, feed on each other. One is that people come to believe, even after they have left school, that learning must mean schooling, something that must be done and can only be done in a school. They think that if they want to learn something they have to go to some place called a school and there get some person called a teacher to teach it to them. Many times people have said to me that they felt their brains were getting rusty, that they hadn't learned anything in a long time, and that they needed to go to some school or university and sign up for a course, as if there were no way to learn on their own. People who were good at school may look forward to this. Most people feel, with reason, that they haven't the time or money to be a full-time student again. Beyond that, most of them learned in school, not just that school is the only place you can learn anything, but that they couldn't learn much even there. They may believe in some abstract way that education is important, and may want all of it they can get for their children. For themselves, the experience was so unpleasant that they want to put it behind them. Years ago, I wrote that many people in their worst nightmares find themselves once again a student in school. Since then many others have said the same.

Many mature and competent adults tell me that to this day they feel uneasy in a school building, as if they were guilty of some crime, but didn't know what. Beyond that, many probably think something like this: "The purpose of education is to get ahead in life. My schooling is over, I did what I did, and it brought me to where I am. I can't rewrite the past, live my life over; it's too late to change all this. I had my chance. My life is decided, and I might as well get used to it and make the best of it. What's the point of talking about going to school to learn more? What difference could it make?"

Another consequence of defining education as schooling is that as we put more and more of our educational resources into schools, we have less and less left over for those institutions that are truly open and educative and in which more and more people might learn for themselves. One example would be the public libraries. In any community, compare the local public library, which serves everybody, with the local public high schools, which serve only a four-year age span. In most places the schools are probably twenty to fifty times as large as the library and spend twenty to fifty times as much money. It is this kind of imbalance that we ought to change. Whatever money we put into institutions should go to those that are truly open, which anyone can use, without preconditions, and for his own purposes. Such institutions are what Illich, Reimer, and others call networks, and the public library is only one very special and perhaps rather conventional example of these. Still it is worth looking at. My home city has quite a good public library system. It is just now building a large extension to the main building; perhaps this will soon change some of the figures I give here. But as of this moment, and for the 14 years I have lived here, there are in the main library only three places at which a citizen can sit and listen to records—whether music, language, or whatever. In the main library there are no tape recorders, either for open reels or cassettes, on which a citizen might play a tape that he had bought or that someone had sent him—perhaps of a meeting, perhaps of people speaking another language. To teachers of foreign languages I've sometimes suggested that they might exchange tapes with students in the country of the language. Students in school can of course usually find school tape recorders on which they could play back such tapes. But for an adult in most cities there are no such recorders, far less ones he might use to make his own tapes.

Some elementary schools I have seen, serving not more than four or five hundred students for a few hours each day, have more record listening facilities than our whole library system. In the schools and colleges of this city there are dozens of language labs, with hundreds of tape recorders. All of these are for people called "students." If a citizen, unable to find a public tape recorder, were to go to one of these schools and ask to use their equipment, even when it was not in use, he would almost certainly be refused. Indeed, in this respect we are moving rapidly in the wrong direction. A young woman in her early twenties told me recently that it is becoming more difficult for anybody to make use of any of the resources of the colleges and universities here in Boston, even when they offer to sign up and pay for courses, unless they are enrolled in a full degree program. The president of Boston University announced not long ago that henceforth all but a very few university functions would be closed to the public.

Though the public library has motion picture films to lend, they have no facilities with which one might show his own films. Thus most of their films go to schools (or perhaps film clubs—a good small network) that already have projectors. Nor do they have still or motion picture cameras with which people might make their own films. But anyone learning a sport, or perhaps many other skills, can be very much helped by watching film loops of experts. Wolverine Sports Supply in Ann Arbor, Michigan, used to advertise such films in their catalog. Other makers of sporting goods, or publishers of sport materials, surely produce them. Certain kinds of musical technique, i.e. of bowing and fingering stringed instruments, might well be shown on such loops.

It would surely encourage many people to try to play an instrument, which they might like to do, if there were a place where they could borrow instruments, and even more important, a place to practice. Most practice rooms are in music schools; people not enrolled can't use them, and few can practice at home. This effectively rules out music for most people—including many children that, at some expense, we taught to play instruments in schools. And people learning an instrument would be helped even more if in the practice room there was a tape recorder (preferably cassette) on which they would record their own playing, and compare it with a recording of the same piece played by their teacher, or some other skilled musician. There is probably more audio-visual equipment locked up and unused in many high schools than is available to all the citizens of Boston.

The same could be said of many different kinds of art and craft equipment. In the last year or two, with no instruction, and by watching a few other people, a friend of mine taught herself a great deal about pottery and made some pots of her own. Many people might be tempted to experiment a bit with clay, get the feel of it, perhaps try to make something on a wheel. But all the necessary equipment is locked up in schools. The only way one can get access to it is signing up somewhere as a "student," which means in turn that some "teacher" will tell how he may use the material, what he may do with it, and so forth. In short, he will have to submit to instruction. For people who want to teach themselves things there are few resources available. The more resources we put into schools, the fewer are likely to be available outside of them. To some extent, this is already happening. Within the past few years many public libraries have had to cut down the hours during which they were open. Many of them are now closed at the only times when working people could use them.

An editorial in the September, 1971, issue of *High Fidelity* tells us:

> As of this coming January 1, according to a New York Public Library announcement, scholars, teachers, students, writers, and researchers from all over the world (and just simply the curious)

Note in passing this faintly contemptuous way of referring to the person educating himself.

> will find the NYPL's research doors closed. From that date, and barring a miracle, there will be no public library access to the music library, the Rodgers and Hammerstein Archives of Recorded Sound, the theater library, or the dance library—all now housed in Lincoln Center—or the science and technology libraries in the main building at Forty-second Street and Fifth

Avenue. (The main circulating and branch libraries will remain open.)

. . . Frank Cambell, chief of the Music Division, wrote to us that "The Research Libraries draw their support from the major endowments, i.e. The Astor, Lenox and Tilden Foundations." (It is a popular misconception that the Library is supported entirely by the City of New York.) The endowment's income is now down to little more than $3 million annually. New York City provides some $600,000 a year for maintenance of the central building. New York State has been appropriating $2.8 million, and fund raising generally brings in another $800,000. This still leaves the NYPL some $2 million short each year.

Not many years ago, soon after Lincoln Center was finished, these arts and music facilities were first opened. We were told proudly that nothing to match these resources could be found anywhere else in the world. It was good that they should have been put into the public library and made available to everyone, even "just simply the curious," instead of being buried for the benefit of a few professors and students in some university where "the curious" are not allowed to go. And it will be a big step backward if these facilities are closed.

Meanwhile, might ways not be found, without closing such doors, to run the library on something less than 9 million dollars or so a year? Does everything that is done there have to be done? Or is it done because those are the kinds of things libraries have always done? Do all books in a library, some of them surely of fleeting value, have to have the same elaborate files kept on them? Why not a paperback division in which, having borrowed one book, all you would have to do to get a new one would be to turn in an old one? The library here almost certainly spends quite a bit of money to keep for its recordings elaborate cross-indexed files that few borrowers ever look at and that in any event are not and cannot be kept up to date. Perhaps public educational facilities such as libraries might be more useful and less expensive if they could learn to run less elaborately than the schools. Why keep files, as if for eternity, on records most of which are so roughly handled that their useful shelf life is hardly ever ten years, often less than five.

After I had spoken to an evening meeting at a large university not long ago, some students invited me to talk further with them at the Student Union, a handsome if rather heavy modern building. In the large main room, below the entrance level, many students were sitting at tables, some eating and drinking, some talking, reading or studying, some thinking. In one part of the room was a cafeteria, in another part a jukebox. On the upper floor were many smaller and quieter rooms that could be used for many different purposes. We went to one of these for our talk. At the large meeting we had been talking about learning resources other than schools, and as we settled down in our comfortable lounge, I pointed out that this building and this room were perfect examples of the ways in which schools have swallowed up not only the learning resources of society, but also much of what we might think of as the ordinary amenities. In no city that I know of is there an Everyman's Union, a place to gather, sit, talk, think, meet one's friends. One can use the library to read, but not to talk, or do anything else. There are, of course, restaurants and bars, but these are often crowded and noisy. People keep after you—reasonably enough—to buy food and drink and to make sure that when you have finished you either order more or leave. There are sometimes parks, but they have few places to sit, and these are not arranged to make conversation easy, and are rarely under any kind of shelter. If you sit for long on the grass, chances are a policeman will come and tell you to get off. There are simply *no* public gathering and meeting spaces. Rich people, at least some of them, have clubs; conventions and business meetings use hotels; but for the ordinary citizen there is nothing.

In this connection, a few paragraphs of an article I wrote in 1969 about the University of California at Berkeley may be to the point:

> Not long after arriving at Berkeley I was invited by a new friend on the faculty to go with him to a noon performance in the university music theater of Purcell's *Dido and Aeneas*. This was produced, played, sung, and danced entirely by the students. It was a beautiful production, up to the highest professional standards, imaginatively and wittily done. I left the hall with my heart swelling and my feet scarcely touching the ground. I looked about

the campus, which, particularly in that section, is very beautiful, with rolling grass and lovely trees, and I had a vision of what that university might be. Seeing that vision, like my friends from the Free Speech Movement, I fell in love with it, and at the same time realized how very far from its promise and potential the university had fallen. I looked about the buildings and the campus and thought what an extraordinary gathering there was here of human knowledge, skill, and talent. How much the university might be, how close it was even now to being a kind of distillation of everything we mean by civilization in its best sense, a collection of so much of the finest things that men have thought and done. I thought what a lovely thing it would be if we could have, here and in many places, such a gathering of man's finest works, and people who knew them and understood them and loved them and could use them, a pool of wealth for everyone to dip into as they needed or wanted. How lovely it was too to walk in broad spaces between buildings which if not always handsome were at least not covered with neon signs and constant appeals to people's greed, envy, and fear. I thought of the streets of downtown Berkeley itself and of the people who lived there—and I often thought of this when the police were on campus—and reflected how seldom if ever they must have had the opportunity even of walking in so spacious and so gracious a place. Why shouldn't a university be like a park, but a park of the mind and hands and spirit as well as a park in space? Why not a place to stretch and refresh the soul as well as the legs?

And with this thought I became painfully aware, then and for the rest of my stay, of the signs sprinkled all over the campus—THIS IS THE PROPERTY OF THE REGENTS AND THE STATE OF CALIFORNIA—something full of talk about trespassers being prosecuted and so forth. I thought to myself, why should an institution supported by public funds not be open to the public? By what right is it run like a private club?

Later I visited the new campus of the University of California at Santa Cruz, a lovely group of small and intimate colleges in the midst of pine-covered hills. I found myself thinking, wouldn't it be nice if there were places like this, where you could perhaps pay (but not too much) to go, for a day or two, or a week, or longer if you wanted, and along with enjoying the air and the view, have access to a good library, a chance to read a book you had always meant to read; a chance to hear and take part in discussions of matters of interest to you; a chance to hear or perhaps sing or play some music; a chance to use some of your talents and skills, or to learn new ones. After all there are hotels and resorts (all too expensive for most people) to which you can go to swim, play tennis or golf, fish, water ski, gamble, dance, or listen to famous night club and TV entertainers. But where was the hotel at which one could make or learn something? Or to turn it around, where was the university at which one could in the best sense be a student not for four years, but just for a week or for a weekend?

There has been much talk about physical fitness, and about the poor physical condition of most adults and many children and about the need for regular exercise. But where are people to do all this? We very much need more public athletic facilities—tennis, squash, handball, basketball courts; softball and soccer fields; running and bicycling tracks and paths; gyms; swimming pools, and so forth. A number of British cities much smaller than Boston have very large public swimming pools, used by all ages of people day and night. Traveling out of London by train in almost any direction, one can see dozens of athletic fields, used by all kinds of amateur groups. Many of the roads in Denmark, in country, suburb and even city, have at their side a narrow path for bicycles. It is encouraging to read that Oregon has decided or voted to spend some money to set up a network of bicycle paths in various parts of the state. Other cities would be wise to begin to develop a network of bicycle routes, if only by painting certain lanes and saying that in these lanes bicycles had the right of way. (And a good thief-proof bicycle rack would help too.) We need many more small parks and playgrounds where children of many ages can go and play with minimal or no adult supervision. The British, the Scandinavians, and the Japanese all have things to teach us here. We need to design environments that will be safe, and in which children will have such a variety of challenges, opportunities, and stimuli that they will be active and happy—and so, learning.

Many of the activities that made or might make our towns and cities into true communities either never got started or have all but disappeared because among other reasons there is no place for such things to happen. For example, a number of years ago, when I was traveling less, I used to play the cello in a small amateur orchestra run by a musician friend of mine. There were perhaps twelve or fifteen of us in the orchestra. We met every week or so, and once gave a small semipublic concert. The leader had worked hard to get the orchestra together, and we all enjoyed very much playing in it. But after a while we had to disband. Why? Simply because in this Boston-Cambridge area, with all its enormous educational facilities, we could find no place to play. We had been renting a room at a conservatory of music, but they needed the room for a group led by one of their own faculty and kicked us out. There was no other place; at least, we could find none. How many other group activities may have ended, or never even begun, for just this reason?

More than once, worried small-college teachers or administration officials, pinched hard by rising costs, ask me what I think the future of such small colleges might be. I say that if they define themselves as places where a student comes to get a four- (or more) year college degree or job ticket, I doubt very much whether they can compete for long with the rich private colleges or the big state universities. But I suggest that they may be able to provide different kinds of resources and services to a quite different and much larger group of people. To a dean of a college near New York City I said, "There may not be many students who want to come here for four years to get degrees. But there might be hundreds of thousands of people within a few miles of here who have a great many things that they might like to do or try to do if there was only a place where they could do it. Perhaps your business will be to provide such a resource."

To this one might reply that the reason so little in the way of learning equipment and facilities, what Ivan Illich calls tools, is available to the general public is that there is so little demand for them. Perhaps so. But how do we know there is so little demand? How can we measure the demand for what does not exist and what most people have not imagined? If people did want such things, of whom would they demand them? What chance is there that their demand would be heard, particularly since at first they might only be a small minority? The bad consequences of schooling feed on and reinforce each other. As people believe more and more in schooling, that learning is something that must and can only take place in a school, and that it is a painful business they are no good at, they act more and more in ways that make it harder and harder to learn anywhere but in school. Thus, as more people learn in school to dislike reading, fewer buy books from bookstores and borrow them from libraries. The bookstores close and the libraries cut back their services, and so we have fewer places in which people outside of school can have ready access to books. This is just one of the ways in which too much schooling works against education.

Another question: if deschooling may bring us many new learning resources, might it not cost us some good ones we now have? The question forced itself on me not long ago when, first in London, and not long after in a country village near Paris, I spent a day each in two of the most delightful primary schools I've ever seen. The London school was somewhat bigger, in a pleasant but not wealthy suburban neighborhood. The French school (my friends there assured me that there were very few like it in France) was in a tiny village. The English school was larger, with seven or eight teachers; the French school only had two. Each, in its own way, was an excellent example of the kind of open or alternative schools I have been writing about. I have rarely been in schools where so many of the children seemed so much of the time absorbed, alive, active, happy, at peace with each other. At the end of my day's visit at the school in London I went away thinking that we certainly don't have to make schools like this compulsory in order to get children to go to them. Then I remembered somebody suggesting to me that while our societies might be willing to spend large amounts of money on school systems most of which were coercive, intimidating, and stifling, and while within such systems we might be able to have *a few* very human and lively and interesting schools, no society would spend much money just to provide pleasant and interesting places for all children to go. A disturbing argument. Is it true that only in the cracks and corners of school systems as we know them will there be any room for schools as good as the ones I saw, and the kind of people who are working in them? Must we then have many bad schools in order to be able to have a few good ones? I doubt that it is true; in any case, it is not a good enough reason.

And I remembered recently a conversation of many years ago. In one of the western states I met the kind of oilman who might have been invented for a satirical cartoon. He was too good, or maybe too bad, to be true. On this occasion he said that all this fuss and expense about education was a lot of damned nonsense. We ought to send kids to school for three or four years to teach them a little simple reading or a little simple figuring and then kick them all out into the world and make them get to work. More education than that just made them into troublemakers.

Some of my friends on the Left have suggested that the movement to deschool society might attract a good deal of this kind of support. It's possible, but not likely. As we cannot make too clear (or often make clear at all) by deschooling we mean among other things that people shall not be judged or discriminated against on the grounds of their schooling or lack of it, or because they cannot do well on school type tests. Deschooling means not only doing away with compulsory attendance laws, the threat of the law, but also doing away with our whole system of diplomas and credentialing, which keeps many young people locked in school long after the law would let them get out. In short, proposals to deschool society come in a context most unlikely to appeal to Stone Age millionaires.

The kind of society that would begin and carry through the sort of program of deschooling that we have been talking about would not be a society indifferent to or contemptuous of children. It would want to find and provide for them as many resources as possible to help their learning and growth. But this does not mean that it would do so in the impossibly expensive ways, including schooling, that we have come to think of as essential, which only bring about the result that most people *cannot* have what all agree everyone *must* have. To the claim that in the absence of compulsory schooling and credentialing we would not have enough money to provide for all children a kind of idyllic "school" I can only say, quite right. If we define learning or growing up as a process which requires that every child get during most of his waking hours the continued attention of specialists who have nothing to do but attend to him, whether we call these people teachers or counselors or playmates or whatever, we say in effect that most children can never grow up. There is no way to provide this kind of experience for more than a tiny minority of children. As we find this to be so, we simply tacitly agree to provide for the great majority some way of growing up that we and they see as inferior. What we must look for instead is a definition of growing up that will not exclude most of the children of the world or our own society. If growing children do need (as they may) some kinds of resources for their lives which are rather different from those needed by older people, we have to find less expensive ways of making available such resources.

9
Schooling and Poverty

What about the argument, heard all the time, that middle-class kids might be able to get along without schools and schooling, but that poor kids have to have them because they are the way and the only way they can "make it" in society. The reasoning behind the argument goes like this. For one poor child, more school and more degrees greatly increase his chance of getting a better job, more money, an escape from poverty. Therefore, if we could only give all poor kids more schooling and more degrees, they would almost all get better jobs and more money, and so escape from poverty. The argument seems to me deeply mistaken. The flaw in it is a matter of scale. What is sometimes true on a small scale may not be true on a large scale. What may work for one person, or a hundred, may not work at all for millions. If we look at poverty on a small scale, from close up, as if through the eyes of a poor parent worried about his kid, we ask ourselves, "How do I escape from poverty, help my kid escape?" The obvious answer is that people who stay in school a long time and get degrees seem to get good jobs, good pay, so naturally, I want my kid to stay in school and get some of these degrees. And I want schools to be such that when my kid does get a degree from them, people will take it seriously, will think that the degree means that my kid is better than a whole lot of other kids. I don't want my kid to go to a school where everyone is a winner, because then the prizes they hand out to him won't be worth anything. I want him to go to a school where there are plenty of losers, many more than winners; then if he wins a prize, it will really mean something.

But this is very different from saying that schools and schooling in general help or can be made to help the great mass of poor kids. In this chapter I want to try to show why I think they will not. If we look at poverty on a larger scale, as if through the eyes of a citizen worried about *all* kids, we have to ask ourselves, "What must we as a society, a nation do to reduce and do away with poverty? What sort of things must we do to help, not one or a few, but all poor kids?"

In writing about this I am going to make use of a few very simple graphs or diagrams. If among those who read this there should be some who think they are afraid of or can't understand math or anything that looks like math, I beg of you, please don't black out or turn away or start flipping pages until the graphs are all gone. There aren't very many. I will explain them. They are very simple, and I will use them in a simple way, not to make mathematical formulas, or anything like that. They will make it much easier for me to say and readers to understand the point I want to make about poverty—that it is not caused by poor people not having enough schooling and cannot be reduced or done away with by giving them much more schooling.

The word "poverty" is too general, too vague. Let me try to make it more concrete by suggesting that it has three parts; employment, income, and material standard of life. A man feels poor and is poor when he has a bad job or no job, lacks money, and can't get the things that he needs. These components of poverty are closely related, but they are not the same. Changing one is likely, but not certain, to change the others.

Anyone who does work that in varying degrees is uninteresting, or monotonous, or machinelike, or below his capacity to think and act, or dirty, or degrading, or dangerous, or physically exhausting, and that seems to lead to nothing better; anyone who feels he has no choice but to do such work, no way of getting out of it, and no prospects of changing it—such a person is poor and feels poor. Sometimes just the sense of being stuck in a job is itself enough to make the job bad. By the same token, half a dozen jobs, none of them very good in itself, might be quite tolerable and even interesting if one could switch from one to another. Another thing—not the only thing—that makes someone poor is that he has not enough money. A third is that the material and physical conditions of his life are bad—he lives in run-down or decrepit housing, in an ugly and decaying neighborhood, surrounded by noise, crowding, bad air, ugliness, crime, without beauty or amenities or community feeling or even routine municipal services.

These components of poverty, as I have said, are related, but not the same. Someone doing work he really loves—an artist, a skilled craftsman, a worker for social change or human betterment, a true scientist, etc.—might not feel poor even if he lacked money and lived in bad material conditions. The fact that he was able to control his own life and do the work he wanted might well be enough to make him feel rich and fortunate. Getting a better job and more money will not necessarily lift a man from poverty if with that money he cannot buy what he needs, whether because it doesn't exist or because he can't get to where it is or because people won't sell it to him. Medicare was supposed to improve the material quality of life for the poor by putting into their hands money for medical treatment. But in fact it did little to improve their health and the quality of medical service they could get. The people who had always charged them more than they could afford for medical treatment now charged them more than ever. The money meant to make poor people less poor served instead largely to raise the income of people in the medical business, almost all of whom were richer than the people Medicare was meant to help.

In the same way, merely raising the incomes of large numbers of people in ghettos would do little to relieve one of the major sources and causes of their poverty—their dreadful housing—unless they could use that money to buy or rent housing that was better. But as long as segregated housing locks racial minorities out of the suburbs and into the inner cities, most of them cannot get better housing, no matter how much money they have. A black family I knew, the father a successful physician, the mother a college graduate and registered nurse, had to search for two years to find housing outside the ghetto. If black people living in inner cities suddenly had more money, the likely quick result would be that the people who own the rotting housing they live in would charge even more for it—and for some time people living in many of our worst slums have been paying more rent per square foot than many white people living in good housing in pleasant districts. When a tenant has not the option of moving, it is easier to raise his rent than to fix his house.

Raising the income of a poor man, whether by getting him a better job or by guaranteeing him an income, will not improve his material standards of life unless something is also done to make available the things he needs, and at prices he can afford. There is ample evidence that the profit or market economy cannot do this or does not want to—they amount to the same thing. Even its staunch defenders admit this. Years ago, *Fortune* magazine, which every month celebrates the extraordinary wisdom and talent of businessmen—in this it has some of the fan magazine flavor of *Sports Illustrated* (it might well be called *Business Illustrated*)—published an article, "Our Enduring Slums," which showed why "private" i.e. corporate enterprise would never be able to rebuild them. The slums have indeed endured. Every now and then—most recently a couple of years ago—there is a new burst of talk about using corporate technology and know-how to rehabilitate the slums. For a year or two there is a little activity and much public relations, and then the corporations retire quietly from the lists. The reason is simple. Nobody wants to compete for the poor man's buck. There is always more and easier money in selling luxuries to the rich than necessities to the poor. The man who has one home and wants another for his vacation can always outbid in the building market the man who has no home at all. To put it another way, in a market economy money goes where money is. Wealth tends to concentrate. Poverty, on the other hand, tends to spread, like a disease. The difference is that diseases sometimes cure themselves. Poverty never does.

Here I would like to introduce a way of illustrating and looking at the distribution of poverty that I will be using throughout the chapter. It is a common enough idea, a version of what is called in statistics a distribution curve, though my way of using it may sometimes be unorthodox. For those readers who may not know about distribution curves, which are simple, I will take a few lines to show and explain one. Suppose we measured to the nearest inch the heights of a group of people, and found the following:

> three people are 5'3" tall
> eight people are 5'6"
> fifteen people are 5'9"
> twenty people are 6'
> fifteen people are 6'3"
> eight people are 6'6"
> three people are 6'9"

We could make a graph, as shown in figure A. Each black dot shows how many people there are of each height. We can then draw a smooth curve connecting the dots. I should say before going on that in real life the figures would not come out so neatly. I made up these figures and picked them so that they would give a curve that looks more or less like what is called a "normal distribution curve." A curve showing the distribution of heights in a large group of people, or of weights, or of the time they would require to run fifty yards, would probably look more or less like the normal curve, since these qualities are distributed throughout the population more or less at random.

But if we were to make a distribution curve for family income, we would get a curve looking roughly like the one in figure B. The curve is not exact, but close. This distribution curve for family income is, as they say, "skewed"—that is, bent out of normal shape, pressed as it were toward the poor end. If money were randomly distributed throughout society, or if in the race to get money everyone had more or less an even start, the curve would look more like the normal curve. The fact that it is skewed indicates very strongly that the money race is not an even race, that some run under handicaps, that it is easier for those who have money to get more money than for those who have none.

What I will now do, and do for the rest of the chapter, is to stand these distribution curves on end, as in figure C, and then make them symmetrical, as in figure D. This curve or shape I will call the income pyramid or, more often, since we are concerned with poverty, the poverty pyramid.

In our first income distribution curve, figure B, we can draw (the dotted vertical line) what might be called a "poverty line." This line is not exact. Where we put it is a matter of opinion and

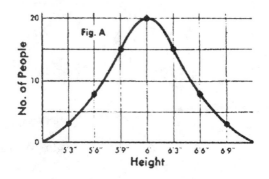

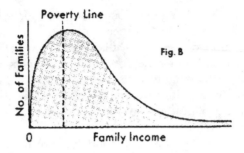

judgment as well as statistics. Also, it is not narrow and sharp, like a line, as if having $4,999 a year meant that you were poor while having $5,000 meant that you were not. Also, the poverty line is not the same for all people, or in all places. It depends on, among other things, whether people can grow some of their own food, or get or make other things they need without having to buy them; on the local cost of living; and on the availability of services—rents are high in my home town of Boston, but public transportation to many areas is good enough so that many people (including me) can live comfortably without a car. It depends on climate—people generally need more money to live in cold climates than in mild ones. And so on. The Bureau of Labor Statistics, I believe, estimates every few years how much money a family of four in a typical city or near-city would need to live at a minimum standard of

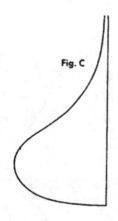

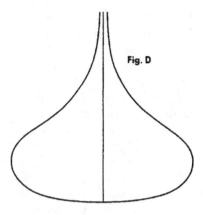

Fig. D

health, comfort, and decency. The current estimate is something slightly over $5,000 a year, but it is a bare minimum at best and makes almost no allowances for amenities or recreation, to say nothing of such common enough family emergencies as sickness, accident, or injury. It is fair to say that most families living under that line are poor and feel poor.

Instead of a poverty line, it might be better to think of a poverty zone, intense at the bottom, shaded off at the top, as shown in figure E.

The income or poverty pyramid has a different shape in different societies. In some of the underdeveloped countries of, say,

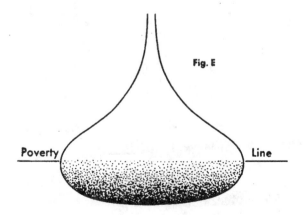

Fig. E

Poverty   Line

Latin America, where a few live in great wealth, a few more hang on in the middle class, and the great majority live in poverty, the pyramid is even more pushed and flattened down toward the bottom, as in figure F. In general, when the poverty pyramid for a country has this flattened down shape, the poverty line will be well up the narrow part of the curve, most people living below it. However, a society that decided as a matter of national policy that it would not have poverty, as for example Sweden has largely decided, would have a pyramid of about the same shape. But in this case the poverty line would be at the very bottom of the curve, and the great majority of the population would be above it, as in figure G. As one society can push most of its people down into poverty, so another *if it chooses* can lift most of its people out of it.

One way to consider the problem of reducing or doing away with poverty would be to ask the question, how can we push up the bottom of the pyramid of figure E to make it look like figure G? The defenders of more and more schooling seem to be saying that since any given person by getting more schooling and degrees can probably (but less probably than a few years ago) rise out of the poverty zone, if we can only get more schooling and degrees to all poor people they will all rise out of it. They are saying—part of the conventional wisdom of the times, and in almost all countries—that poverty is an educational problem that can be cured with massive doses of more schooling. I want to try to show in this chapter—this is what all the talk about pyramids is leading up to—

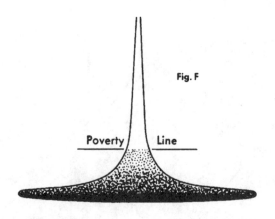

Fig. F

Poverty / Line

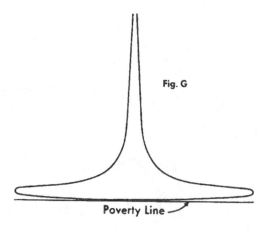

Fig. G

Poverty Line

that this is not so. Poverty on a large as opposed to small scale is not an educational problem; it cannot be cured with doses of more schooling; more schooling for all those people in the poverty zone will not lift more than a few out of it, and then largely at the expense of those just above it; and billions of dollars spent to provide more school services for the poor will, like the Poverty Program in general, enrich the middle-class people providing the services much more than it will enrich the poor.

To show why I believe this to be true I am going to have to talk more about poverty and pyramids of poverty. I say pyramids as a way of coming back to something I said before, that poverty has three components—employment, income, and material standards of life. We can imagine and make a pyramid for each of these. They will look roughly but not exactly alike. They mean different things, and we can learn different things from them.

The employment pyramid (or job pyramid) I have drawn in a slightly different way. Instead of making it a smooth curve, I have drawn it as a series of boxes. The pyramid (fig. H) shows very roughly how "good" jobs, not so good jobs, "bad" jobs, and no jobs are distributed. Box A represents the top class jobs; Box B— very good jobs, but not quite so good; and so on down. The black box at the bottom of the pyramid represents complete unemployment. The shaded box just above it represents part-time employment, odd jobs, casual or seasonal labor, etc. All the boxes above

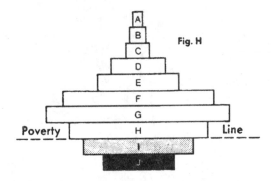

Fig. H

the dotted line represent full-time jobs, going from the least desirable jobs in Box H up to Box A. The width of each box represents
the number of these jobs available in our present economy.

This pyramid is also made up—a guess, though I think not a
bad one. Whereas there is, somewhere, in some office or report, a
real or official income pyramid, there is no job pyramid. There is
no way to draw it accurately, since what it shows in the up and
down direction is the goodness or badness of jobs, and these,
which depend on how people feel about them, can't be accurately
measured, or perhaps measured at all. The relative sizes of the various job boxes or job classes may not be quite right. Perhaps some
should be wider or narrower. What I want to show in the figure is
that there are many more "bad" jobs than "good," relatively few
jobs that people would choose for themselves or their children if
(1) they could get any job they wanted, and (2) they had so much
money they didn't need to work.

In an underdeveloped or very rapidly expanding economy,
the number of jobs of a certain class is primarily determined by the
number of people who are able to do them. If a new country is desperately short of typists, it is true on a large scale as well as a small
that learning to type will automatically move you up the job pyramid. It then makes at least some sense to say, "We should teach
children clerical skills in school, so that they can get better jobs."
The jobs are there, waiting for people to fill them and do them. If a
new country wants to build roads and needs but does not have
civil engineers who know how to build them, it makes at least
some sense to say that the bottleneck is in the schools, in the lack

of trained people. There is still the larger question—why do we need such fancy roads, why not build the kind of roads that people already know how to build? But I don't want to take that up here. In a country which is short of all kinds of labor, and particularly many kinds of skilled labor, education in the sense of skill training can pay off, not just for the individual student, but for large numbers of students, and the society as a whole. Again, this leaves open the larger question—if we are training someone to do a certain work, would it not make sense to train him as close to the work as possible, so that he can see the need, meaning, and use of what he is learning? But again, I will not take that up here.

In a highly developed and indeed inflated economy like our own, the situation is different. The number of jobs that are available in any one of those job boxes has nothing to do with the number of people who know how to do the job. When aerospace engineers with high qualifications and much experience have no work, with no prospects in sight, training new engineers is not going to increase the number of these jobs. Even on a very small scale, a single student is not likely to better his chances by getting a degree in an overcrowded field. Eighty percent of the graduating class of one teacher training college I know of did not get jobs as teachers. And we certainly are not going to help any large group of young people to escape poverty by training them at great expense in these unwanted skills. Schools are theoretically supposed to adjust their priorities, to some degree, to take account of the jobs in the job market. But they are always too slow, there is too much time lag, they are always hard at work training students for what was needed yesterday or five or ten years ago. At our present rate of training teachers, we should by 1980 have almost four times as many teachers as teaching jobs. In short the schools, whether by what they teach or the amount of degrees they give out, *do not determine and cannot change the shape of the job pyramid*. The number of jobs that exist, and the goodness or badness of these jobs and the amount of money they pay, are independent of the schools, the things they teach there, the number of people who are learning them.

Thus, cleaning the streets of New York City, which now requires a high school diploma, is not a better job than it was when it didn't require the diploma. Raising the school requirements of the job has not made it more interesting or cleaner or better paid. All that has happened is that some people who once might have been able to get that job now are no longer able to. They either get an even worse job than that, or no job at all. Who are these people for whom getting a dirty, undignified, and physically strenuous job has been made more difficult than before? They are mostly black, Puerto Rican, and above all poor.

Consider another question. Can schooling do anything to make more fair the *distribution* of good jobs, and bad, among all racial, ethnic, and social groups? Let us look again at our job pyramid. We know that black people make up about 12 percent of our population. If such jobs as there are were equally distributed among different groups, or if a black kid had as fair a chance as anyone else at getting a good job, then blacks would hold about 12 percent of the jobs in each of those classes or boxes—12 percent of the best jobs, 12 percent of the worst. But of course this is not the case. Blacks have much less than 12 percent of the good jobs, and more than 12 percent of the bad ones, or of no jobs at all. The same would be true, to a greater or lesser degree, of any of a number of other groups—Chicanos, Puerto Ricans, Indians, Orientals, whites of non-WASP descent, children of poor parents. The employment pyramid for each of these groups, like their poverty pyramid, is much more squashed down toward the bottom end. What they would all like, if they can't have all good jobs, is their fair share of such good jobs as there are.

On a small scale, the question becomes, how can an individual worker or would-be worker move himself up the job pyramid. There are only two ways. One is to find a job that exists now, and that is better than the one he has (or that his father or mother has), and take it away from whoever has it, or might have it. In this case he wins, but somebody else loses—gets a worse job, or none, instead of a better one. The other is to take the job he now has, and make it better, or get it made better. In this case, nobody loses—the job itself has improved, and thus to some small degree the job pyramid has changed its shape. On a large scale, only the second of these two options is possible. There are only so many vice-presidents, or shop foremen, in a company. We could not, however much we wanted, multiply by a hundred that number of vice-presidents or foremen. But we could, *if we wanted,* find many ways to give all workers more variety in their work, more control over both its nature and its pace, and more effective voices in decisions that affect their work and their future. We could, in short, change the shape of the job pyramid by improving the quality of the work that many people are doing right at the place where they are now doing it.

Some of this can be done by raising wages—pay is, after all, an important part of what makes one job better than another. But we can only do this to a point. Imagine a wage or pay pyramid. It would look like the ones we have already drawn. High-paying jobs would be at the top, low at the bottom, the width of the pyramid would show how many of each there are. We can try to push up the very bottom of the pyramid by raising the legal minimum wage and extending it to cover more workers, and we should. But while this would improve the pay of some jobs, there is a very good chance that it would wipe out many other marginal jobs altogether. Some low-wage employers would begin to find it cheaper to use fewer workers and more machines; others would find ways to get around the law; others would simply go out of business. We can see that in any individual company, or the country as a whole, there is a limit to how high we can lift up the bottom of that pyramid. We could squeeze the narrow part of the pyramid down somewhat— most top management is overpaid and overpensioned, and this increases many workers' bitter and angry sense of being unjustly exploited—why should I work my ass off to make him rich? But even if we pushed top management salaries down to a more reasonable level, this would make available only a very small amount of money to raise the pay of most workers—not enough to make any real difference. If an individual company were to try to lift its entire wage pyramid, raise everyone's pay, its costs would soon go up so fast as to put it out of business. When an entire society, or a large part of it, tries to do this, whether through wage legislation or union negotiated agreements, the result is soon an inflation that wipes out what everybody has gained. We can make the wage pyramid flatter, shorten the distance between top and bottom, and as a matter of justice it would probably be wise to do this. But we can't do very much to lift the whole pyramid up in the air.

To this conventional wisdom replies, "Oh yes we can! We can make our whole economy more productive, by making all workers more productive, by spending money on research and capital investment so as to put more powerful and efficient tools in workers' hands." This is the "growth" argument. Nothing but economic growth will wipe out poverty, and therefore the first and most important task and duty of the political economy of the nation, however organized, however labeled, is to get the highest possible rate of economic growth. This is one of the few truly worldwide religions of our time—or we might say that combined with Science, Efficiency, and Bigness, it is *the* new world religion. Every country, every government in the world, whatever political labels it may put on itself, whatever it may declare its true or ultimate purposes to be—Freedom, or Profit, or the People, or the Revolution, in the short run dedicates itself to Growth, and views and deals with the human beings under it only as means to that end. In all but at most two or three countries in the world (if that many), whatever they call themselves—Socialist, Capitalist, Communist, Peoples' Democracy, etc.—if we were to complain to someone in a position of power and authority about some government or industrial policy on the grounds that it dehumanized and trivialized people, made them into machines, just in the interests of growth; if we were to say, "You must change the conditions of that person's work to make it more interesting, more varied, to make him feel more like a man and less like a machine, even if doing this might cut down on growth"—if we were to say this, the official or manager or commissar, to whom we were speaking would angrily say, in effect, "What are you, some kind of a nut?" He might say this in bureaucratic language; he might in some cases and places call us a Commie Nut, in others a Bourgeois-Romantic or Capitalist-Imperialist or Counterrevolutionary or some other kind of nut. But nut we would be. To deny or even question the all-importance of growth is to attack Truth itself. Much safer these days to deny the existence or importance of God.

To be fair, the argument for growth has some truth in it. Certainly, in the developed countries, at least, growth has made large numbers of people far more rich, comfortable, and secure than earlier ages would have dreamed possible. And if it has not done away with poverty, it has largely done away with many forms of it. People in developed countries do not often die anymore of malaria or smallpox or typhoid fever or of being kicked by a horse, or drowned in a fishing boat—though more and more seem to be dying earlier of a new and more difficult plague, cancer, and the oldest of plagues, war. What we might call "growth freaks," now the overwhelming majority of the world's people, often like to say that in developed countries even poor people have things like cars and TV that in earlier times emperors did not even dream of. True; but if that is meant to imply that poor people today are richer than emperors used to be, the argument is just plain silly. What rich people have always been able to buy with their money is something that poor people never get and always need, and that no amount of growth alone will ever give them—space, freedom of choice, the right not to be pushed around, privacy, and above all the certainty that most people they come in contact with will not violate their dignity, will treat them with at least the appearance of respect. A person is not poor because he does not have what no one has ever dreamed of. But he is indeed poor, and bitterly poor, if he does not have, sees no chance of ever having, what is constantly waved under his nose as something that every self-respecting person has, ought to have, and must have. If growth has truly done away with some old and painful forms of poverty, it has created some equally painful new ones.

In a developed country, growth by itself may enable many people who already live above the poverty line to rise higher and higher above it, to move into the middle and even upper-middle classes, to thicken the thin neck of the top of the income pyramid. But there is much evidence that growth, by itself, does very little for the people at the real bottom. The growing economy simply leaves them behind. The new (whether useful or not is another question) goods and services it provides, the poor cannot afford; the new jobs it provides, the poor do not get. Indeed, it may make their poverty worse, by destroying many of the institutions and services they need, and by turning one-time luxuries into necessities hopelessly out of reach. In most cities, and indeed almost anywhere in the country where most people once rode passenger trains, buses, streetcars, etc. and now drive their own cars, people who can't afford or can't drive a car are much worse off than they used to be. In cities without good public transportation, it takes a car even to *look* for work. What is someone without a car to do? As has been widely noted, more and more city jobs are moving out to the suburbs. But because of antipoor and antiminority segregation in suburban housing, because the suburbs have little low-income

housing and will not allow it to be built even when the money for
this is available, the poor city people who used to have those jobs
cannot follow them. Because public transport between suburb and
city is planned for the people who come *into* the city to work, city
people cannot get to suburban jobs. It is common for black women who earn their living and support their families by doing
housework in suburban homes to have to spend many hours a day
getting to their jobs, much of this simply waiting, in weather good
or bad, for the next bus or streetcar or whatever to come along.

As I said earlier, growth doesn't help a poor person if the new
goods or services it provides are not the ones he needs, and if the
new jobs it creates are ones he can't get. Examples come to mind.
In recent years the snowmobile business has boomed. How does
this help poor city people? They can't use them, and except for the
few that live near snowmobile factories, they can't make them.
There has also been a boom in, let us say, the ski business, or the air
travel business, or the motel and convention business. But except
for a very few more black people working as stewardesses or at the
airline ticket counters, or in the motels, these growth businesses
entirely by-pass our poor. To this the reply used to be that when
any part of an economy grows, everyone benefits ultimately, if only
indirectly. Even if no black people make skimobiles, the people
who do make them eventually buy something that black people make. In the first place, this is no help to the black or other
poor people who, having no jobs, do not make anything. In the
second place, it is untrue even of a great many poor people who
do have jobs, since these all too often low-paid service jobs—cleaning, dishwashing, etc.—are outside the mainstream of the economy. Moreover, the man who builds a vacation house, and neither
employs any black labor nor buys anything that black people make,
helps to bid up the price of the things that would be needed to
build new inner city housing or to repair the housing already there.
Growth in the automobile industry has not only destroyed most of
the alternatives to owning a car, but also has enormously increased
the cost of owning a car itself. The days when people using a few
simple tools and cheap and easily available spare parts could keep
an old jalopy running for years are gone. The cars today are made
to wear out; they are difficult to fix and adjust, requiring tools so
specialized and expensive that poor people could not afford to

own them; and the spare parts themselves are expensive, even when they are available. And so on. Growth, in and of itself, does not necessarily improve the position of poor people; at some point, it may make it much worse. We are well past that point. Indeed, large numbers of people with supposedly good paying jobs in strongly unionized industries have found that over the last ten years their income has not kept up with the rising costs of what they need. In short, it is not just the poor who are getting poorer. People who thought they had escaped from poverty are beginning to feel themselves slipping back.

There is another and more fundamental and intractable reason why we cannot count on growth to solve or much reduce the problem of poverty. It is that we can no longer afford the kind of growth that until now we have taken to be right, necessary, and inevitable. We cannot afford any longer to pursue the goal of the ever higher gross national product. The cost in the destruction of our environment is too great. We learn more clearly every day that a higher GNP means not a better life but more garbage, noise, and pollution. We learn more clearly every day, not to say see, hear, and smell, what our modern economies, their products, by-products, and waste products, are doing to the biosphere, the complicated and delicate network of interconnected life of which we are a part and on which we wholly depend. More news comes in every day, all of it bad. No need to repeat any of it here. We never hear, except from people we have good reason to believe are lying—advertising people, the Atomic Energy Commission, etc.—that something we thought was harmful is, after all, harmless. Quite the contrary. Hardly a month or even week goes by without our discovering that we have loosed some new poison into the environment, or that an old poison is proving even more lasting and deadly than we had feared, or that what had seemed a trivial consequence of our acts is in fact far-reaching, dangerous, and often irreversible.

Perhaps someday we may see the world that Buckminister Fuller talks about, in which we will have learned enough about the laws of life, of our planet, and of the universe to know how to work with them instead of against them. In such a world, by making full and wise use of the inexhaustible energy resources of the sun and tides, we may be able to maintain a permanently high material standard of life for all men, without damaging our home planet Earth. That world is not here now, nor is it even within sight. To make it we will have to develop, often from scratch, altogether new sciences, technologies, political and economic institutions, ways of looking at life and work. We will even need new words, or new ways of using old ones. Consider our use of the word "production." Over many millions of years of time the sun poured energy into green plants, the energy was stored in their stems and leaves, they were covered up in upheavals of the earth's crust, and under heat and pressure they were turned into petroleum. Now we dig holes in the ground, take up this accumulated and stored up energy, and burn it up into smoke. This process we call "oil production." Every time we pump a gallon of oil out of the ground and burn it up, we say we have "produced" another gallon of oil. This is crazy talk. We should be saying that we have *destroyed* or *consumed* or *used up* a gallon of oil. Indeed, we might very well say that what we call the productivity of a modern economy is the speed with which it can turn irreplaceable raw materials into indisposable junk.

To make this new world we will need a new science of economics, in which we will measure the cost of anything we do, not in the traditional terms of the amount of trouble and resources needed to do it, but in terms of how doing it affects the environment. Our motto will have to be that of the good woodsman— Leave Things as You Found Them or Better. We will have to find and make laws and institutions that will require everyone who wishes to do something to pay whatever it will cost afterward to obey that woodsman's motto, to leave our planet in at least as good shape as he found it. We will have to learn ourselves, as some young people seem to be learning, the kind of reverence for Earth and all living things on it that was to some degree embodied in the culture and religions of people that we have sneeringly called "primitive." We will have to learn to think of Earth, not just as a hunk of real estate to drive our cars on or to exploit for whatever we can get out of it, but as Mother Earth, our true mother.

Meanwhile, we are badly stuck with old habits, old ways of thought, and the deadly consequences of what we are doing. President Nixon said that he was not going to change the American economic system no matter what it might do to our environment.

A marvelously and comprehensively ignorant remark—and typical not just of him but of what large numbers of people, in any country in the world, would say. Give up my car, or TV, or whatever, for the sake of the life of the Earth? Never! It calls to mind the famous comedy dialogue:

> A: Hands up! Your money or your life!
> B: Take my life—I'm saving my money for my old age.

Or the wonderful Jack Benny version of it, in which the command is followed, not with an answer, but with about twenty seconds of thought-packed dead silence. We are all living in that silence. Not only do we not know how to save Earth, our planet, our home, our spaceship, our mother; we are not really sure we care enough even to want to save it. I have to assume that we will want to, otherwise there is no point in writing this book, or in worrying about schools or poverty, or in doing anything else. And in proportion as we become serious about saving the earth, we are going to see that one of our problems must be, not how to increase our economic activity year after year, not how to raise that GNP ever higher, but *how to level it off and turn it down,* cut it in half, and in half again. For it seems quite clear, and more so every day, that the earth will not be able to survive for many more years even as much industrial and economic activity as we have right now.

Business and industry, sensing the beginnings of a new public concern, are beginning to make soothing sounds about conservation and the environment. But anyone who follows these matters closely knows that this is mostly lies and public relations, aimed only at preventing exactly the kinds of supervision or control of industry that will someday be necessary. Lumber companies talk about sustained harvesting of timber while clear cutting forests that will never be replaced, on land that once exposed to rainfall may be made wholly barren by leaching (washing or draining away of nutrients and minerals) within a generation. Oil companies talk about clean exhaust from cars while planning tankers ten or more times the size of those involved in our most serious oil spills to date—tankers so large and unwieldy that it will take half an hour to bring them to a full stop. The chemical companies put out more and more packages and containers, indestructible as they are useless, that will clutter up the landscape for no one can guess how many thousands of years, or prepare and peddle ever more destructive and long lasting pesticides. And so on. In a very different kind of society, with a great deal of new knowledge, new technologies, and above all new attitudes, economic growth might be healthy or at least tolerable. Now, as we are, knowing no more than we know, it is destructive and suicidal.

One more word on this point. Recently a number of people have begun to say that people concerned about the environment were not concerned about poverty, were indifferent or even hostile to the poor, and that any improvement in the environment was going to come at the expense of the poor. This is a very ill-considered and short-sighted view. The poor will always suffer more than anyone else from a degraded environment, as they suffer most now, because they are least able to counter it or escape it. Much of the food which is most dangerously contaminated with poison is cheap food, poor people's food—i.e. fish. It may not be long before most prudent city dwellers will start buying bottled water or installing in their homes not just air conditioners, but elaborate electrostatic and chemical filters, to take dangerous particles and chemicals out of the air. The poor will not be able to afford such things, but will have to continue to drink polluted water and breathe polluted air. Business, having made the city unfit for people, finds later that it is unfit even for business, and pulls out, leaving the poor unable to follow. *Time* recently printed a joke about Detroit that might well be about any one of a number of other cities: "Will the last corporation to leave Detroit please put out the lights." Whatever makes a place bad, city or country, makes it most bad for the poor. When everyone else can leave, the poor have to stay.

Even if what I have said about growth were not true, or even if we were as ignorant and unconcerned about the environmental costs of growth as we were twenty years ago, it would still be true that the kind of growth we have known for a generation and more, and most of this under national governments committed to the idea of fighting poverty through growth, has done very little to change the shape of the job pyramid. For all our trillion dollar a year GNP, we have not done away with unemployment, or increased very much the number of good jobs, jobs that people are glad to do. For most people in our society work is drudgery, what you have to do to live, perhaps a punishment for not having been smarter or done better in school. If this has been so little changed by the last generation of growth, there is little reason to suppose that it will be changed much by the next.

This brings me back to the point I made earlier, that as long as the overall shape of the job pyramid is not changed, as long as the numbers of good, fair, and bad jobs remain about what they are, any poor person who moves up to a better job is going to move up at someone else's expense. He may make it. But that someone else is almost certain to be someone only slightly less poor than he is. When we try to apply on a large scale what works on a small, if we try, through schooling or otherwise, to move large numbers of people from the lowest job boxes up into higher ones, the result is to put poor people and working-class or lower-middle-class people in competition for jobs that are scarce and good jobs that are scarcer yet. This makes them each others' rivals and enemies, and prevents them from forging the kinds of political alliances that would make real large-scale change possible. It is grimly ironical and even tragic that our minority group poor should be most feared and hated by the very people whose friendship and support they must have if they are ever to make any real improvement in their lives. And it's a great day for the rich when they can make the poor think their true and worst enemies are those who are even poorer.

Since large numbers of poor people can only rise up the job pyramid at other poor people's expense, and since we are very unlikely to raise by much the present pay scales of most jobs, let us look at the other alternative—the ways by which we might improve the quality of the jobs we have. Job quality, what makes a job better or worse, has many components. One has to do with safety. For many people, work is safer than it used to be, but not for all. Our mine safety laws, for example, are still grossly inadequate, and far too many miners are injured and killed in mine accidents that better or more strictly enforced laws would have prevented. Many migrant farm workers, as Cesar Chavez has often pointed out, must work in fields that have recently been dusted or sprayed with chemicals very dangerous to man, and many people have become sick, and some have died, because of this. Where work is safer, it is almost always because of a combination of strong unions and tough safety legislation. The same could be said of comfort and cleanliness. Better lighting, places to sit while working, cleaner air, floors, and rest rooms, regular breaks—all of these were won through hard bargaining or through legislation. One reason it is hard to improve the quality of some of our worst jobs, the jobs many poor people do, is that so many of these poor are not under the union umbrella, and that since they seem to threaten the scarce jobs now held by union members, the unions have tended to be more interested in keeping them out than in getting them in.

But what makes so many jobs bad, what makes so much modern work into hateful drudgery, is that it is so dull, so machinelike, so unvarying, so undemanding. The worker has so few choices or decisions to make, so little control over his work, even in the most immediate sense, so little opportunity to use his intelligence and abilities. One of the best books I have ever read about modern work, and one very aptly titled, was *The Making of a Moron,* by Niall Brennan, now unhappily out of print. At the very beginning, he tells us:

> The director of Mental Hygiene in Victoria, Australia—Dr. Catarnich . . . wanted to find out whether there was any way in which the subnormals under his care could be put into useful work . . . (he) found that there were very few industrial occupations beyond the ability of subnormals.
>
> So much, we might say in passing, for the notion that all this schooling is needed to train a competent labor force.
>
> . . . The Australian Department . . . took five young morons, placed them in a special hostel, and sent them out to work for RCA. . . . A year later, the Works Manager (said:) "In every case, these girls proved to be exceptionally well-behaved, particularly obedient, and strictly honest and trustworthy. They carried out work required of them to such a degree of efficiency that *we were surprised they were classed as subnormals* for their age . . ."

He continued:

> . . . It may be good to discover that in a modern industrial plant there are mental processes which can be performed by a boy with a mental age of less than eight years, and with a severe lack

of muscular coordination. It may be fine for the boy. But what were the "normal" adults doing in this same process before the crippled and retarded boy came along to do it for them? No really normal person can afford to ignore the frightening implications in the discovery that many "normal" men and women are working in jobs at which subnormals are equally and sometimes more efficient.

Later Brennan writes:

The unpleasantness of a job depends solely on how many of the parts of man are being used and how well they are being used.

One of the best jobs he had he describes, in part, as follows:

Laboring is not the simple thing it seems to be. It is still the most common of man's works, but it is never the same ... Jammed in among a score of similar businesses in Melbourne's Victoria Fruit Market was a wholesale fruit business which employed me for several weeks ...

The efficiency and morale of this shop were tremendous. No man knocked off before the day's work was done, and the day's work was so erratic that it might be anything from six to twelve hours. Work began as early as each man could get to it. . . . The first man began at 4 A.M. and all the staff had arrived by 6:30 A.M. Knock-off time varied from 12 noon to 4 P.M. . . . The task consisted of loading and unloading vehicles of every size from auto-trucks to five-ton semi-trailers; stacking, restacking, moving crates, packing crates, delivering, and for the elite of the store, bargaining, buying, and selling. . . . A desire for and need of order was the essence of their work. In a limited area, stacks had to be neat and accessible. Every man knew the origin and destination of everything he handled. They were proud of the fact that they worked hard, that they were doing a man's job.

Again, they could not be replaced by machinery in any way. [My note: perhaps now, in our day of computerized warehouses, they could.] What machines they had *were completely subordinate to them.* [Italics mine.] As a business it was an honest business. . . . It was a shop which—honestly—supplied food, thereby adding a necessity for its existence to its business integrity . . . (it) was a shop which called not so much for a skill—the work was nominally unskilled—as for *intelligence and initiative.* [Italics mine.]

Intelligence and initiative are exactly what are not called for and indeed not permitted in most of the jobs that people do. And workers are more and more being turned into machine *tenders* instead of machine *users.* It is discouraging to read this eloquent, original, in some ways old-fashioned and (the same thing) radical, and deeply Christian and indeed Catholic book. He hoped that he would see work become more human and less moronic; almost everywhere in the world we have moved the other way.

The matter of the honesty and integrity and usefulness of the business is also important. Harvey Swados worked in auto factories for some time, and then wrote *On the Line,* an excellent book of short stories about auto workers. In the book, or in an article about auto workers and auto plants, he once described some of the ways in which workers sabotage the cars they are making—seal up a bolt, or a banana skin, inside a rear fender, jam a nut on a bolt so that it cannot be unthreaded. One of the reasons the workers hated their work and their products so much is that they knew the cars were not meant and not designed to be good, but to be sold, to wear out, to be replaced. The pressure on them was to keep the line moving and to turn the cars out. They were not encouraged or even allowed to take extra time to fix something that they had seen had gone wrong, or to do something well instead of badly. Denied any chance to work as well as they could, (in Brennan's phrase) to use all their parts and use them well, they quite naturally did the reverse, worked as badly as they could. From a good friend who is related to a foreman in an auto assembly plant, I hear that the problem has if anything become worse. Not only absenteeism and high turnover, but drug abuse and deliberate sabotage are serious problems in many large factories.

There are, happily, some exceptions to this. Perhaps more companies and employers will learn from them. One example is the Avanti company in South Bend, Indiana. As some may remember, the Avanti was a very fine sports car made by Studebaker during the last years of its corporate life. When Studebaker went out of business, some men who loved the Avanti and wanted to keep it going bought the rights from Studebaker and continued to make the car. But they do not put it together on a conventional assembly line, in which the car moves along past first one worker, then another, each of whom performs one or two operations on it until it is completed. Instead, as I understand it, the car is assembled by two teams of workmen, one of whom put all the mechanical parts—engine, steering, transmission, suspension, etc.—on the chassis, and the others of whom put on the body, wiring, upholstery, dashboard, carpeting, etc. Each team of workers is in charge of its own work. They may rotate jobs or in other ways change the order or rhythm of what they do. When the car is finished, these two teams can look at it and think, "It's a good car, and we built it, we put it together." Some may say, "Avanti only builds a few hundred cars a year, but such methods would never work in a big factory." Quite recently I read that the Saab company in Sweden, who in addition to making one of the world's most sophisticated jet fighters make one of the world's best small cars, has made very much the same kind of change. A more recent story says that Volvo plans to do the same. I have not seen their new process described in any detail, but I gather that, as at Avanti, their cars are assembled by teams of workmen who stay with the car throughout the entire assembly and who have a large measure of control over their work. From the little I have read I judge that many people in Sweden, in business, government and elsewhere, are deeply concerned with the moronic quality of so much modern work, and are seriously looking for ways to make it more interesting, varied, and human. No educational task is more important. Not just our politicians, businessmen, and union leaders, but also our educators, should pay close attention to the progress of this movement in Sweden. It is a waste of time and money, as well as a cruel deception, to talk about providing good education for children if the central experience of their adult lives is going to be pointless, stupid, stupefying work.

One educator, with whom I talked about these things recently, gave me a strange reply. His argument was, in effect: There's nothing we can do to change the character of modern work. The trends of the past generations, which have taken more and more initiative away from workers of all kinds, robbed them of any control of their own work, removed them further and further from whatever product they were making, in a word, alienated them from their work—these trends are going to continue. We can't stop techno-logical progress. Work is going to get more and more automatized, computerized, planned and controlled from the top. At the same time, people are going to have more and more leisure time. Our purpose in education must be to educate them to make more and more creative use of their leisure. Many educators probably share this view—that work and play, or work and leisure, are and must be separate; that work is by definition something that we don't want to do and do only because we must; and that it is foolish to talk about making work meaningful. These views seem to me mistaken and dangerous. If carried far enough, they lead to a world such as Kurt Vonnegut, Jr., portrayed in his early novel, *Player Piano*—a few people doing all the meaningful work needed to keep the super-computerized society running, the rest leading lives of emptiness, unhappiness, and anger.

What is wrong with the educator's argument is simply this. People do not live their lives in pieces, even though they may think they do. As Brennan rightly pointed out, what we do in one part of our lives carries over into the others. We do not and cannot lead moronic, machinelike lives for eight hours a day, or even six or four, and then turn around and for the rest of the time be aware, intelligent, responsible, creative. Even if the hours of work are greatly reduced, most people, however much they may dislike their work, are going to think of it as the most purposeful and serious thing they do. If it seems empty and pointless and stupid, so will much of the rest of their lives. The workers Brennan knew and de-scribed who found nothing important in their work found nothing important anywhere else in their lives. If they lived at work only to get money, they lived outside only to spend it—even their sex was nothing more than a kind of consumption. Whoever sees himself in his work as only a maker or seller of junk is likely to see himself in his leisure as only a buyer and user of it, like the young cabdriver I once talked to who told me that he was doing three jobs, two full-time and one part-time, all of them by his description dull and stu-pid, because, as he said, "That's the only way you can buy a house, drive a big car, live good."

But it is probably in Yugoslavia that large numbers of industrial and factory workers have for some time had the most effective con-trol over their work, and of their factories themselves, making many decisions that in a traditionally run factory (whether Capitalist, Socialist, or Communist) would be left strictly up to management. I do not know what kinds of things these workers' councils have decided, or how they decide them, or where their powers begin and end. It seems something that we ought to know much more about—at least those of us who are interested in improving the quality of work, and hence of the lives of many working-class and poor people.

What steps might be necessary to begin to make some such changes here? We will need two things, at least: much greater union pressure on management, and, even more important, much more democratic control of unions by the workers themselves. From Samuel Gompers on down, most American union leaders have strongly denied the right of workers to make important decisions about their work, let alone the running of the factory or corporation itself. Let management manage the business, has been their cry. Our job is to get out of management the highest possible price for our labor. In other words, labor unions no less than management have from the beginning treated labor as nothing more than a commodity and workers as nothing more than people who sold their work. This was the great betrayal, the great sellout, and by their own leaders, of the American working man. From the rhetoric of these leaders, one might suppose them rivals, adversaries, even enemies of management. In fact and in effect many of them are much more partners of management than rivals. As much as management, they want to deny workers effective control over their work, prevent them from gaining an effective voice in the management of the enterprise. Like management, they worry about how to keep those people down there on the factory floor in line. Such accounts of union meetings as I have read, particularly meetings at which the rank and file challenged the leadership, sound remarkably like corporate stockholders' meetings. In both, the leadership assures the members that it knows best and that whoever doubts it is probably an enemy of the organization. In both, democratic control is more theory than fact. All this will be hard to change, even if and when workers want to change it. In part, it is an educational job—and I don't mean something to be done in school. Working-class people and poor people must, as they once did, educate themselves. In *Hard Times,* Studs Terkel's wonderful book about Americans in the Depression, he quotes a number of old union organizers and radicals as saying that when they were young working men talked and thought a lot about economics and politics, but that now they only talk about sex and baseball. To whatever extent it may be true it is a great loss, not just to the workers but the whole society. We will probably not see very much real or lasting social reform until many people in the working class, and among minority groups and the poor, think hard and talk widely about what might be a better society for all, and not just for Us, or *Me* or even *my kids.* The idea, "I want to have more than you" is not much changed or ennobled by being turned into, "I want my kids to have more than your kids." It is all too easy to use our children as a cover and excuse for our own greed.

The public, too, will have to be educated. Most people these days are very hostile to the idea of strikes, of any kind, for any reason. Also, most people are used to the idea of bosses and being bossed, to the corporate-military model of human organization, and tend to regard as rather queer or dangerous anyone who objects to it, or says something else might be possible. If workers and their unions organized a strike on the issue of greater control by workers over their work, or greater worker participation in management, it seems likely that an overwhelming majority of the public would be strongly against it—and such a strike could only succeed with broad public support.

All I have said so far seems to assume two things, which most people believe. The first is that in a normal or proper state of affairs, except for emergencies and disasters, people will get their incomes through jobs. The second is that it is possible, at least in theory, and in practice if we could only find the right way to do it, for a modern economy to provide enough good jobs so that everyone will have an adequate income. But I don't believe either of these things, and would like to take some space to say why, and what I think needs to be done about it. We have reached a time when we must begin to untangle, or think how to untangle, three ideas that we have been used to having lumped together—livelihood, jobs, and work. Until now most people have felt that a person's *livelihood,* what he needed to support himself, and his family if he had one, should depend on his having a *job,* a position in which he got paid for doing some *work,* something that he didn't particularly want to do but that someone wanted done.

For many people, this goes beyond politics or economics. It is a matter of morality. They think it is wrong, immoral, and something very close to criminal to get money in any way except in payment for doing a job. On the other hand they often make some very odd exceptions to this. Many of them see nothing wrong with people living on inherited money, and would certainly object strongly to any suggestion that rich people not be allowed to will all their money to their children. Many who do not hesitate to say, "Why should I support some lazy bum who won't work?" like to gamble, see gambling as a perfectly legitimate way of making money, and if they should strike it rich, would see nothing morally wrong with the idea of giving up their job and living on their winnings—though in fact many people who do win the big prize in a sweepstakes go on working because they don't know what else to do. Many of them see nothing wrong with making large sums of money on land speculation, or on such common enough tricks as buying up parcels of land where inside information says a highway is going to be built. Many are not at all offended by corruption, bribery, cheating, or swindling public or private. They have been taught to believe that life is a jungle, that everyone is the natural enemy and rightful prey of everyone else. When they speak of politicians as "a bunch of crooks," they are as likely to speak with grudging admiration as resentment—they would take a piece of the action if they could get it. By this light, cheating someone is just a matter of outsmarting him. If he'd been smarter, it wouldn't have happened. He should have looked out for himself. And anyway, if you hadn't done it to him, he might have done it to you. It reminds me of a grafitto on the wall of OTHERWAYS, a radical school that Herb Kohl and friends started some years ago in Berkeley. On one of the big brown sheets of paper tacked to the wall for that purpose, one student had written in bold letters:

DO UNTO ME
AND I'LL DO UNTO YOU
RIGHT BACK

Perhaps their feeling boils down to this. Work is a moral obligation, but as with other moral obligations, if you can get out of it and get away with it, that's fine—more power to you. But it's not fair just to refuse to work and then get treated the same as the people who are working. If you want to get out of working, you should have to go to some trouble and take some chances to do it. And in all likelihood the serious gambler or swindler or corrupt politician or even the outright thief thinks that his gambling or swindling or making deals under the table or stealing *is* his work.

Behind these rather confused attitudes is the thought: if everyone's livelihood did not depend on a job, no one would have any reason to work, no one would work, and the work would not get done. "In the sweat of thy face," says the Bible, "shalt thou eat thy bread." Everyone could see that this made sense, that without the sweat there would be no bread. For most of man's history this has been the case. There was always a labor shortage. There were never enough people to do all the work that clearly needed to be done.

But under a modern economy this is no longer true, and this way of linking livelihood with jobs makes no sense. In this richest country on earth we find ourselves in a strange position. Many people and their families lack a decent livelihood, live in poverty and squalor, because among other reasons they cannot get *good* jobs. The word "good" is important; one half the people on welfare *are* working. The reason we cannot provide good jobs is that there is not enough work to be done. People say all the time that this thing or that must be done "for the sake of the economy," "to keep the economy healthy," or "so that the economy can provide jobs." Until very recently no one in the world would have said or understood such things. A storm might wreck men's ships and ruin their trade or fishing; droughts or floods might spoil their crops; diseases might kill them and their animals; a bitter winter might exhaust their supplies of fuel. But that in the absence of such calamities, and in the midst of wealth, men should suffer and starve because something called "the economy" was "unhealthy" would have been beyond imagining. It is a kind of madness to say, as we now do all the time, that we must support this project or that industry, bring them into our communities, and allow and even encourage them to destroy our resources and pollute our air and water, simply because this will "create jobs." A truly grotesque example is the town, whose name I have forgotten, that recently worked hard to *per-*

suade the army to build a nerve gas storage depot near them because "it would be good for the economy."

Another case in point is the now defunct SST. Many people in Seattle, where it was to be built, argued and fought for this monstrosity, not so much because they really believed it was useful or needed or economically viable, but only because if it were not built fifty thousand people at Boeing, and in consequence many other people in the area, would lose their "jobs" and thus their livelihoods. In short, we are told we must build the SST, or that failing any one of a thousand things like it, so that some people may have a roof over their heads, clothes on their backs, and food to eat. But no one can *eat* an SST, or wear it, or live in it, or even make money from it. Our modern economies, in which it seems normal and sensible to think in such roundabout ways, have lost all touch with reality, with human nature and human needs.

In England not long ago the Conservative government decided to stop underwriting or subsidizing the Upper Clyde Shipbuilders in Scotland, and thus, in effect, to close them down. The Labor MP Anthony Wedgewood-Benn angrily protested this decision. In a TV interview he said among other things, first, that every other leading shipbuilding nation was subsidizing its shipbuilders, and secondly that if the shipbuilding industry closed down many people would be out of work and that it would be even more expensive to find some other way *to transport jobs* to Scotland. When we talk of the expensiveness of "transporting jobs," we are surely a long way from the times when we wanted people to have jobs so that necessary work would get done.

Not long after *The Times* of London wrote:

> There are three different kinds of objections which can be raised against the Cleveland (potash) mine: visual spoilation of countryside so beautiful that it has been designated a National Park. . . . It is possible to argue that the visual invasion of any national park by large-scale industrial buildings is a contradiction of our whole countryside policy and to be resisted. It is not easy to argue that when it is known that, in an area with some 10 percent unemployed to which *it has proved exceedingly difficult to attract new jobs,* [Italics mine.] the mine would employ 600–800 people, a good proportion of them local.

An article, "The Surprising Seventies" by Peter F. Drucker, in *Harper's*, July, 1971, says in part:

> ... During each year of the next decade, we will have to *find jobs* for 40 percent more people than in each of the past ten years.
> ... If we hope to succeed *in creating a vast number of new jobs* for the young people coming into the labor market during the years just ahead, the country will have to find a great deal of new capital somewhere. For every additional job requires a capital investment. This is particularly true of the *jobs we need the most*—jobs for highly educated people who are supposed to work with knowledge rather than with their hands. [All italics mine.]

Such talk is crazy talk. What became of the notion that we had to send all those people to college because there was all that skilled work out there that needed to be done and that only college graduates could do? On the one hand we hear endless talk about "society's need" for highly educated (i.e. schooled) people. And in the next minute we are told that we must find vast amounts of capital in order to create new jobs so that these expensively schooled people will have something to do that will make use of their expensive schooling.

More Drucker:

> A computer operator can't work without a computer. A doctor can't function efficiently without a substantial investment by somebody in a nearby hospital, equipped with everything from X-rays to artificial heart-lung machines—not to mention the costly equipment in his own office and in the laboratories on which he depends.

We have to ask ourselves, in the light of this sentence, what does it mean to say that a doctor functions "efficiently?" And I naively thought that a business bought a computer to help do its work more efficiently, and then looked for someone to run it. Apparently business must buy more and more computers to make work for computer operators.

A writer (or editor) needs not only his own typewriter, but an investment somewhere in printing presses and the facilities for nationwide distribution of books and magazines.

But we had writers before we had any of these things, didn't we?

An atomic physicist may need at least part time access to a nuclear accelerator costing billions. A professor needs not only a classroom, but a good library, perhaps a laboratory, and probably housing for his students. . . . So on the average a "knowledge job" in the American economy today whether in business, education, or government—requires a prior investment of something like $20,000.

In like vein, a science publication I saw recently—I think the British magazine *New Scientist*—spoke of the extraordinary expensiveness of "providing jobs" for research chemists. So we have to spend large amounts of money—wasting the earth—to provide expensive training for chemists and the like, and then spend still more money—still further wasting the earth—to "provide jobs" for them. In short, we are increasingly destroying the earth to spare people from the guilt of feeling lazy and to give them the comforting illusion of being useful. Even poor countries are locked into this strange way of looking at things. In the December 30, 1971, issue of *New Scientist* is an article about the underdeveloped countries entitled "280 Million More Jobs To Find." Jobs to *find!* One expert, Prof. Hans Singer, estimates that the real unemployment figure in the developing world is now about 25–30 percent and rising rapidly. Clearly the notion of the "job," of making people's livelihood depend on getting paid for work, is not only an inefficient and unfair way to distribute the wealth of a society, but also it does not even succeed in getting the needed work done.

Tens of millions of Americans lack a decent livelihood because there are not enough good jobs for all who need and want them. We have no hope of providing these jobs. There is not this much work to be done, or at least we cannot see how to turn the work that does need to be done into what we call jobs. Vast numbers of people have needs unmet—needs they might in many cases meet for themselves if they were helped or even allowed to do so.

Their needs are not met because their demand is ineffective, because they have so little money that they cannot pay anyone to meet their needs, cannot turn the work of meeting their needs into a "job." The poor may someday be able to build or rebuild their own housing; they will never be able to pay workers much richer than they are to build it for them.

Suppose for a moment that we agree to take as useful and necessary, in their present form, *all* the goods and services now provided by our economy. If all the people and institutions providing those services were working as hard and efficiently as they could, we would need many fewer man hours than we now spend to get the same work done—perhaps as little as two-thirds as much. Many of what we think of as 40 hour a week jobs might become 20–25 hour a week jobs. This is not just a wild speculation; *Life* recently had an article about the four-day work week, in which more respectable thinkers than I predicted it would soon and in many places become a three-day work week.

This much assumes that the goods and services provided by our economy, that add up to make the GNP are necessary to our well-being, and are provided in the most efficient possible way. But such is far from the case. Much of the GNP serves no need at all, other than the need for job, career, status, wealth, and power of those who provide it. Nobody *wants* to read advertising or to see TV commercials. Few people would have asked to pay, or if asked would have agreed to pay for the space program, the hydrogen bomb, nuclear submarines, MIRV, or the Asian War, to name only a few.

Another large part of the GNP meets human needs that are wholly artificial, needs that can only be created and maintained by psychological pressure—intense, unrelieved, and destructive—"If you do not use our product, you will go right on being what you are now—ugly, smelly, friendless, sexless, loveless, a joke, a disgrace, and a failure." But for this merciless pressure most of the cosmetics would stay on the drugstore shelves, the high style clothes on the racks, and the wild-animal named cars, power mowers, snowmobiles, etc. in the dealers' lots. No sensible person believes anymore the lie that industry gives the public what it wants. If people really wanted the kinds of cars that Detroit makes, why would they have to keep bombarding us with ads linking these cars with rich men and "sexy" girls?

Finally, those human needs that are real—housing, clothes, clean air and water, nutritious and unpoisonous food, transportation, health, learning, recreation, sport, repose, space, beauty, companionship, society, communal experience, and effective citizenship—are almost all and always defined so that they can only be supplied by certain people, if at all, and then in the most round-about, cumbersome, and expensive ways. As Kenneth Boulding has rightly pointed out, the size of our GNP is a measure only of the *trouble* we have to go to in order to meet the simplest needs and get the simplest things done. It is a measure, not of our economy's efficiency, but of its inefficiency.

It is hard for most of us, snowed under with the lies of our politicians, propagandists, public relations and advertising men, to see how extraordinarily *inefficient* our economy has become. Consider Denmark. The Danes live much as we do. They are not ascetics. They like their pleasures. A British economist estimated not long ago that for their economic system they command, per capita, only about one-twentieth of the resources we do. They have little or none of the coal, oil, or other fuels, hydroelectric power, minerals, or timber that we have; they have less arable land per capita, and almost none of that of very high quality; and they have comparatively little of the scenic, cultural, or historical resources that bring many tourists to Switzerland, France, or Italy. But their average standard of living, even measured in strictly economic terms, is close to ours; in less economic terms, it may well be higher. And thirty million or so Americans are poorer than the poorest Dane, and live in a squalor and misery that they would not put up with.

It is in large part because our economy is so much based on fear—the fear of being destitute—that it is inefficient and by nature inflationary. It creates featherbedders, monopolists, and racketeers. When a man's livelihood depends on his having a job, he will create if he can a situation in which some human need—to learn, to build a house, to fix the kitchen sink, to get a haircut, to cure a headache, or whatever—is defined in such a way that he and a few like him become the sole suppliers of it. In short, he wants to corner the market. The more effectively he can do so, the better his livelihood will be. This is why the *median* income of doctors is now about $40,000 a year. Buckminister Fuller has rightly said that it would pay us many times over to give all construction workers a good lifetime pension—$15,000 a year—buy them off, so that we could begin to work seriously on the really vital task of building efficiently the housing we so desperately need. The fear that may once have made our economy run now keeps it from running.

I have offered a guess that we could do the work we now do in two-thirds of the time or less if we did it as well and efficiently as we could. This would give us a work week, for those working, of 20–25 hours. But we protect these work weeks, these jobs, these livelihoods, by excluding in various ways many of our people from the job market—the young, the old, a great many women, millions in the armed forces, and millions of unemployed. The young we shut up in schools. The old we force out of the job market with "retirement," which for many people comes at 50, not 65, and which forces many people against their will into idleness and poverty. We exclude women from many jobs and we make years of useless schooling a requirement for many jobs that could be done as well or better without it. If everyone who wanted to could do a share of what we now consider "the work," how long would they have to work to do it? Twenty hours a week, or more likely, fifteen or ten. And if our economy became truly humane and efficient, if we quit the business of meeting nonneeds, or of creating needs so that we could meet them, or defining real needs so that they could only be met in the most expensive ways, the average work week might be less than ten hours. If we define "work" in the old Puritan sense of something unpleasant we have to spend a large part of our time doing whether we like it or not, most people will not have to "work" at all. Whatever truly unpleasant or dangerous work there is we can divide up fairly among many people, or pay so much for that some people will be glad to do it, or learn how to do it with machines. Work for most people can then become what it should be—what they do because it seems worth doing.

In our society we go to great trouble to preserve *the moral purity* of work. We do not care much whether work is useful, and we are scandalized by the thought that it might be interesting, pleasant, even joyful. We cling instead to the belief that work should be unpleasant, disagreeable, boring; that it should take up most of a man's waking life; and that he should do it only under the pressure of greed and fear. But we preserve this moral purity of work for a minority of our people only by denying to all the rest the possibility of working at all.

In a time of scarcity people quite rightly called idleness a curse. The curse of our time, perhaps soon a fatal one, is not idleness, but work not worth doing, done by people who hate it, who do it only because they fear that if they do not they will have no "job," no livelihood, and worse than that, no sense of being useful or needed or worthy. We used to try to make people afraid and ashamed not to work. Now we not only do not need such people, we cannot afford them. In their frantic need to keep busy, to promote more and more useless growth, they will destroy the earth. In their need to protect their own livelihoods, they will block at every possible turn all our efforts to make our economy more efficient, less wasteful, less destructive—that is, truly economical and conservative.

It would be the most hard-headed political and economic realism for us to guarantee and provide to *every* American, man, woman, or child, an income on which he can live decently and comfortably, whether he has a "job" or not. He can then do whatever work he does, not out of fear of want, but because it interests him and seems worth doing. The much discussed so-called Negative Income Tax might well be an easy and sensible way to do this. Then we can begin to open up all these corporate, professional, institutional, and occupational monopolies that make people's lives so difficult and expensive, and so much out of their control. We can at the same time work on another fundamental and urgent economic task. As I have said, it clearly won't help people much to raise their incomes if even then they can't buy the things they need, or if the cost of everything they buy goes up faster than their income. How can we make, more efficiently, at less cost to the environment, more durably, less expensively, the goods and services that people really need. How might we redefine some of these needs so as to make it possible to meet them at less expense? More important yet, how can we make it more and more possible for people to make themselves many of the things they need. These are some of the questions that Paul Goodman (and perhaps others) for many years, and more recently Ivan Illich and Everett

Reimer in their writings, have been asking us to think about. Most people have put this off, finding it easier to call such ideas "idealistic," "romantic," or "impractical." Now that the world of the so-called practical men is coming down about our ears, being swallowed up in poison and junk, we had better think while we still can. To put all this another way, we need to find ways constantly to *lower* the poverty line, that is, to *reduce* more and more what it costs to live a decent, comfortable, and human life. This would be the mark and test of a truly efficient economy—how *little* a person in it would need to live well.

It must be clear that much of this will require large-scale government action and support. The kind of serious thinking, research, planning, and investment that we will need to move ahead on some of these problems, to find and make, for example, really efficient forms of housing and transportation, will require the kind of effort that until now we have reserved for atomic bombs, moon shots, supersonic planes, and the like. Our research priorities are all wrong. In the face of a serious fuel and energy crisis, with the ocean itself in grave danger from ever greater oil spills, and the air more and more seriously polluted from the burning of fossil fuels, we are spending almost nothing on research to find economic ways to use the great energy of the sun, the winds, the tides, and the natural heat of the earth. (NOTE: The January, 1972, issue of *Environment* has much interesting material on this.) We are not even spending much money on what I would have thought would be the technocrats' darling, the development of thermonuclear power—though if the Russians get to it we will get to work in a hurry. We need vastly better ways to store and transmit energy, so that we may easily collect it in one place and use it in another. We are spending almost no money to find ways of using our enormous quantities of animal waste. Issue Number 10 of *Mother Earth News* (see Appendix) tells how an Englishman, Harold Bate, has developed a simple process for using animal manures to generate methane gas, which may then be used to drive conventional internal combustion engines (more cleanly, more efficiently than gasoline, and without emissions), heat houses, and do other work. The yield is surprisingly high; from three hundred or so pounds of high-grade (chicken) manure, he was reported as getting the equivalent of about sixty U.S. gallons of gasoline. Even if the fig-

ure were too high by a factor of ten or twenty, this opens up exciting possibilities. In 1966, the man in the Department of Agricul-
ture who had the task, *unaided,* of finding out what to do with
enormous quantities of animal wastes produced in our agricultural
industry, reported that our more than ninety million cattle produced about 13 tons of manure per animal per year, or a total of
over a billion tons. If we could convert any large part of that to
methane, it could take the place of the gasoline that we now use.
This would very much reduce dangerous auto emissions, would reduce the need for huge tankers, destructive pipelines, etc., and
would make useful waste products that are now almost wholly useless and indeed harmful, since we simply dump most of them into
our waters. But no one I have heard of in this country, or even in
Britain, where gasoline is scarce and very expensive, is looking seriously into this. This has less to do, I suspect, with sinister plots by
the oil companies than with the fact that while fooling around with
nuclear reactors is scientifically respectable, fooling around with
chicken, cow, etc. manure is not.

In other important areas we do nothing, or lag behind. We
urgently need new forms of high-speed ground transportation. For
years the French have been working on a centrally mounted, air-
supported, jet or electric powered monorail, that can travel at
speeds close to 200 mph. By now, as I write, they have a full-size
pilot model built and running on 25 miles or so of track, and they
may be very close to building some lines for actual use. A German
company, Messerschmitt-Bölkow-Blohm, of Munich, is working on
an even more advanced type, magnetically supported, to travel at
about 300 mph. Very little such work is going on here. Our own
Department of Transportation is keeping in touch with what these
other countries are doing, but it hasn't the money to do much
more than that. If we are going to subsidize aerospace companies,
as we are, why not put them to work on something useful like this,
instead of wasting money on space shuttles and similar junk? Nor
has there been any large-scale research and development of something else we need equally badly, a small, low-cost, low-powered,
passenger driven, coin or token or card operated electric car for our
cities. In the October issue of *Harper's,* Charlton Ogburn, in the
article "A Modest Proposal" suggested in considerable and sensible detail what such a car might be like—as it happens, very like

the car I have had in the back of my own mind for several years. The auto industries are, for the most obvious reasons, not going to develop or build such a car. But it would cost the government a lot less to develop and build it, or prepare plans and/or kits from which it could be built locally, than it regularly spends on complicated weapons systems, half of which turn out not to work or are never used, or that it spends to bail out incompetent and bankrupt aerospace companies.

The list could go on. The Swedes are well ahead of us in research on the preventing of pollution, on the recycling of industrial and human wastes. They have developed, for example, a vacuum sewage system instead of our water-carried gravity system. This saves water and reduces the amount of piping needed to carry sewage. It also makes possible far more efficient ways of purifying water for reuse, and turning wastes into compost or fertilizer. This vacuum system has been licensed to an American company—National Homes Corporation—and is being installed in a large housing project in Washington, D.C. But we should be looking into these things ourselves, not waiting on other smaller and poorer countries to find out for us what we need to know.

What we have to do, then, is to change many of the research, development, and spending policies of the government. This means that much of our task is political. We have to create, bring together, organize a public demand for these changes. We have to make and build political alliances between groups that now see each other only as rivals and enemies. This means in turn that we have a lot of educating to do. We can't do it all in schools (though these matters should be discussed there). We must use all the means, all the media, every possible channel of talk and print in the entire society. Only in this very broad sense can we say that the problem of poverty is in part a problem of education.

10

Deschooling and the Poor

A poor parent might well say, "All that stuff might be okay, but my kids are going to be old before any of that gets done. I'm worried about them right now, and I want to do something right now to get them ahead, and the only place I can see to push is school." In the same way, people who work with poor kids often say to me, "Listen, when I am working with some poor kid, I haven't got time to worry about changing society or deschooling or any stuff like that. I'm going to tell that kid to go to college and I'm going to do everything I can to get him there, so *he* can have a better chance to make it in society."

Fair enough. But suppose we had known, back in the early 1930's, a young working-class man or woman, working in some then nonunion factory. Suppose this young person had just begun to hear about the unions that were trying to organize the plants. Suppose he was thinking of joining, or even helping them to organize. Suppose we then had said, "Listen, now, you don't want to go fooling around with that union. If the company finds out, they'll fire you sure as hell. What's more, they'll blacklist you, and you won't be able to get a job anywhere else. You'll just ruin your future messing around with them. Stay out of it, work hard, do what you're told, keep your nose clean, and with a little luck you can get yourself promoted to foreman and maybe in time something even better than that." Wouldn't that have been good prudent advice? Of course it would. And what would have happened to industrial workers, where would they be now, if that advice had been followed, if some people hadn't been willing to stick their necks out, risk their own chances, for the sake of many others?

What schools say to poor kids today is very much like what antiunion employers used to say to workers then: "What do you want a union for? Anyone who works hard enough can get to be

165

president of this company." There was some truth in it; in those days (but not now) some poor kids did work their way up to the top of the company. But that road was only open to a very few people. For most it offered no hope at all. Today the message is, "Work hard in school, do better than all these other kids, get that degree, and you'll make it in society." True enough, but again, only for a very few. There are no comfortable spots in society sitting there unoccupied, just waiting for some deserving poor kid to come along and occupy them. There is no great surplus of good, high-paying jobs and big stylish houses in the suburbs. The comfortable and pleasant and powerful places in society are *occupied,* and the people who are in those places are not going to move out of them and down in society just so that poor people can move up and in. There is a kind of crazy Adam Smith way of looking at things beneath this idea that if every poor parent tries to get the best schooling he can for his kid, and every poor kid in school works as hard as he can for himself, the result is going to be something better for all poor kids. It is just not so.

In all I have said so far I have allowed for the sake of argument that on a very small scale, for any one poor kid or a small number of kids, doing well in school and getting school credentials may help them rise in the world, and therefore, that on a very small scale it makes sense for a poor parent or parents to press for more and "better" schooling for their children. Though the first part of this statement seems true, I doubt very much whether the same can be said for the second. It might be true if the schooling race— the race for scarce credentials, tickets giving access to higher places in society—was a fair race, with black and white, rich and poor kids competing on equal terms, and if after the race was run the prizes were distributed fairly. Neither is true. Schools would favor rich kids over poor even if they wanted to treat all kids equally—and they don't want to. And the prizes that poor kids get when they do occasionally win this crooked race are not worth as much as the prizes handed out to the rich. The poor kid has to struggle harder for his diploma and it is worth less to him when he gets it.

In short, I don't think the schools are or can be made into a kind of springboard or ladder to help poor kids rise in the world. Instead, I think that schools and schooling, by their very nature, purposes, structure, and ways of working are, and are meant to be, an obstacle to poor kids, designed and built not to move them up in the world but to keep them at the bottom of it and *to make them think it is their own fault.* The odds against not just all poor kids but any poor kid being helped rather than hurt by school are enormous. For the parents of poor kids to put all their hopes into getting good schooling for their kids seems to me to have about as much chance of paying off as putting all their money into sweepstakes. They would almost certainly be wiser to put their time, energy, and political muscle into getting the obstacle of schooling out of the way of their kids, instead of trying to turn it into what it was never meant to be and with the best intentions in the world never can be.

A story in the January 10, 1972, issue of *Newsweek* gives a very good example of what I have in mind. It describes an eighteen-year-old black, Hunter Nicholas, who recently presented a research paper to forty members of the American Federation for Clinical Research. The story reads, in part:

> Nicholas is the finest and youngest flower so far of an informal program that was started three years ago at Boston City Hospital by Dr. Gary Huber, chief of Harvard University's pulmonary unit at the hospital's Channing Laboratory for Infectious Diseases. Huber's program doesn't even have a name, let alone a fancy acronym, but its purpose is to expose interested young people to medical procedures and give them positions of genuine responsibility in a research laboratory. The program has no funding and seeks none. It also lacks entrance exams and admission criteria. Huber, as a one-man screening board, looks for motivation, not academic credentials, in the dozen or more teenagers who volunteer for work in his laboratory each year. "We underestimate what young minds can do," he says. His own motivation is a belief that the fifteen year grind of conventional medical education can do terrible things to a student's head. "It's a crazy way to train people. You usually put them into a lock step of learning by rote during what ought to be their most creative period."
>
> . . . Nicholas' project was a modest one . . . [it] sought to quantify the loss of resistance to infection, rather than to speculate on the ultimate mechanisms of that loss. But any researcher,

let alone an 18-year-old, could take professional pride in the work, which involved histology, the use of laboratory animals, statistics, X-rays, and radio-labeled bacteria.

. . . Nicholas is eager to give credit to Huber's program. "This is really revolutionary, you know, it's really going against the system." And so it is. The system dictates that a medical student do intellectual drudgery for at least eight years, that he delay the beginning of his practice until he's in his mid-30's and overschooled, underexperienced, often exhausted and sometimes only five or so years away from his first heart attack.

The most revolutionary of Huber's notions is that high-school students can do useful, original research, even though their overall knowledge of medicine is limited. He feels that Nicholas probably knows more about the effects of radiation on lung tissue than 97% of the doctors in the world. "Getting to be really knowledgeable about a specific aspect of research may involve reading and digesting 50 or so papers. That's a finite number. It can be done. Research isn't all that special," Huber insists. "You don't need the education. You just need to know how to think."

Before looking further at the many ways in which schools discriminate against the poor, let me try to make clear what I mean, and what I do *not* mean, when I talk of a deschooled society and alternatives to schooling. Some people take a deschooled society to mean a society exactly like ours, but with school attendance noncompulsory. Others take it to mean a society without any schools, or indeed any planned and organized learning arrangements at all. Neither is even close to what I have in mind. A "schooled" society is not just a society full of schools, or one in which many people for many years have to go to school whether they want to or not. It is not just a society in which the state, which has not yet made everything its business, has made education its business—and indeed as far as many people are concerned, its monopoly. It is, of course, both of these things. But beyond that it is a society in which most of the tools and resources of learning are locked up in schools. It is a society in which it has been made very difficult to learn or do many things outside of school, and almost impossible to get official credit or recognition for having learned or done them.

In a schooled society you have to go to school to learn something. But even there you cannot learn just what you want to learn. You can only learn what they want to teach, and in the order and manner in which they want to teach it to you. Most of what they teach is strictly placed and locked in what Ivan Illich calls a graded curriculum, a sort of ladder of learning. This ladder is very hard to get on and off. As a rule, a learner may not take a step on that ladder unless he has taken many steps before it (all in school) and unless he is willing to take (again in school) many steps after it. Suppose you find that a school is teaching something you want to learn, and you go there, money in hand, and say, "I want to come here for a year (month, week, day) and learn that." They will tell you, "No, you can't do that, you have to learn or prove that you have already learned (in school, of course) many other things *first,* and you will also have to learn many other things *besides.* Where are your prerequisites? How do we know you are good enough to learn here? What previous schooling have you had" (not "What have you done, what do you know?")? "Where are your transcripts, your diplomas? Are you a candidate for a degree? Which one? And so on . . ."

Suppose you are a student at a school and want to learn something they are not teaching. One day you find that some other school is teaching it. You say, "I want to go to this other school and learn this thing they are teaching. Will you give me credit for it?" In almost all cases, their answer will be No. The other school probably wouldn't let you learn the thing they are teaching anyway. They would say, "If you want to learn something here, you have to be one of *our* students and learn all the other things *we* are teaching." Learning, in short, comes in packages—four-year packages, sometimes twelve-year packages. You may have a choice of packages, but you always have to buy a whole package, or get nothing. A strange procedure. Obviously it has more to do with merchandising than with learning.

This we want to change. Conversely, by a deschooled society we don't mean a society without any arrangements and resources for learning. Ivan Illich in *Deschooling Society,* Everett Reimer, in *School Is Dead,* and I in this book, among others, have suggested what some of these resources and arrangements might be, and others will add many other ideas to the list. We don't even mean a society without any schools. Some things—languages, music, dance—may be better learned in a school than in any other way, or may even require a school. If some people like schools and learn well there, let them by all means go to schools. If some people think they cannot learn anything unless they pay a teacher to teach it to them, let them by all means find and pay their own teachers. But in a deschooled society nobody would be compelled to go to school, neither by the law nor by the threat of joblessness, poverty, discrimination, and exclusion from society—all of which are in force today. No one would be punished or disadvantaged for not liking schools, not finding them good places to learn, and not learning there, or for wanting and trying to learn in other ways. No one, whether for lack of money, previous schooling, or any other reason, could be denied access to the opportunity and resources to learn or try to learn whatever he wants to learn. No one could have his right to learn made to depend on his first being able to pass some sort of test. Thus, it is fair and sensible to say that anyone who wants to drive a car must first pass a driving test, to show that he can in fact drive it. But it would not be at all fair or sensible to say that he must pass a test before he can even try *to learn to drive*. In sum, a deschooled society would be a society in which everyone shall have the widest and freest possible choice to learn whatever he wants to learn, whether in school or in some altogether different way. This is very far from being a society in which poor kids would have no chance to learn things. On the contrary, poor kids, like poor people, and indeed all people, would have many more chances to learn things and many more ways of learning them than they have today. It would be a society in which there were many paths to learning and advancement, instead of one school path as we have now—a path far too narrow for everyone, and one too easily and too often blocked off from the poor.

It is sad that the poor have found it so nearly impossible to imagine, far less demand or make, arrangements other than schools for their children to learn in—arrangements that might be many times cheaper and better. For we have known for years now that schools do not work for most poor kids. They learn little or nothing there, except perhaps to think that they are incapable of learning. Many of them get more frightened, hopeless, defeated, stupid, angry, and self-destructive every year they stay there. Some come out not knowing things they knew when they went in. George Dennison, Daniel Fader, James Herndon, Nat Hentoff, Jonathan Kozol, and by now a host of others have written eloquently on this point. And this is nothing new. It was just as true when the poor children in our country were nearly all white, and it is equally true where the people are all of one color or race.

In most schools and school systems, in this and a number of other countries, poor children are in a great many ways discriminated against, humiliated, and often brutally treated. Wherever schools allow what they call "corporal punishment," by which they mean the practice of allowing teachers, on whatever pretext they may choose, to assault and beat children, it is poor children who get beaten the most and the worst. Indeed, even for the severest offenses, upper-class children are rarely beaten at all. In all schools and school systems that divide children by so-called ability—tracking as it's called here, streaming as it's called in Great Britain—the poor children are almost all and always in the lower tracks. Studies have often shown an almost perfect correlation between family income and school tracking—rich kids at the top, poor at the bottom. Furthermore, the poor kids are put into the lowest track almost from the moment they enter school. Once in, they have little chance of getting out. Teachers of low tracks have often told me that even when a student was doing very good work the school would not allow them to give him a high grade, on the grounds that if he were capable of doing that good work, he wouldn't be in the low track. That he had been in the low track almost from the first day he entered school was dismissed as irrelevant.

An even more horrifying example of the way this discrimination works in a *kindergarten* class can be found in the article "Student Social Class and Teacher Expectations: The Self-Fulfilling Prophecy in Ghetto Education" by Ray Rist, in the August, 1970 issue of the Harvard Educational Review. The kindergarten teacher described, after only eight days of school, and entirely on the basis of appearance, dress, manners, in short middleclassness, divided her class into three tracks by seating them at three separate tables, which remained fixed for the rest of the year. One of these tables got most of her teaching, attention, and support; the other two were increasingly ignored except when the teacher told them to do something or commented unfavorably on what they did. Worse yet, the children at the favored table were allowed and encouraged to make fun of the children at the other two tables, and to boss them around.

Some of this has changed a little, for a number of reasons—bad publicity, poor people's militancy, the growing crisis of schools in cities and out—but it is not likely to change very much. One reason is simple and hard to escape. The schools, particularly the schools where poor kids go, are filled with people who don't like poor kids. Almost everyone I know who has had wide experience with inner city schools has found this to be true. The reasons are many, having to do with social class, background, life-style, charac-ter, temperament, taste, and sex. Race seems to be much less im-portant. Some very good teachers of poor, minority kids have been white, while some of the worst have been people from their own race, new migrants from poverty into the middle class. In *The Way It Spozed to Be,* James Herndon gives us this description of Mrs. A., who substituted for him in his class for a month:

". . . She thought that what these kids needed was to learn to conform to the ordinary standards of American society, morals and language. She also thought that too many teachers, faced with these children—just give up on them, considered them hopeless, wouldn't give them a chance.

It wasn't surprising that we had so little to say to each other. She believed my classes were a mess because I was white and they were Negro kids and so I thought they weren't worth making an effort for. I thought she was working hard to help them in a way that hadn't ever helped them, wouldn't help them in the future, and was in fact cementing them into failure, rebellion or apathy. She thought I couldn't imagine them ever being tolerable stu-dents or responsible citizens. I thought that she, a middle-class Negro woman in a lamb's-wool sweater, had less contact with these students than I, knew less about them, mistrusted them more, thought less of their capabilities, and disliked them, as they were now, utterly."

Daniel Fader, in *The Naked Children,* tells of a teacher who called a student, one of Fader's five friends, "a jungle nigger." Of her, he says, "I knew the teacher, and I knew how well she deserved her reputation for a vicious mouth. . . . No one in the school who had any prolonged contact with the woman had escaped her mouth." But, as he explained to the children, it would do no good for him to complain about her, because he was white and she was black.

Far more damaging are the teachers—very often the same teachers—who, believing that poor kids can't learn anything and don't want to learn anything, don't try to urge or help or encourage them to learn anything, preferring to settle instead, when they can get it, for peace and quiet. Herndon, in *The Way It Spozed to Be*, describes a *teacher*, Mrs. Z., white, who on the grounds that she had been taught while young only to speak to ladies and gentlemen, and that her black students were not and never could be ladies and gentlemen, *did not speak* to them, ever, all year, and refused to allow them ever to speak to her—sending them from the room if they did. All the teachers told him that the best way to keep the children quiet was to have them copy paragraphs from the board—never mind what was in the paragraphs. And the school itself made a bargain with one particularly unruly boy, that they would at the end of the year read out his name as one of the winners of the citywide spelling contest if he, hanging around school though never attending classes, would not make any trouble while he was there. The bargain was kept; the principal, whose bargain it must have been, duly read out his name to the unbelieving students; but the boy couldn't spell and both he and all the other students knew he couldn't. Daniel Fader describes other such teachers. One let students sit silent and ignored in class day after day, month after month, as long as they did not speak up, and so bother her and her two or three "good students." Many other teachers were given enough copies of the daily newspaper so that every student could read his own, but instead of using them or letting students use them left all the papers untouched in the back of their classrooms. When that secret was exposed by the man who later collected the papers, one teacher had her students spend the last few minutes in class messing up the newspapers so that other people would think they had been using them. Jonathan Kozol describes, in *Death at an Early Age*, how every time he began to provide for the black children in his classes the kind of enrichment or special materials that white children were used to having, and indeed every time he found something that the black children were really interested in, he was told by the school authorities to stop using it. For, after all, if teachers have been saying for years that these children can't learn and don't want to learn, and then someone comes along and shows that they both can and want to, it threatens the other teachers' alibi. It is easier and safer to go on teaching the children in ways that you know won't work, because they never have worked, and then to go on blaming the children.

Many such teachers will be in our schools for some time, or at least as long as we have schools. For a while, it looked as if it might be changing. Under the pressure of the Asian War and the draft, many more young men began to go into teaching. Also, many of the education students were far more politically minded, and critical, than earlier students. They saw teaching, not as a clean and respectable job with long vacations, the trappings of professionalism, and a pension at the end, but as a way to challenge and change society. But the numbers of such people going into teaching will almost certainly decline. Our Asian War, though it may go on forever as far as Asians are concerned, may soon be largely over for most young American men, who will not have the incentive they had for going into teaching. Also, our critical and change-minded young may turn away, as many are turning, from the idea that the schools are now a good place to work for major social change. Most important of all, the sudden and very great surplus of teachers will make it easy for most schools to keep out and weed out the kind of teachers who want to rock the boat, or even those who are able to make contact, alliances, and friendships with poor kids.

Schools and school people, even those who do not dislike poor kids, discriminate against them in another way, more kindly, less contemptuous, but probably more destructive. These people— and there are many of them—really want to help the kids. But they believe that everything in the life of a poor kid—his home, his family, his street, his neighborhood, his speech, his friends, his values, his way of dress, his tastes, virtually everything he knows, does, and likes—is a kind of disease of which he must be cured as a precondition of learning or becoming anything. To educate a poor kid, for such people, does not mean—what Paulo Freire would call "awakening of consciousness"—taking him where he is, helping him understand that, and then helping him grow from there further and further out into the real world that surrounds him. It means, in effect, trying to make him over into an altogether different kind of person. I remember once hearing a very able and intelligent chairman of a school board in one of our largest cities say with real distress, to explain the learning troubles that many poor children were having, that many of them came into the schools not knowing what a dining room was.

Fader shows us how the teachers in a Washington, D.C. junior high school, many of them black, resisted in many ways, and after a brief acceptance slowly sabotaged and abandoned a reading and writing program—the kind he described in *Hooked on Books*—that really worked. They agreed it worked—children who had never read were now reading. But they were reading what they liked! How can that be educational? Education, and particularly education of poor kids, means making them over, improving them. Since this process demands that from the beginning the children deny who they are, they resist it. Of the matter of Standard English, and the refusal of black children to learn it, and their more striking refusal to use it even when they have learned it, Fader writes:

> Children of white immigrants knew they had only to assume the clothing of the dominant group—in large part, its language—and they could live undetected in its midst. Knowing that lifelong masquerade to be beyond them . . . black and brown children see no reason for wearing clothes that give them neither warmth nor camouflage. . . . They know that standard English isn't worth its cost; they know that they may not be able to prevent their minds from learning it, but they also know that they can prevent their mouths from speaking it. They know that it is better repressed because it has no place in their lives. Who but a fool practices for a contest to which he will not be admitted, a struggle in which he will not be allowed to compete?

Much of what the schools work hardest to teach poor kids, and penalize them most for not learning, has nothing to do with any real knowledge, competence, understanding, or skill. Defenders of schools constantly ask whether I would want to be operated on by a doctor without any training, or willing to cross a bridge built by someone without any training, etc. Of course not. Nobody says that people can or should practice medicine or build bridges without some kind of training. The question is whether the training they now get is in fact the most efficient and most productive training that they could get, and beyond that, whether such training is best given in a school. I doubt that it is, just as I doubt that most of what practicing surgeons or bridgebuilders know about their work was learned in a schoolroom. But it certainly doesn't matter to me whether the person who takes out my appendix, builds the bridge I cross, or whatever, says "ain't" or not, speaks Standard English or not (one of the best doctors I know does not), uses four-letter words in his speech, wears funny clothes or haircuts, or shares my tastes in books and music. But these are the things the schools think they have to teach *first,* and the children who don't learn them, or refuse to learn them, or pretend not to learn them, are never allowed to get far enough up the school ladder to have a chance to learn how to take out appendixes or build bridges. In short, what schools demand of poor kids, as a condition of being given a chance to learn some skills that might get them into the middle class, is that they act as if they were already in it. This is not just difficult, but unfair. It is not hard to learn to act rich if you are rich—a little money can wear away a lot of rough edges. But it is damn tough to have to learn to act rich when you are not rich and have no prospects of getting rich.

Much eloquent material has already been written about this. Working-class children in Great Britain who had done well in school, and so received scholarships to grammar schools and universities, were terribly cut off from the places from which they had come, from friends and families. They were self-exiled from the society of their growing up, without having another society in which they could feel welcome and at home. In a private secondary school I have taught black kids who felt the same strain, who told me that many of their old friends would no longer talk to them, looked at them as an outsider and enemy. In Mexico not long ago a young architect, born and raised in a small and remote country village, said to me that for him a condition of being an architect or of even being allowed to study to become an architect, was that he learn to act, talk, dress, and indeed think and feel in such a way that he was totally cut off from that village and all the people he had known there. When he goes back, as he does every so often, they see him as an outsider.

Even more recently I spent quite a part of one evening in Denmark talking to a student at a university there. She was an unusually tense and anxious person. Perhaps eased by Danish beer and the sense of a sympathetic listener, she said things to me that most of the time she might well have kept hidden. Having grown up in a low-income, working-class family, and being unusually good at school, she was pushed along into fast classes and eventually into the university. In this process she had learned to be deeply ashamed of her parents and everything about them—and was even more painfully ashamed of herself for being ashamed. In spite of feeling that she ought not to, and even trying not to, she could not help despising—her word—her parents' way of speaking, their ideas, their interests, everything about them. I suggested to her that the schools she had gone to had worked hard to make her feel this way, so that the fault was more theirs than hers, but this didn't help much. As Illich and Reimer so well put it, school teaches above all the superiority of the schooled, and one of the very first and most important requirements for getting ahead in school and rising in the world is that the student accept this myth as true. In other words schools require of poor children, as a condition of getting more schooling and a chance to learn what might help them get rich, that in fundamental and important ways they destroy themselves or cooperate in their own destruction. And even then the schools do not guarantee to deliver what the child has so heavily paid for.

We cannot say it too often. Schools, far from being the means by which poor and minority group kids may escape discrimination, are instead a very powerful instrument of discrimination. A society that discriminates against such people can do so more easily, more invisibly, and with greater impunity in schools than in almost any other place. A poor man accused of crime may not get a very fair shake in court, but at least he has some chance of seeing a court. But a student charged with doing wrong in school, and threatened with punishment that may affect his entire future, has not the slightest chance of defending himself. This gives the schools a very powerful weapon, which many of them do not hesitate to use. They very commonly use the threat of lowering a student's grades as a way of keeping him in line, and as a way of making him submit to humiliation and abuse. Not long ago I talked to a number of students from a high school, in the northeast section of the country, in which many teachers very frequently, in the hearing of the black students, refer to them as "niggers." If they protest or react, they get demerits, or are suspended. They are often suspended for the most trivial or even imagined violations of school rules. On one occasion, a black girl was suspended for several days—I should add that most of the stories the students told me were confirmed by older white people who often visit the school—because, having obtained permission to go to the washroom, she objected and refused to leave when a white cleaning woman tried to order her out. One might ask, since these students don't like school and are not learning much there anyway, why wouldn't they welcome an opportunity to get away for a few days. The trouble is that the school, having ordered the student to be absent, then routinely gives him zeros for his classwork for all the days he missed. There is no way to get these zeros off the book, to make them up, and they get averaged in to make his grade. This is, of course, absolutely inexcusable. Grades tell us little enough, as it is, but if we must use them, the very least we can do is use them to measure academic work and not as a disciplinary threat.

Not long after my talk with these students, I talked for a while to the director of admissions at the state university—the only one most of these students could ever afford to go to. I asked him why some of these students, unquestionably bright and capable of doing college work, could not be admitted to the university on the basis of a high school equivalency exam, or some other kind of test, ignoring their high school grades, which had been so often lowered for disciplinary reasons. He said, in effect, that the legislature and the public would not stand for it. Access to state-supported higher education, in their view, has relatively little to do with ability or potential. It is a reward for good behavior.

Schooling discriminates against the poor in another way, for another reason. Schools are expensive, more expensive than most people imagine who are not paying school bills, and more expensive all the time. I have already described how everything in the present situation, in the competition among students for more schooling, and the competition among schools for "higher standards," reputation, and prestige, combine to drive the cost of schooling even higher. And schools are expensive for another and more fundamental reason. Ivan Illich best expressed it one time in conversation with some students. He said that for a very long time men had been learning knowledge and skill within institutions. In the shoemaker's shop the apprentice shoemaker learned to cut and sew leather, to make shoes; the apprentice painter learned about canvases, pigments, paints, in the master painter's workshop; the apprentice mason and builder learned about stone, stone cutting, and building from the master builder; even the apprentice philosopher learned about philosophy by being around his master when he was practicing it. But, though each of those institutions produced learning, that was not their main task. The shoemaker's shop was there to produce shoes; the painter's studio, to make paintings; the mason and builder's shop, to make buildings; and so on. It is only recently, at least on a large scale, that man has come to think that learning best takes place in an institution that doesn't produce anything but learning. Hence the expensiveness of schools. They are expensive because they are wasteful and unproductive.

Some people at a big state university were not long ago showing me around one of their new campuses. They told me proudly that only a few years before there had been only a few thousand students here; now there were 22,000, and there would soon be many more than that. Everywhere new buildings were up, surrounded by the raw earth left by the bulldozers. These were usually not far away, digging up the earth for other new buildings. Looking at all this expensive activity, and in a community which like most American communities is short of good housing, I had a quick fantastic vision. I imagined myself the guide for a visitor from outer space, showing him around various parts of our society, and telling about what people do here. I imagined him coming with me to this campus, looking at all the buildings and activity, and saying, "What do people do here?" The answer that came to my mind was, "Well, as a matter of fact, they don't really do anything." Those 22,000 students—what were they doing? Most of them were on campus to get a piece of paper that (they thought) would enable them to do whatever they were going to do next, when they got out of school. Most of them, if given the piece of paper, would leave immediately and do that next thing. Most of them, if they left right away with paper in hand to do that next thing, would do it about as well as they will do it after many more years on this or some other campus. Others of the students are here because they don't know what to do next, or because they want to put off, for as long as they can, whatever they will do next.

Meanwhile, one might say that all those students are learning something. Perhaps they are. But they will not long remember more than a small part of it, or use or benefit from more than a small part of that. They are learning this stuff to pass exams. Most of them could not pass the same exam even a year later, to say nothing of ten years later. And, if some of what they learn should someday prove useful, they would probably have learned it ten times faster when they needed to use it and thus had a reason for learning it. The anthropologist Edward Hall told me not long ago that when he first started working as a dendocrinologist (determining the age of pieces of wood by the patterns of the rings) he had to make statistical correlations between the rings of one specimen piece and another, and learned easily in a couple of weeks what most college statistics courses take months or more to teach.

By contrast, I think of a really effective educational institution—the submarine on which I served during the latter part of World War II. Because we were at war, and because the submarine service was expanding, and because there was, in the navy as everywhere, a shortage of trained and skillful people, everyone on board that ship was advancing in skill, rank, and responsibility many times faster than he would have in peacetime. In every department, the experienced men passed on their skill to the younger ones. When an engine, or compressor, or electric motor, or piece of radio equipment or whatever, had to be taken apart and fixed, the men who knew how to do the work made sure that men who didn't know were watching and helping them do it. They explained as they worked; whenever they could, they let the younger man turn the nut or the screw, remove the part, take the reading. We had to train our younger men for several reasons. The older man might be sick, or hurt or killed at sea, and we would have to depend on the younger. More likely, the more experienced men would be taken from us to fill more responsible posts elsewhere, or to make up the core of the crew of a new ship. Also, it was very good for morale to have the higher positions filled by men who had, so to speak, grown up on the ship. Seeing the men just above them learn and advance rapidly gave the younger men a strong incentive to learn. And the older men themselves had a strong incentive to pass on their skill. They were not worried about the younger men "taking their jobs" away from them. There was no reason to hoard their skill or turn it into a mystery. On the contrary, there was every reason to have the younger men as skilled as they could make them. It meant that if we got in a real emergency and had to fix many pieces of machinery or equipment all at once, there were plenty of people who knew enough to do it, so that we could get it done quickly. It also meant that the routine work, heavy and hard enough, of keeping a complicated ship running could be more evenly spread around, instead of resting largely on the older men.

All this made the ship, like the submarine force in general and beyond that the navy as a whole, a most effective school. But what made it most effective of all was that it was not *just* a school, not even primarily a school. It had other and more important work to do—in our own case, to find Japanese ships and sink them and at the same time to keep them from sinking us. This gave a great seriousness to the learning. When, in the middle of the China Sea, we had to pull a cylinder head off one of our main engines, we were not pulling it so that young machinists could see what it looked like. We were pulling it because that engine was not running right and had to be fixed, and fixed right, and right away, for the difference between having three engines and four might be the difference between life and death. Men learned as they worked, and the lives of everyone on board ship constantly depended on both the work and the learning being done well.

To a great extent, what was true of our submarine, or the U.S. Navy, was true of the whole country. We suddenly needed, urgently, quickly, many highly skilled people. We found very soon that almost any person with a skill, if he wants to, can teach it very quickly to anyone else who wants to learn it. We also found that almost anyone who wants to learn a skill, and knows that as soon as he learns it he can use it, can learn it very quickly. We found that whole lists of skills, which people had said could be learned only through years of slow experience, could in fact be learned—like writing and reading—in a matter of weeks. We found that skills are learned fastest when learned closest to where they will be used.

Thus we needed welders for our shipyards and light metal workers and riveters for aircraft factories. Did we with vast effort and expense introduce Welding and Riveting into the curriculum of our high schools, and say—as we do for Reading and Mathematics—that nobody could get a diploma unless they had passed years of courses in Welding and Riveting? Did we tell people who wanted to learn to rivet and weld that they could not learn it unless they learned a lot of other things first? Did we ask to see their high school diplomas and transcripts? Did we set up some kind of job corps to prepare them to learn riveting and welding? We had no time for such foolishness. We took the people we wanted to have learn to rivet and weld to places where riveting and welding was going on, and we put them in contact with people who already knew how to do it, and we said, "Show these people how to do it, and when they can do it, put them to work."

This seems to me the model of a sensible educational system for a poor community, a poor minority group, or a poor nation. They are in a position very much like that of a ship, or a nation at war. They can't afford the luxury of people "making it" at other peoples' expense, or of separating learning from work and the rest of life. They can't afford to require their skilled people to decide whether they will use their skill or teach it and spread it around; whether lawyers or mechanics, professionals or craftsmen and artisans, they must do both at once.

Instead of this, the poor have only schooling. What does this cost them, specifically the college degree, that so many of them have been trained to think they must get. The Kiplinger magazine, *Changing Times,* published in May, 1971 an article called, "Colleges With Openings," which gives a clue. It listed 57 colleges, and for each gave average yearly expenses per student for tuition and fees, and for room and board. The tuition and fees expenses were further broken down for in-state and out-of-state students. The table below shows the number of the colleges listed for which the expenses fell in the given range:

Cost in Dollars	Tuition and Fees in State	Tuition and Fees Out of State	Room and Board
under 1,000	8	3	12
1,000–1,500	5	6	43
1,500–2,000	11	15	2
2,000–2,500	21	21	——
2,500+	12	12	——

The median cost, in tuition and fees, whether for students in or out of state is between $2,000 and $2,500 per year. Many of the colleges in the highest bracket are small private colleges to which perhaps black students or other poor students might not be attracted, so that we might put the median tuition expenses at close to $2,000 per year. The median expense for room and board is between $1,000 and $1,500, but closer to $1,000, though only two of the colleges listed had room and board expense under $800 per year. From all this we can get a rough estimate—it costs about $3,000 per year to go to college, for tuition, fees, and room and board alone. This does not take into account transportation to and from college, or in the college community, or books, or any other such living expenses as clothes, recreation, etc. To be sure, some colleges are cheaper, like the teachers college I spoke of, but their degrees are to just that extent worthless. They do *not* guarantee jobs.

The cost alone is enough to put college—to say nothing of graduate school—effectively out of the reach of most of the children of the poor. To be sure, there are scholarships—but most of the scholarships now given out, according to a report I read not long ago, go to children with family incomes of $10,000 or more; children from families with incomes of $3,000 or less get almost none. In any case, there are scholarships only for a few. The American middle class will not allow itself to be heavily taxed so that poor and minority group's kids can put their own children out of jobs. If we had no way to discriminate against the poor but this, the mere expensiveness of schooling, it is hard to see how we could find a better.

Someone wrote not long ago that schooling had made it easier for people to rise in the world now, because people are picked for jobs by qualifications instead of connections. The trouble is that they are not picked by qualifications, but by school credentials, which are something quite different, and which cost so much that few poor kids can afford to get them. It was once possible for a poor kid to start at the bottom of a company and work his way to the top. It wasn't easy, and it didn't happen often, but it happened. Walter Chrysler, among others, began his career as an apprentice machinist on the factory floor, where to start his training he was given a square, some kind of ruler, a file, and a lump of metal, and told to file the metal to a one-inch cube. There really was a path, if a long and narrow one, from buck private in the corporate army all the way up to general. Not any more. No one would even be considered for the management training program of a big company unless he had at least a four-year college degree, and in many firms, to have a shot at a top job one needs more than that. In short, in the race for good jobs, it costs 10 or 15 thousand dollars, and often much more, just to get up to the starting line. If we add the money the student might have earned had he not gone to college, that figure becomes 30 thousand dollars or more.

Schooling does not make it easier for poor kids to get the credentials that would admit them to good jobs. It simply keeps raising the amount of credentials that poor kids have to get. It is much easier, by raising the school requirements of a job, to shut poor kids off from it than it is for them to get that additional schooling. Nowhere in our society are the school requirements of jobs going down. Through these requirements we are constantly closing down, not opening up, the work and career opportunities of the poor. As fast as poor kids learn to run the school obstacle course, already much longer and tougher for them than for kids of the middle class, we find ways to make the course still longer. It is a great way, among other things, of burning off the political energies and anger of the poor. We can keep them busy for years scrambling and competing against each other for a scarce handful of degrees, on the chance that they may then get jobs that in most cases could have been done just as well without the degrees. Nor are poor kids free from discrimination even when they get the degrees. They still need the connections. Where before they had to run one obstacle course, now they have to run two.

At the end of this there is no assurance that the degree will get the job. Of some sort of academic conference or meeting, Judson Jerome writes:

> . . . some 1700 Ph.D.'s between the ages of 25 and 30, with a sprinkling of older ones, all with worried looks on their faces, vied for 250 college level teaching jobs. No one really expected to get one.
>
> The mood among the young applicants . . . most of whom are on the prowl for a job, is one of despair. It is somehow very hard for them to accept that after seven or eight years of hard work, study, and deprivation [my note: and about $30,000], their doctorate degree isn't worth the paper it's printed on.
>
> One said she didn't want to settle for teaching on the high school level [my note: there's now a surplus there too]. . . . "Besides, I probably couldn't get a job in high school. I'm overeducated."

Sometimes the word is "overqualified." In either case, as I have said earlier, it's a word that young people had better start thinking about. A school credential can close doors as well as open them. And it's not much easier to lie that you haven't a degree than it is to lie that you have one. People want to know what you did with all those years.

The poster on the subway—paid for (why?) by the Advertising Council of America—says:

> DROP OUT NOW—PAY LATER
> *The cost is only low wages and unemployment.*
> *To get a good job, get a good education.*

But the schools cannot make good anymore on their promise to deliver "good jobs" to those with their diplomas, and least of all can they make good their promise to poor kids.

There is still another argument put forward in defense of more and more schooling for the poor. Not long ago an able and dedicated professor left a highly successful career at one of the prestige universities to become dean of a small black university in the South. He did so, and urged others to do so, because he said black people needed to go to college to get the skills that were needed in their communities. This is a remarkable statement. When we think of what most people learn in colleges, the kinds of degrees they get and the work they do when they get out, and then think of what we know about the needs of black and other poor communities, it is hard to see how these are going to fit together. A black community might be able to use a doctor or lawyer, but why does it need and how would it use the "skills" of a holder of a degree in any of the Liberal Arts, or almost any of the Social Sciences, or for that matter even in Physics, Chemistry, or Engineering. True enough, such skills may help those who own them to *escape* the black community. But as I have said, this escape route is open to only a few. And in any case, this dean is not talking about escape. He is saying that the few blacks who do get credentials can then help all the others.

It is by no means even certain that what poor communities need most are doctors and lawyers. What might be much more useful to them would be something like army medics, or the pharmacist's mates we had in the navy. When a submarine went on war patrol in World War II, the health needs and problems of a ship of eighty men, which could be and occasionally were serious, were in the hands of a pharmacist's mate, usually a young man with a high school diploma and perhaps two more years of training. The general quality of medical care in the armed forces is considerably higher than it is for the general population, and certainly for the poor. Yet a great deal of the medical work done and treatment given in the armed forces is done and given by people with much less training than those who do this in the civilian world. It is not necessarily or at all true that more and more training means better medical and health care. When we say that only a doctor can treat many minor ailments and injuries it does not mean that they will be treated better; it means that for a great many people they will not be treated at all. Most poor people can't get the diagnoses, advice, and simple treatments that in many cases might be enough to keep them well. The result is that most of them don't get to a doctor until they are seriously ill.

Thus large and increasing numbers of women die prematurely every year from cancer of the breast or uterus because this was not detected sufficiently early. The tests for detecting these cancers, according to an experienced nurse I know, are very simple. It would not be hard to train large numbers of women, with no other medical training, to make these tests, either for themselves or for many other women. To do so might prevent many premature deaths and save large amounts of expensive and often futile medical treatment. But, for the most natural reasons, the medical profession does not want to make the techniques widely available.

We could say much the same thing for lawyers. What poor people need is more knowledge of the law, or easy ways to get that knowledge; more access to the resources of the law when they need help; a better understanding of their rights and opportunities. Some of these needs are now being met by legal aid societies and the like. The November, 1971 issue of *Boston* Magazine, in an article, "What's a nice young law student like you doing in a neighborhood like this?", describes the work of the Boston Legal Assistance Project. Eighty law students assist in "helping people with low incomes solve their legal problems and obtain what they are legally entitled to." Three-quarters of the students receive for their work a full course credit toward their law degree. Above the students are 50 full-time attorneys, all salaried, 32 paid by federal government, 10 paid by VISTA, 6 on fellowship. "Roughly 25 percent of the cases concern domestic relations; 30 percent landlord-tenant disputes; 10 percent consumer problems, including debt, bankruptcy, and fraud, and the remaining 20 percent are cases of miscellaneous nature."

The article describes one student's work with one family:

The Johnson family lives in Dorchester. Two attorneys from the Boston Legal Assistance Project visited them and discovered that four of the six children were sleeping on the floor. The gas was about to be shut off; windows were broken; the furniture was collapsing. Although the Johnsons had received notice of a cost-of-living welfare increase, the additional funds had not been delivered in a year and a half. The mother simply couldn't make ends meet. She was afraid to contact her Welfare Department worker—whom she hadn't seen for three months—for fear that she would be cut off completely from any assistance at all.

The Legal Assistance workers asked the Johnsons and the Howards to make a list of the basic furniture and clothes they needed. The next morning they accompanied Mrs. Johnson to a furniture store to select what she needed and could afford within the limits of her welfare payments. Their next stop was the Welfare Department. The long-absent worker granted her a food order, made arrangements to pay the overdue gas and electric bills and approved the furniture requests and estimates. The Department also agreed to review the Johnson's family budget and see that they received a cost-of-living increase.

This is good work, and these are good people doing it. But why do we need lawyers to do it, or law students, or even college graduates? Why can't poor people do it, or learn to do it, themselves? There are, of course, important differences between lawyers and law students on the one hand, and poor people on the other. They have assets that the poor do not have. But these have very little to do with knowledge of the law. The difference is that poor people are demoralized and frightened, and the law people are not. It is that the law people think they can get things done and change things, and the poor people do not. Schooling had a lot to do with making this difference, with making those poor people much less confident, much more resigned and passive, than they might have been. To be sure, lawyers and law students have more clout than poor people. When they step into the welfare office, people snap smartly to attention—these guys have connections, they can make noise, make trouble. The remedy for this is for poor people to get themselves more clout. After all, this project is almost entirely paid for by the Office of Economic Opportunity in Washington, and the well is running dry. What happens to the poor when it runs dry, or when, as in California, the governor puts heat on Washington to get the program turned off in his state? There are many more poor people than there are lawyers, let alone lawyers with a sense of social responsibility. Why should so many have to depend on so few? How long can they afford to?

Why should the law be such a mystery? My friends in Norway have on their bookshelves a book—a thick book, but one book—called *Norwegian Law*. It may not have all the law of Norway in it, but it has enough so that the citizen can find out for *himself* what the law says to and about him. Many of the things poor people really need to know about the law are not that obscure, and many of the problems they have don't really need to go to court. They need some kind of legal equivalent of pharmacist's mates, that they could pick from among their own number and train themselves. They need for one thing, protection against the kind of fraudulent installment contracts they are so often talked into signing—and it is a disgrace to the so-called legal profession that so many people trained in the law should help to write such contracts, and so many others help to enforce them. They need a place where they could go to find out, in plain language, what a contract means and what it binds them to do. It might be a good idea if we had a law saying that anyone asked to sign a contract could write down what *he* understood that contract to mean, and that the person offering the contract would have to sign that statement and endorse it as being correct, before the contract could be binding. In other words, if I want you to sign a contract, one of my duties is to explain it to you clearly enough so that you really understand it. The common law has long held than an agreement or contract was not binding when based on force, when signed under duress. Why should a contract be any more binding when based on misunderstanding, or as is more likely, on the intent to deceive and defraud?

And why couldn't we have something like an Everyman's dictionary of widely used legal terms, so that people could find out what the law said and meant? Why couldn't those who write the laws be put under a legal obligation to write them clearly. I understand and accept the need for writers of laws to use what is called "court-tested language." But it would surely be possible to provide that when someone writes a law, he must append to it a paraphrase, stating clearly and in nonlegal terms what the law intends and means. I can see no reason to excuse any writer of a law from this obligation; if *he* cannot say clearly what the law means, who can?

Such proposals, to spread out among the people much of the knowledge and skill now held by and reserved to professionals, these professionals quite naturally strongly oppose. They call it "the Dilution of Professional Practice." Exactly. A perfect phrase for it. It *needs* to be diluted. It has become so strong and expensive that poor people, and by now much of the middle class, can no longer afford it, and thus can no longer get any good out of it.

In any case, most of the skills that black and other poor people get, useful or not, expensive or not, *don't* stay in the community. The point was brought home very vividly in an article I read not long ago, a report of a symposium on community organization. One man said that one fact, more than any other, made community organizing terribly difficult, almost impossible. Most of the black or other minority group people who were able to get schooled, trained, skilled, and credentialed, soon stopped working in their own communities. They might still live there, but their work was done outside. The reason was simple. Almost no poor person who has gone through the struggle and sacrifice needed to acquire a high-paying skill *can afford to give that skill away for nothing*. In other words, he must take his skill into the white middle-class community where people can afford to pay for it. Most poor people who become highly schooled are lost to their own communities.

A *New York Times* story, about an increase in violent crime at the north (i.e. Harlem) end of Central Park says in part:

> The reasons that law-enforcement officials give for this escalation of violent crime include growing narcotics use, the continuing migration of untrained jobless men from the South and from Puerto Rico, and *the exodus of middle-class Negroes from Harlem, where they have been a stabilizing influence.* [Italics mine.]

And the article on the Boston Legal Assistance Project said:

> "Black people, in most cases, will prefer a black lawyer to a white one," a BLAP attorney relates. . . . But it's only a partial solution, and a more complete one is difficult. "With the offers that black law school graduates get," the attorney says, "they're not often about to turn back to the same kind of life they've just left."

Evidence of this can be found everywhere. In an article in the magazine section of *The New York Times* of Sunday, January 2, 1972, Nathan Glazer points out what I had not known and would not have suspected, that in the worst slums of our cities, not just the white but also the black and Puerto Rican population is declining.

Those who can get out, do. An editorial in the January, 1972 issue of *Ebony,* entitled "Let's Keep the Inner City Black," urging successful blacks *not* to move out of the ghetto, says, in part:

> ... The ghetto becomes a wilderness. The ambitious and successful are moving out and no one is moving in.
>
> The ghetto of today ... consumes itself. Addicts prey on their neighbors for a TV, a camera or radio that they can sell quickly to get dope. Older men push dope to children who later push dope to those younger than themselves. ... Experienced thieves back a truck to a door and move out an apartment of furniture in the broad open daylight. ... Blacks in the more affluent sections of the ghetto must take recourse to metal doors, chains and bars ... to protect their household belongings. ... The black ghetto is allowed to chew itself to bits and then come the bulldozers, urban renewal (either public or private) and, eventually, whites take over the land.
>
> Too often, now, the black man is nearsighted when it comes to the slum ghetto. ... What is needed now in slum ghettoes is black men who are willing to stay and fight to develop their own neighborhoods. And they should be helped, not only by the blacks in the slums but by the blacks who have "escaped" the slums to more affluent ghettoes or the integrated suburbs. ...

How far we are from any such development can be seen from a most eloquent article in the January, 1972 issue of *Harper's,* "Soul in Suburbia," by Orde Coombs. He makes the point over and over that successful blacks, those who have "made it," get as far away as they can from those who have not, and do not want to be bothered or reminded of them. Coombs (himself black) writes, in part:

> With the onset of black power and the call to black unity, a new kind of black bourgeois duplicity has set in, for the middle-class black can now seem relevant to the black struggle, while remaining aloof from the battle. It has become fashionable for blacks to say that they are involved in helping other blacks. A myriad of organizations understaffed, underfinanced, and manned by the black bourgeoisie are indeed trying to rekindle black hope. But I

wonder if the past is really past. When I commented recently on the expensive clothes of a colleague who worked with the poor, I was told: "I'm getting mine now. It's not that I'm selling out my soul, it's just that I'm bettering my body."

. . . The bright and pessimistic wife of one of the growing cadre of black bourgeois problem-solvers who traipse from city to state to federal agency talking about "the needs of the people" (said) "They *talk* about helping, and they feel a bit more guilty than their fathers in being so openly materialistic. But they cannot really identify with poverty. All these young management blacks have become white liberals."

Later . . . my bourgeois friends rapped about how their attempts to help poor blacks had been met with hostility and scorn. . . . And then someone said, "We're going to have to leave the real work to our children. They are the ones who have always lived with black consciousness, and they will make all black people one." And another, his voice shaking with emotion, said, "We've got to build the economic futures of our children, and with money under their belts, they can take up the fight for all black people." I listened that night as black people pledged their children to the black nation while they remained safe and on the periphery of danger. . . . I asked a doctor, an old internist, if he thought that his peers should be redirecting their efforts towards the black poor. He said, no, then his face grew somber: "Have you thought about how hard we have had to work for what little we have? We cannot lead, Mr. Coombs, because we are tired people. . . . They say the younger guys are closer to their consciences, and that they will work with the poorer Negroes, but I don't believe it. . . ."

Most bourgeois blacks have . . . left the hard task of organizing to those less talented than they. They have been seduced by the American myth of individualism and have come to believe that their salvation lies in individual conquests of poverty.

This is not an argument against such conquests. Anyone who lives in a poor community and wants to get out has a right to do so, and is entitled to all the help he can get. Anyone who gives that help is doing good work. But we ought not to fool ourselves about what we are doing. Helping a few get out does nothing for the many who remain locked in. The poor person who "makes it" helps only himself, and the school that helps him "make it" helps no one but him. In poor communities as in poor countries, large doses of schooling do not create leadership, but an elite, which is not at all the same thing.

Perhaps this story will make clearer the difference. A couple of years ago, talking about these matters with some students at a local women's college, I got into an argument with a young black student. Like so many others, she said that all this talk about deschooling or free schooling or whatever was only for rich white kids. She and other poor and black kids needed schools just the way they were, with regular required courses, exams, grades, diplomas, and so forth. Only by such means could she get to law school, become a lawyer and so gain the power to help her own people. That she would get into the prestige law school she said she was aiming for, or gain there the power she was looking for, seemed to me very doubtful. For all her knowing and cynical talk about "the system" and its institutions, including law schools, she seemed to know very little about them, and saw the law only as a kind of Magic Dirty Trick that whites had long worked against the blacks and that she would now learn to work against the whites. I doubted if this notion and vision would sustain her through many thick books about torts, equity, and the like. But that is by the way. What I tried, without success, to say to this spirited and angry student was that the school machine, if all went well, would someday stamp WINNER on her forehead, and perhaps even give her the power to do something for black people. But this school machine at the same time would go on stamping LOSER on the foreheads of a thousand or ten thousand other black kids. Doing so, it had robbed them, even in their own minds, *above all in their own minds,* of the power to help themselves. I said, "You say you need to become a lawyer so that you can have the power to change things. Fine. But where does that leave the ninety-nine percent of your fellow blacks who will never become lawyers? The system that declares you powerful by the same token declares them powerless, wholly dependent on you and people like you. Frankly, from the point of view of your community I think it's a damned bad trade, and I doubt very much that anything you will be able to do, even if things work out as you hope, will even come close to making up for what their schooling has killed in them of their intelligence, curiosity, resourcefulness, hope, confidence, and self-respect."

She wasn't convinced. I didn't expect her to be. Since she struggled so hard to get as far as she did, I hope she makes it the rest of the way. But again, particularly since the law schools are now overapplied to by 5 to 1, that is not a road that very many can take.

Our poor people are not going to be helped much by a few such highly trained leaders and helpers—even if there was not something terribly condescending about their help. They need, first, much better—cheaper, more widely available, more effective—arrangements and resources for learning all the things they may want and need to learn, from writing and reading at one end to practical medicine, economics, and law at the other. They need a much freer, less restricted, less expensive access to what opportunities there are in society. Above all, they need a society in which there are many more opportunities, a society committed to doing away with poverty and to making available and possible an active, interesting, and useful life to all its members. These are above all political needs, ends, goals. None of them are things that schools and schooling can provide.

11
Reading Without Schooling

"Maybe there's something in what you say," a poor parent might reply. "Still, if the schools don't teach my kid how to read, how's he ever going to learn?" Well, the schools aren't teaching a lot of kids how to read right now. Many learn without being taught. There's no question here of giving up the Good in search of the Perfect. What we are doing now is not working very well. What can we learn that might help us do better?

The northeastern part of Brazil is one of the great poverty areas of the world. Most of the people are tenant farmers or share-croppers. They own nothing. They must pay even for the water they get from the landlord's well. They live in the most wretched poverty, in isolated villages virtually without print. They have none of the books, newspapers, signs, or TV advertising that surround almost all children in modern society. Some years ago a Brazilian educator, Paulo Freire, and colleagues trained by him, were able to teach large numbers of wholly illiterate adults in these villages to write and read in a few months, and at a cost of $25 per person. Most of our schools spend $200 or more per pupil per year to teach literacy. At the end of six, seven, ten years and $1,500 or more worth of work, not only do many of our children not read as well as these Brazilian peasants, but also many of them have become so demoralized that they think they are incapable of learning anything.

When Freire and his co-workers came into a new village their first step was to try to get the villagers to come together in a meeting, to discuss their lives, interests, needs, problems, and concerns. Many people were afraid (like many people in the United States) that if they spoke out in public they would get in some kind of trouble. Many more felt that since nothing they said could make any difference in their lives, what was the use of saying anything?

Why even think? Better live out your short and wretched life in a kind of numbed resignation. Freire describes the culture in which such people live (the culture of poverty is in a sense worldwide) as the Culture of Silence. Words are not used because they would be wasted. His first step in trying to teach these villagers he called "the awakening of consciousness."

When the meetings first began, the villagers talked diffidently, ashamedly, as even many middle-class Americans talk when they have to speak in public. How could anyone be interested in their thoughts? But as they talked, they gained courage, put more of themselves into their words, spoke with passion and conviction. In this talk certain words began to appear, key words, what Freire calls "generative" words—they generate ideas, and they generate syllables out of which other words can be made. Freire would write these words down and show the villagers how to write them, and by writing them, take hold of them, own them, possess them, have them for their own use. Once they reached this point, the rest was relatively easy. From this beginning they were able to help these villagers become functionally literate in evening classes after a hard day's work, over a period of roughly eight weeks.

Some might say, "But after all, Freire *had* to have schools to do his teaching in." The answer is that in three critical respects his "schools" were altogether different from the schools we know and have, and that I and others, in our talk of deschooling, want to get away from. In the first place, they were not compulsory. In the second, they neither required nor gave any credentials. In the third, they did not lock the student into a prescribed sequence of learning determined in advance.

Clearly our national reading problem is not a necessary problem. Reading is easy. It can't be said too often. It is easy. And yet large numbers of children seem not to be able to do it. What has gone wrong? A great deal has been written about this, some of it nonsense, some of it very important truth. Dennison's *The Lives of Children;* Herndon's *How to Survive in Your Native Land;* and Fader's *The Naked Children,* all throw useful light on the problem. All of them underscore in many ways what Dennison said about one illiterate and defeated twelve-year-old:

José had failed in everything. After five years in the public schools, he could not read, could not do sums, and had no knowledge even of the most rudimentary history or geography. He was described to have as *having* "poor motivation," *lacking* "reading skills," and (again) *having* "a reading problem." . . .

By what process did José and his school book come together? Is this process part of his reading problem?

Who asks him to read the book? *Someone* asks him? In what sort of voice and for what purpose, and with what concern or lack of concern for the outcome?

And who wrote the book? For whom did they write it? Was it actually written for José? Can José actually partake of the life the book seems to offer?

And what of José's failure to read? We cannot stop at the fact that he draws a blank. How does he do it? What does he do? . . . Is he daydreaming? If so, of what? Aren't these particular daydreams part of José's reading problem? Did the teacher ask him what he was thinking of? Is his failure to ask part of José's reading problem?

Once, when I was trying to explain or teach fractions or something to a fifth-grade boy who had always done badly in school, I felt that though he was giving me the appearance of attention, his mind was elsewhere. I stopped explaining, and as gently as I could, said, "What are you thinking about?" He came to with a start, and perhaps surprised into honesty, said, "I was thinking about how when I flunk math my father is going to beat me." Clearly, when someone is worrying about things like that he can't do much thinking or learning about math, or reading, or anything else.

Printed words are an extension of speech. Reading is conversing. But what if this larger world is frightening and insulting? Should we, or should we not, include fear and insult in José's reading problem?

José's reading problem is José. . . . We need only to look at José to see what his problems are: shame, fear, resentment, rejection of others and of himself, anxiety, self-contempt, loneliness.

None of these was caused by the difficulty of reading printed words—a fact all the more evident if I mention here that José, when he came to this country at the age of seven, had been able to read Spanish, and had regularly read to his mother (who cannot read) the post cards they received from the literate father . . . in Puerto Rico.

I agree with Fader that many, perhaps almost all of the children that schools call nonreaders can in fact read. But, as Herndon points out, either they can't do *in school* what they can do everywhere else, or, as Fader suggests, they refuse to do it—refuse to read *in* school, or *for* school, just as many of them refuse to use the Standard English they have in fact learned. On another point I tend to disagree with Fader. I don't think that it is just around fourth grade that children begin to get turned off school; it has happened to many children I know, rich and poor, as early as first grade. And I doubt very much that those children who do read were "taught" to read or indeed helped very much in their learning by anything that school did; they learned more in spite of school than because of it.

In the last three of my earlier books I have said why I think most of what we do about reading in school, at whatever grade, is harmful, and what we might do that would be better. To what I have said before let me add this. Almost everything we do about reading, in school or out, hides the vital fact that writing is an extension of speech, that behind every written word there is a human voice speaking, and that reading is the way to hear what those voices are saying. The mother of a nine-year-old told me that when the author of a book that her child was reading came to their town, she arranged for them to meet. Introducing the child to the woman, she said, "And this is Mrs. So-and-so, who wrote that book you're reading." The child stared at the woman, astonished, for a few seconds, before she finally said, "Do *people* write books?" In her experience words were simply there. They appeared as if dropped out of the sky. They were as independent of people as the stars.

I strongly suspect that we would have many more good readers than we have, and many fewer reading problems, if for all chil-

dren under the age of ten or even twelve reading were made illegal.
Almost all the children in this country, rich or poor, all but those
few growing up in isolated pockets of rural poverty, live in a culture of print. Every day they see outside of their schools, hundreds
of printed words on signs, posters, billboards, packages, newspapers, and on the TV screen—probably many more than they see *in*
school. As long as children continued to see those words, there is
no way that we could prevent them from wanting to know what
they said and meant, or from finding ways to learn this forbidden
knowledge and pass it along to others, just as they now find ways
to learn and pass along many things we would prefer them not to
learn, including the Word Which Is Never Misspelled. (At least, in
the thousands of times I have seen it written I have never seen it
misspelled—and surely no child was ever taught by an adult, least
of all a teacher, how to spell it.)

It is, after all, how we treat people, not what we tell them,
that most affects what they do. Our acts carry a hidden message
much stronger than anything we say. What we say to children is
that reading is fun, reading is important, they'll like it, and so on.
But everything we do about reading carries hidden messages that
are quite different. We all of us, teachers, parents, the government,
society as a whole, seem to children to be saying two things. The
first is, "If we didn't make you read, you lazy good-for-nothing,
you never would—but we *are* going to make you." The second is,
"Reading is so difficult and so complicated and you are so stupid
that unless we lead you into it tiny step by tiny step, like a blind
man being led down a rough path, you'll never be able to figure it
out."

Many children, fortunately, simply ignore these messages.
They see other people reading around them, they are curious
about these words, and they learn to read, as they once learned to
talk. Many of them learn before they ever set foot in a school
building—why have we never tried to find out how many such
children there are? Still more probably teach themselves to read
while they are at school, in between underlining and circling things
in workbooks. But some other children, unfortunately, hear the
grownups saying to them, "We are going to make you learn to read
whether you like it or not, not for your reasons but for ours." -

To this they reply, "Oh, you are, are you? Well, we will just see about that." I have tried to teach children who have come to see reading as a power struggle between them and the adults. A child who feels this way about reading will not *let* himself learn to read, will resist understanding if he feels it coming, will deny or conceal such understanding as he already has. I remember a very bright second grader who was in some sort of combat with his very bright and overpowering mother. We were working alone; he had become impossible in class. I had a lot of letters, printed in color, cut out of one of the Words in Color charts, and was moving them around to make words and syllables. Children are curious, so I was often able to beguile him into looking at these letters and playing some of my games with them. We would go along for a while, and I would begin to think, "Aha, he's beginning to get it." Then he would begin to think, "Hey, what's happening here, I'm learning to read and I don't want that," and he would slam on the brakes, refuse to go on, play stupid, give deliberately wrong answers, try to get me to talk about other things—which I sometimes did, until I could get him to play with the letters again.

Many children get the other message, that reading is terribly difficult, that they are too stupid to learn it, that they cannot reach out and take hold of it and make it their own, but must sit passively while someone who "has" reading pours it into them, or perhaps injects it into them, like a doctor giving a shot. Once people look at learning this way, as something someone else will do *to* them, there is no chance of their learning anything. A man once told me that his child was having trouble learning to read even though she desperately wanted to learn. I said, "That word 'desperately' is the key to the trouble. We don't learn difficult things desperately. When we learned to speak, we did not 'desperately' want to learn it, we hardly knew we were learning it, it was part of everything else we did." What this desperate child desperately wanted was not to learn to read but, as Dennison once so well put it, *to have learned to read*. In other words, she wanted to escape from the stigma and shame of being a nonreader. But it is that very shame that more than anything else prevents her from learning to read.

Maybe we need to say "Illiteracy Is OK." Maybe we need signs and buttons saying ILLITERATE POWER. For to make not knowing something a disgrace is to make it certain that many people will never learn it. This gives us a clue why forbidding reading, making reading illegal would be so much more likely to produce readers. If we seriously tried to forbid reading, we might say things like: "If I catch you reading, I'm going to punish you—yell at you, send you to your room, spank you, no supper, can't play outside, etc." But the hidden message would be loud and clear—"Reading is fascinating, there's all kinds of exciting, secret, and forbidden stuff in there, you'll really like it. And you smart little devil, you, I know you, if I turn my back on you for just ten seconds, you'll be in there reading away, in spite of my having told you not to, so I'm going to have to watch you like a hawk." Thus the child would get the idea that reading was both fascinating and easy, and that people who were in a position to know judged him more than competent to master it. Master it he would.

All this is fanciful, of course. But there is something useful we might do. We could just cool it for a while. We could try to learn what experience ought by now to have made plain, that learning to write and read is much simpler than many things children learn for themselves, something that anyone with a good reason for learning it can master it in a matter of months or even weeks. Above all, we could try to revive or to keep alive in children the sense that learning to read is not external to them, somehow lying outside them, but is instead within them, a natural extension of their own powers.

People have asked, "If schools didn't teach reading, how else would anyone learn it? What kinds of arrangements might we make, other than schools or school-like places, to help people learn to read? What might be both better and cheaper?" Paul Goodman once suggested that we pay a small extra salary to many kinds of workers and craftsmen, such as garage mechanics, in return for which they would agree to let some kids hang around while they were working, and answer any questions they might ask about what they were doing. This gave me the idea of what we might call "reading guides." They would be volunteers. A reading guide would not have to do his guiding all the time, only as much of the time as he wanted, fitting it in along with the rest of his life. College or high school students, or even younger children, if they

could read, could be reading guides; or housewives; or older or retired people; or librarians; or parking lot attendants; or anyone else
who in his daily life might come into contact with children or other
nonreaders. The guides would wear some kind of identifying arm-
band, hat, button, etc. so that people wanting information could
easily spot them. The understanding would be that when a guide
was wearing his sign anyone who wanted could ask him either one
of two kinds of questions. He could show him a written word and
ask, "What does this say?" and the guide would tell him. Or he
could say to the guide, "How do you write such and such a word,"
and the guide would write it for him. Nothing else; that's all a
guide would have to do.

It should cost almost nothing to get such a program going.
We might have to spend a little money for the identifying signs,
but even this is not necessary; people could make their own. We
might have to spend a little money to get the word out about the
program, to get people to volunteer as guides, to let other people
know what the guides were for. What about testing the guides? No
need for it. There is no reason why a guide should be able to read
or write every word he might be asked. If he is asked a word he
doesn't know, he can say, "I don't know that one, you'll have to
ask another guide." A school, a church, a group of parents, or students themselves could start such a program. Indeed, the work
could be started without an organized program. Anyone who reads
these words, likes the idea, and wants to make himself a reading
guide can make his own sign and become one, even if no one else
does. Others may later follow his example.

In many cities people, usually young people, have set up what
they call "switchboards"—phone numbers that people can call to
get various kinds of help or information. Following this example,
we might have a reading guide switchboard. The number would be
listed in the phone book, and perhaps shown in other places. A
caller could call the number, and as before, ask the switchboard either one of two kinds of questions. He could spell the word, and
ask the switchboard what the word said, or he could say the word,
and ask the switchboard how to spell it. Older people might be
glad to take such calls, or invalids, or people otherwise shut in. It
would give them a little contact with the world, and a true sense of

being useful. Parents in low-income neighborhoods might also take turns doing this.

It would probably not be very difficult or expensive to build a kind of reading machine, which would work like this. On the front of the machine would be buttons, labeled with the letters of the alphabet. Let us suppose that someone comes to the machine wanting to know what the word C-A-T says. He pushes the C button, then the A button, then the T button. Then he presses another button, perhaps green in color, marked READ. Inside the machine, some kind of guiding mechanism leads a playback head to a small piece of recording tape, on which someone has previously recorded the spoken word "cat." The playback head moves over the word, the signal is amplified, and through a loudspeaker at the front of the machine a voice says "cat." If the client wants to hear the word again, he presses the READ button again. Again he hears the voice, and so as many times as he wants to hear it. When he is ready for another word, he presses some kind of CANCEL button, then pushes the buttons for his next word, pushes the READ button again, and as before hears it as many times as he wants to. Such machines would have to be loaded beforehand with a prerecorded selection of words, and possibly, syllables. It would probably be simpler to limit them to words of not more than five letters. If someone dialed in a group of letters that did not make a word or one that was not in the machine, a dial that says NOT IN MACHINE, or perhaps just "?", could light up. These machines could be in schools, but it would be better to have them in many other kinds of public places—drugstores, supermarkets, libraries, bookstores, airports, bus stations, YMCA's, neighborhood houses, churches.

We might also have another kind of machine, using a continuously repeating endless loop, like some advertising displays at airports. This machine, perhaps using sound films, perhaps slide film synchronized with a tape recorder, would flash words on a screen while over a loudspeaker a voice read the same words. With such a machine we could run through sets of word transformations, like the Pop-Ups that Caleb Gattegno (see Appendix) has prepared for TV, in which we see how changing a word, one letter at a time, changes the sound of the word. These machines might run continuously, or at the push of a button.

Several makers of equipment for schools now make a reading machine that works like this. The student has a card, with a word or words written on it. On the card is a strip of magnetic recording tape, on which the sound of a voice speaking the word has been recorded. (It might be the student's own voice.) When the student drops the card into the machine, a magnetic playback head moves across the strip of tape, and the sound of the voice reading the words comes out through a loudspeaker. These machines are expensive, much more so than they need to be. As usual, the schools that can most easily afford to buy them are the ones whose students need them the least, and indeed they are generally used not to teach reading but to "teach" foreign languages. But such machines, which already exist, could be put in many places in low-income areas. Children, or older people, who could not afford to buy the machines, could afford to buy some of the cards, or better yet, since even the cards are far too expensive, improvise some of their own. They could go into a store or library or community center, where such machines were located, and make up (or have made up for them) and later use, their own reading cards.

Or we could put into various places, for children to use, cassette tape recorders, which are widely available and much less expensive. A child could have a story, or a list of words, and a tape cassette onto which the story or words had been dictated, by him or someone else. Then, whenever he wanted to look at the words or story and hear them read at the same time, he would only have to drop his cassette into one of these available recorders. Some schools already have such recorders, but again usually not the ones whose pupils need them most. Schools in poor areas are not likely to buy such equipment, and are in any case not a good place for them. They should be out in the community, in places less shut off and threatening than city schools have come to be for most children. Of course, this suggestion supposes a community which is not so demoralized that people will steal these reading aids to sell, or smash them up just for spiteful satisfaction. Perhaps if organizations based in and run by the community itself had these machines, theft or vandalism would be less of a problem. There might be small storefront reading centers, where people, or even one person, could act as guides, run a reading switchboard, and show people how to use the reading machines. Or, if no storefront can be found, or if there was no money for rent, a friendly store owner, or a neighborhood church, might set aside a small space, perhaps just enough for one table and chair, for a mini-reading center. Or such a center might be run during the day in someone's apartment, with an older person doing the work. Or, at least during nice weather, a mini-reading center might be set up outdoors in parks and near playgrounds. Or someone selling ice cream, hot dogs, and pop might dispense a little reading information along with the food. Or there might be a readmobile, a mini-center in the back of a converted small truck, or even a car, traveling to different neighborhoods, with a schedule so that people would know when it was coming.

Or we could do things cheaper and simpler than this. We know what kinds of things, put up on the walls of the classrooms, may help children to read. Why have them only in classrooms? Why not paint some of these things on the walls of buildings, or on the sidewalks? Why not post in the windows of stores pictures of things, with the name printed underneath—CAT, RAT, HAT, BAT—or a series of phonically regular sentences, like those we can find in Leonard Bloomfield's book, *Let's Read*. Why not put signs—labels—on many of the things children see in the streets—STREET LIGHT, LAMPPOST, FIRE HYDRANT, CURB, STREET, DOOR, WINDOW, BRICK WALL, and so on? In short, let the whole community take the responsibility and initiative in educating its young, instead of turning the job over to a few specialists of doubtful competence that in many cases the community doesn't trust anyway.

Many poor and minority group people are demanding better reading programs in their schools. They might be wiser to try to get more branch libraries in their districts, or better yet, neighborhood storefront libraries or traveling bookmobiles, with newspapers, periodicals, and paperbacks—the kind of reading material that we know kids like to read. What's the point of having kids learn to read if after they've learned there's nothing *to* read. How many adults would read if every time they wanted a book they had to go two or three miles into a completely different part of their city? Access to reading matter, not reading methods, is the name of the game. And yet, many libraries are cutting down their services, not building them up. In one small city I know of, in many ways an intellectual and cultural center, the public library has for years made its newspaper and periodical room, the most important of all its facilities for young people, permanently out of bounds to high school students, on the grounds that when they come in they talk and disturb older readers. A giant backward step. A stupid "solution" to an unreal problem. And a man from one of the mountain states told me not long ago that in his community and others he knows, the local poor people, mostly Chicanos, are not allowed to use the public library *at all,* cannot even get a card to borrow books.

From the fuss we make about reading, one might think that this was a country of readers, that reading was nearly everyone's favorite or near-favorite pastime. Who are we kidding? A publisher told me not long ago that outside of three hundred or so college bookstores, there are less than one hundred true bookstores in all the United States. This is not to say that these are the only places in which one can buy a book. But there are less than one hundred stores in which selling books is a main part of the business, in which there is always a reasonably large, varied, and up-to-date stock of books, in which the people working there know at least something about books, and in which if the store does not have a book, a customer can order it and be fairly sure that he will get it in a reasonable period of time. Since most American communities do not have even one bookstore, why not have the local schools run a community bookstore? Colleges have their bookstores; why should school systems, most of whom have more students than any college, not have theirs? There is no question of unfair competition with local merchants; in most communities nobody is seriously selling books. If there should be someone in a community struggling against heavy odds to run a bookstore, why not give him some help—some space or a branch somewhere in the schools, student helpers, perhaps a mobile bookstore?

We have hardly begun to touch the possibilities of television in helping children learn to read. Caleb Gattegno (teacher, educator, author of *What We Owe Children* and other books), has been pointing out for years that in a phonic language, in which written symbols stand for spoken sounds, there is clearly *no connection* between knowing the alphabet and knowing how to write and to read. To write and read a written phonic language one must know the connections in the language between written letters and spoken sounds, and so be able to convert written words into spoken ones and vice versa. I can do this reasonably well in three languages in which I do not know the letter names at all. Knowing the names of letters is useful to dictate the spelling of words, or to write them from someone else's dictation. Knowing the order of letters is useful for looking things up in dictionaries, phone books, and so forth, though if you don't know the order you can get it from the books themselves. But neither piece of knowledge has anything to do with reading, and in English, at least, there is good reason to believe that learning the alphabet is not a good first step in learning to read.

We need to make clear to children that writing is an extension (as well as a compression) of speech, that behind every written word there is a human voice speaking, and that reading is how we hear what those voices are saying. It would be far easier with TV than for a teacher in a classroom to make this clear and vivid—when the watching children hear a voice speaking we could at the same time show the words, *as they are spoken,* appearing in print. Figures in animated cartoons could have word balloons over their heads, as in comic strips, a convention which the children probably already know. When live figures are speaking, the TV screen could often be split, with the words appearing at one side—a teleprompter in reverse. It would do a great deal for children's reading if all the people who make the commercials that are shown along with or between children's programs would make frequent use of this device—the voice speaking, the word appearing, letters synchronized with sounds, perhaps showing the word two or three times. It wouldn't take much of this before children would know what it is essential for them to know—that written letters stand for spoken sounds, and that the order of the letters in space from left to right corresponds with the order of sounds in time.

Since children sense their littleness and want to be larger and more potent, the idea that through writing they can make their voices reach further and last longer could be made very exciting to them. Thus we might split the TV screen, and in part of it show a child talking, telling a story, or a dream, or perhaps children talking to each other, while on another part of the screen their words would appear as they speak them, in type or in print. We might hear a child telling a story, and on another part of the screen see the story being simultaneously typed on a primary typewriter, perhaps speeding up the film of the typing enough to have the letters keep up with the child's voice. We might show other ways of getting speech into writing, a child telling a story, an older child writing it down. This would give the viewers something they could do at home. We could use the compressed time of film to do something hard to do in real life; we could ask a child to say a few words, show them written down, and then, while the memory of the child saying them was fresh in the viewers' minds, we could show many people seeing this piece of writing and all reading the same words for it.

It would be helpful to reveal to children that all the writing they see about them began as someone speaking. Thus we might show people talking about what should go into a poster or ad or TV commercial, see them writing it on a sketch pad, see a rough sketch of the ad or poster, and at last see the final product in print. With compressed time we could show very vividly the transition from spoken words to words written where a great many people could see them. Imagine for example, a foolish commercial for a soft drink named, let us say, Choke. We see some people sitting around a table, drinking, exclaiming, smacking their lips. One of them says, "Wow, this stuff is great. What'll we call it?" Someone else says, "Got just the name. Let's call it Choke." They all laugh. (I've seen worse commercials than this.) We see a sketch pad, a voice says Choke, as it does a pen writes the letters. We see a bottle, the voice says Choke, the letters appear on the bottle. Same for a bottle top. Same for a can, a six-pack. Same for the case the bottles come in, the truck that carries them around, the side of the truck, a big poster. At the end, maybe, two people drinking. One of them says, puzzled, "What's the name of this stuff?" Perhaps fade out there—the children will supply the answer. My point here is not that I am trying to con children into drinking more soft drinks—they drink too much of them now—but only that it should be easy to produce TV commercials, which children watch and like, in ways that along with selling a product would get across important information about reading.

We might show a great many possible ways of writing things, with pencil or pen or felt-tipped pen or typewriter, with ditto or mimeo, with printing, with electric signs, even with skywriting. We could show children tricks by which they could teach themselves to write. A small child could ask an adult (or an older child) to write some words for him; the adult, using a heavy felt-tipped pen, could write the words in very large letters; then the child could put a piece of paper over these and, by tracing them, make his own writing. Or we could show an electric primary typewriter, with the keys colored to show the typist which fingers to use, show someone putting little pieces of the proper colored Scotch tape on the child's fingers, then show the child learning to touch-type. Of course, many viewers would not have a typewriter at home, but this might lead them to put some heat on the schools to get typewriters. We might show a child, at first typing very slowly, using the touch system, then an older child typing somewhat faster, and so in a continuum of skill up to a very fast expert typist. From this children would see that what they could at first do only very slowly they might before long be able to do very rapidly, with all the new power this would give them.

But whatever we do, there is one thing we must *stop* doing—sounding out words or syllables one letter at a time. I am dismayed to find, in the programs I have seen, that *Sesame Street*'s big brother, *The Electric Company,* is still doing this. The smallest unit of speech that we can *say* in isolation, all by itself, is the syllable. With a very few exceptions, we do not *speak* isolated letters or letter groups or graphemes, and it is therefore foolish, useless, wasteful, confusing, and harmful to try to "teach" children how to "read" them. What cannot be spoken cannot be read. We speak syllables, so we must read syllables. People in *The Electric Company,* like millions of teachers and adults before them, talk as if there was some natural and logical connection between the sounds "kuh-a-tuh" and the sound "cat." There is none. To go on talking about the *sounds* of single letters is, with very few exceptions, the worst thing we can do for the children we are trying to help.

While I'm talking about TV, let me say a few words about how it might help children learn about numbers. Teaching children to count is not a good way to introduce them to the world of numbers. They tend to think that numbers are a kind of procession of mythical figures, dwarfs maybe, always walking in the same order, the first named One, the next Two, and so on. Even if they have been "taught" to "count" a group of objects by touching them in order, saying "One, two, three . . ." they may not realize at all that the number is a way of talking about the quantity of objects before them. Later, they may think of all arithmetic as a set of complicated and mysterious ritual dances done by these number-dwarfs, without rhyme or reason or connection with anything else.

For any given number, visually, without words, we could show many of the properties of the number: whether it is prime or composite (that is, whether it has factors, two numbers that will multiply together to make it); if it has factors, what they are; how many ways it can be divided up into *two* subgroups; how many ways it can be divided into even more subgroups; how we can use the notation of arithmetic to express these properties. Take the number 8. We can show that it is composite; that it can be arranged in rows of two, or four, that it has the factors two and four; that we can write this $4 \times 2 = 8$ or $2 \times 4 = 8$; that it can be divided into two subgroups of 7 and 1, or 6 and 2, or 5 and 3, or 4 and 4; that these can be written $7 + 1 = 8$ or $1 + 7 = 8$ or $8 - 1 = 7$ or $8 - 7 = 1$, and so on. For the number 7, we could show among other things, that it is not composite, but prime, that when we try to arrange it in more than one row, we always have one left over or too few. We could show children figuring this out, so that children watching at home could work out the properties of other numbers without having to wait to see them on the program. All this could be easily done on TV.

We can also use TV to show what numbers are for, how people use them in the world, and how children might learn to use them. Numbers are for measuring. We can show adults measuring things in the real world. Adults or older children could show younger ones some of the tools or devices we use to measure with, and how to use them—ruler, tape measure, scales, thermometer, barometer, clock, watch, stopwatch, metronome. We might show some of what we do with these measurements, how we write them down, what we use them for, what can we find out from them. From time to time we might measure the heights and weights of some children, and make graphs of them, and show the viewing children how to make graphs of their own height and weight. We could show children how to hear and measure the rate of their own heartbeat.

For all we spend on remedial reading programs why have we so little to show? A poster I saw not long ago may give us a clue. It had been prepared by, and for, an organization with a name like National Library Association, and was taped to a window in the library of an expensive private school. The text of the poster was printed over and around a close-up photograph of a torn paper bag, with part of a gun sticking out. The heading, in big type, said "Pick Up a Book Instead of a Gun." In a pasteurized version of ghetto talk, the text said in effect, if you read books all kinds of goodies are waiting for you, if you don't you're going to pick up that gun and get into trouble. There is a deep, perhaps unconscious, certainly self-defeating confusion and hypocrisy in that poster. For of course it was not addressed to poor ghetto kids. The voice behind the words was not speaking to them. The sign was not where they could see it. It was in a rich school, and the voice was speaking to the rich kids there and their rich parents. Its real message was, "You'd better give us some money, so we can get those poor kids reading books, because otherwise they're going to be picking up those guns and causing you all kinds of trouble." In other words, reading is sold to the powerful people in society as a way of pacifying the poor. But these feelings will not be kept secret. If we think that it is important to get poor kids reading, not for their sake but only for ours, they will find out, and refuse.

This chapter, which opened with Freire, must close with him. The idea that inspired and informed all of his work, and made it work, is that education for the poor and powerless cannot be effective unless it seems *to them* to offer a real chance of increasing their power to change and better the general conditions of their lives.

True education doesn't quiet things down; it stirs them up. It awakens consciousness. It destroys myths. It *empowers* people, as Dennison so well put it, to think and do for themselves. The Brazilian dictatorship understood this very well and drove Freire out of the country. They did not want the poor empowered, and so they could not have them educated. The lesson for us is that unless we want the poor empowered, we *cannot* have them educated. Education as pacifier has always failed, is failing, and is bound to fail.

12

Schools Against Themselves

Many people, including friends I love and respect, say that we must put all our eggs in the basket of school reform. We *have* schools, they say, we always *will* have schools, and all we can do is work, one little step at a time, to make them slightly better. Then, maybe generations from now, schools will be really good places for children.

Well, we certainly have schools, and we are likely to have quite a few of them for some time, so it makes sense to try to improve them. But the fact that we *have* an institution or condition, be it schools, jails, poverty, cancer, or war, ought not to bar us from asking ourselves, "Should we have it? Do we want to have it? If not, how might we get rid of it, and what else might we have in its place?" And even in the here and now it seems to me foolish to put all our hopes for a truly educative society or enlightened way of rearing children into the basket of school reform. To ask or expect the schools, *given their present functions, given our present understanding of education,* to be innovative and imaginative as a whole, consistently, and in the long run seems to me to be asking for the impossible. People have been working at reforming schools for years. Not many of the ideas of today's school reformers are new. This is not the first time people have talked as if we were at the dawn of a new age of humane schooling. Why have we still so far to go?

Not long ago, a man I have known slightly for some years came up to me in great agitation and asked for advice. Without waiting for an answer, he began his story. A woman, a good friend of his, was having a terrible problem with her child at school. The child was getting good enough marks, but he was behaving so badly that he disrupted the entire class. The teacher had already called the mother several times. A suggestion had been made that they take the child to see a child psychologist, and perhaps even

213

give him some drugs. Over and over again the man said how frantic the mother was, how the school kept telling her that something *had* to be done about this child, whose behavior was causing such terrible problems. With visions of a thirteen- or fourteen-year-old boy on a rampage, hitting out in all directions, I said, "How old is the child?" My friend looked taken aback by this question. After thinking a moment, he asked his wife, "How old is N——?" His wife said, "He is six."

Six! I thought to myself, what in the world can a six-year-old do in the classroom that can throw all these adults into such a panic. I tried to get in some further questions. What is the child doing, I asked, that is causing such a disturbance? Persisting through all his talk, I eventually got an answer. What this six-year-old was doing to cause such an uproar was only this—he likes to get up out of his seat from time to time and go talk to his friends. He refuses to stay seated. At first I could hardly believe my ears. Was it really no more than that? Apparently, that was all. Otherwise, as my friend described him, the child was lively, sociable, attractive, and has many friends.

At one point my friend said to me, "We think the child may be hyperactive." I assured him, on the basis of what he had told me, that he was almost certainly not "hyperactive," and that in any case, such a diagnosis could only be made by a very few highly specialized people on the basis of elaborate tests, which the child had not been given. There was no question at all of the child hitting other children or fighting with them or throwing tantrums. He just likes to talk to people—hardly a serious offense, particularly since he does his school work very well. When I could get in a word or two, I tried to convince my friend that the only problem was that this lively, energetic, and personable kid had had the bad luck, like many other kids, to get a first-grade teacher who like many other teachers believed that six-year-olds ought to spend a very large part of their waking hours sitting down, motionless, and quiet. I said that many times at teachers' meetings the program chairman has explained to me that we had to break after an hour and a half because, "You can't keep teachers sitting for longer than that." Was it reasonable or right to expect a six-year-old to sit still for most of the day? But none of this, of course, seemed to make any impression. This child may all too soon find his way into the hands of experts who will find something they can say is wrong with him. (They certainly won't say that anything is wrong with the teacher or the school.) At the very least, he will be convinced that because he dislikes these school rules and doesn't want to obey them all the time, he is in varying degrees bad, queer, and sick. (A month later, I learned that he was being given drugs, which have "solved" the "problem.")

For all the talk, experiments, federal funding, special programs, revolutions in education, and so forth of the past years, most of our schools have changed very little. New evidence of this comes in every day, on a scale large and small, from students, parents, and teachers. Not long ago a lady whose child is in the fourth grade in a "good" school system in a rich suburb of one of our large cities, told me this all too typical story. One day the child was seated at her desk, working at something, and without thinking put one of her feet up on the rung of her chair. The teacher spied this and flew into a passion, bawled the child out in front of the class, and then ordered her to sit on the floor under her desk for an hour. This child had been getting along very well in school. She had not been a troublemaker in class and had not had conflicts with this teacher. Naturally she was amazed by this outburst. Just as naturally, she was not eager to go back to school the following week. A friend in another city, whose child goes to another "good" school tells me that the children there are not allowed to run at recess, and that a teacher stands outside the building with an electric megaphone, shouting first at this child, then that, "Stop running! Stop running! No running over there!" But there is no need to add to what Charles Silberman has pointed out, and in such detail, in *Crisis in the Classroom,* that a large number of our schools are joyless, repressive, mindless. What is puzzling, though, is why they are and why they resist so well efforts to make them something else.

Why is it so hard for schools to move forward, and so easy to slip back? Visiting school systems and talking with school people in many different parts of the country, I often hear about interesting new programs. But just about as often, I hear another story. "We had a good program going here a few years ago," someone will tell me. "We were running the schools in a more flexible, interesting, and humane way, using new materials, or breaking free of the old patterns, or getting out of the building. The kids were really excited, really happy, really learning." But then, apparently, something happened. The parents complained. The money ran out. The superintendent left for another job, or was fired. Or a new school board was elected. Or the teachers didn't like the program and whittled it down. Or this, that, or the other. And now things are getting back to the way they always were. *Crisis in the Classroom* has not been out very long, and already some of the school changes and developments cited there as most hopeful have lost much of their original spirit or are in real danger of being done away with altogether. Many times in recent years I've read about some very interesting and hopeful development in schools, only to learn, often within a year or two, that it had come to an end. Thus, Daniel Fader [in *The Naked Children* (see Appendix)] tells how, with much effort and with the essential help of some of the children, he was able to persuade the faculty of a junior high school in Washington. D.C. to adopt a reading program called "Reading in Every Classroom," which had previously been very successful at a training school for boys in Michigan (see *Hooked on Books* in Appendix). At first, many teachers refused to work with the program. Others pretended to, but did not. But slowly, often because of the help of the students, more and more of the teachers were won over. By the end of the year the program was an unquestioned success. The students were reading voraciously, and everyone was enthusiastic and happy. By the final faculty meeting, the opposition had dwindled almost to nothing. But then, as he was collecting his papers and getting ready to leave, one of the teachers stood up to speak.

> "We've made a lot of changes around here. Some of us swear we're never going to go back to teaching the way we did. We say we'll never use the old textbooks again, and we mean it. But what will we do when we can't get newspapers, magazines, and paperbacks? What will we do when there's no one coming around every week to support us and no one to get us money for all these new materials? I wish you'd tell me that." . . .
>
> "I don't mean to sound like I'm not happy with what we've done. I am, and so are a lot of others. There's some who wouldn't

be happy with anything, but they're not the problem. The problem is . . . I mean, we've all seen a lot of new programs come and go. We don't want to see this one end up like all the others. But it will. I know it will."

It did. Slowly, perhaps inevitably, it ended up "like all the others" . . . one important factor in the program's decline was the departure of every member of Cleo's original gang. . . . A leaderless campaign for pleasure-in-literacy ground slowly to a halt in the school.

Consider that last sentence a second. In a school manned by thirty or more adult so-called "professionals," a program that was an unquestioned success, that everyone agreed had done what needed to be done and had never been done before, became "leaderless" because *five students* left the school. What a shameful admission of adult weakness, laziness, incapacity. No surprise to the students, though. In the spring of the following year Fader had his last visit with his two friends, the leaders of the little gang of five. He writes:

Yes, they both knew what was happening to "English In Every Classroom" at Garnet-Patterson. I wasn't either surprised or disappointed, was I? Cleo was amazed that I was feeling a little of both. Hadn't I said that the reason for putting the program in Garnet-Patterson was to show that it would work in a public school the same way it worked in a reform school? That's what I said and that's what I'd done. Nobody expected it to last; after all, she said, nothing ever does.

A sad and prophetic ending to a most beautiful book.

To be sure, some of the people running schools or teaching in them are people who ought not to be there. They do not like or trust children. They do not like their work with them. They see their main task as getting children ready for a life and work which they themselves find dull, pointless, and oppressive. The schools, like other institutions, have their share of what Edgar Friedenberg calls "control freaks," people who really like pushing other people around and enjoy the splendid opportunities schools give them to do it. We might understand why schools are the way they are, and why it is so hard to make them better, if such people were a majority in the schools. But they don't seem to be. By now I have met and talked with large numbers of teachers, principals, superintendents, curriculum planners, and school board members in many parts of the country. Some I don't like or agree with. But I am constantly impressed by the number of intelligent, perceptive, life-loving people I meet. Why, on the whole, do they seem to have so little effect? Why is the percentage of really good schools—enlightened, flexible, humane, inspired and inspiring, exciting, life-enhancing—so much lower than the percentage of school people who would like to have them? Most of the people who feel they're trying to run their classrooms, schools, school systems in this way feel that they're working against long odds. They talk as if with a lot of luck they might for a few more years be able to go on doing what they're doing. But they rarely talk as if they believed that they can hold whatever gains they make, and move on from them. To some degree, this may reflect the pressures of a society in which few people believe any longer in human dignity or freedom, or experience them in their own lives. But there is more to it than that.

Some people say that "the system" is responsible. This is not very helpful. What is there about this particular system that makes humane reforms have such a short and uneasy life, that makes it so hard for those in it to do well, so easy to do badly? I think the answer is plain enough, and that we would see it if we did not keep turning our heads away from it. Universal compulsory schools are not and *never were meant to be* humane institutions, and most of their fundamental purposes, tasks, missions, are not humane. Our schools, school people, and above all school reformers are ineffective because they are working at cross purposes, because most of what they give with one hand they have to take back with the other. Of the many tasks they have been given to do, some they cannot do alone, some they cannot do well, some they ought not to be doing at all. But above all else, these tasks are in conflict with one another. Good or not, necessary or not, unavoidable or not, they cannot be done together in the same place at the same time. The more we try to do of some, the less by necessity we can do of the others.

There is one prime legitimate, humane mission or function of the schools—to promote the growth of the children in them. Call this the educative mission. This is the mission to which every true teacher must be dedicated. We want to do what we can to help every human being grow and develop in every way to the fullest extent of his capacity—in among other things awareness, responsiveness, curiosity, courage, confidence, imagination, resourcefulness, patience, generosity, sympathy, skill, competence, and understanding; in the ability to see a wide range of choices, to choose wisely among them, and to recognize and change choices that prove to be unwise; in a strong sense of his own freedom, dignity, and worth, and of those same qualities in others. To help people grow this way is the work that good teachers want to do, and it is the hope of doing it that brings many able and dedicated new people into teaching.

But—and here is the rub—the schools have other missions, other functions. They acquired them slowly, over many years. Perhaps nobody ever planned deliberately that they should have them. Perhaps many people now in schools wish they did not have them. But they are there. One of these we might call the custodial function. Society demands of schools, among other things, that they be a place where for many hours of the day, many days of the year, children or young people can be shut up and so got out of everyone else's way. Mom doesn't want them hanging around the house, the citizens do not want them out in the streets, and workers do not want them in the labor force. What then do we do with them? How do we get rid of them? We put them in schools. That is an important part of what schools are for. They are a kind of day jail for kids.

Many teachers get very upset and angry when I speak of schools being in the jail business. They say, as I would once have said myself, that they personally are *not* in the jail business. They don't feel like jailers, and they are not running a jail. Perhaps not. But the fact remains that if their students did not go to school, and within that school to their class and even their desk or seat—if they did not do that they would go to jail. This, as Herndon and Dennison point out, is what compulsory school attendance laws mean. They do not mean that society says to young people, we would like you to please go to school. Society says, if you don't go to school, we are going to put you in jail—a real jail with bars in it. For most children, school is the better choice. Most, not all—*The New York Times* once told about some boys in South Carolina who, offered by a judge a choice of going back to school or going to jail, unhesitatingly chose jail. But these are still exceptions, still a minority, though a rapidly growing one.

If people object to the word "jail" we can use another. Try "corral." It has a nice OK Western sound, with a John Wayne twang to it. Call our schools day corrals for children. The point is that people want them there because *they don't want them anywhere else*. There is further evidence for this in high school equivalency exams. When recently I heard of them for the first time, I was very interested. Many young people in school are suffering great damage to their intellect, character, and spirit, and any way we can find to help some of them escape this damage is all to the good. I thought perhaps the high school equivalency exams might be one such way, that it might enable a young person to study at home, or at least, when he had learned enough to pass the exam, not have to attend school any longer. But the laws of the states and territories about these exams prevent this. All have a limitation on the time at which a student can take the exam. The State of Maryland says you must be seventeen years old. Twelve states or territories say that you must be eighteen; 19 that you must be nineteen; 12 that you must be twenty, and 3 that you must be twenty-one. Many say specifically that no one may take the exam until his class has graduated from high school, or even until a year after it has graduated. These are remarkable requirements. Quite obviously, the law does not mean to let someone get out of high school by showing that he has already learned the things high school is supposedly trying to teach him. Quite obviously adult society has other reasons for wanting young people to stay in high school. We want them there because we do not want them anywhere else. This task or function of schools, the custodial or jail function, the task of keeping young people out of everybody else's way, is quite obviously not a humane function. It is an expression of adults' general dislike and distrust of the young. It is and must be in conflict with the humane function of true education, of encouraging and helping human growth. Whatever we may tell them, we cannot make learners feel we have confidence in them, or make learners have confidence in themselves, if by the way we treat them we show clearly that we do not trust them and do not want them. Moreover, as every classroom teacher knows, any time some student or students *feel* that they are in school, not because they want to be but only because a superior force has compelled them to be there, they are not very likely to learn anything. What is more, they will probably act in a way that makes it very difficult for anyone else to learn anything. As must be clear by now, the schools spend an enormous amount of time, money, thought, energy, and trouble trying to deal with the increasingly large numbers of children who really don't want to be there. They would be wiser to make available other, more interesting, more worthwhile things for these children to do.

The fact that our students are in school whether they want to be or not—and do not have the option of leaving—has still another disadvantage. It makes it all but impossible for us to get from them the kind of feedback from which we might learn to do our work better. If school attendance were not compulsory, and some or many of our students in a particular school or a class stopped going, we would know right away that we had to do something. We would have to think very seriously, as some schools already have, about how to make our school a stimulating and life-enhancing environment for children. Within our schools, we would find out, as we probably cannot in any other way, which were our good teachers. Perhaps the learner's judgment of his teacher is not infallible, but it is certainly better than anyone else's. Proposals for merit pay are and will remain at best useless and at worst harmful as long as some administrative superior judges this merit, or as long as we try to measure it by such things as achievement test scores.

At a meeting not long ago a man asked me whether or not children might shun "good" teachers for more popular ones. His question implied that the really good teacher, because "tough," is likely to be unpopular. This is very seldom the case. Children like learning, and they like being around people who can help them do it. We do not have to worry about children flocking around the kind of adult who puts on an act so as to gain their approval or to be popular with them. Children do not as a rule like such adults.

But even if it were so that a particular teacher, because of odd appearance or eccentric manner, was shunned by children in spite of having useful things to show them or help them learn, in a free learning environment there would be a natural corrective for that. Children have a very good communication system among themselves. They eagerly pass along to each other news of good things. If a few children tried out this odd person, as some, being curious, probably would, and found that he had interesting things to offer, they would tell their friends. "Hey, you know that funny looking Mr. X. Well, I talked with him the other day, and he's really neat, he told me all kinds of interesting things (or showed me this or that)." At any rate, as I said, nobody is likely to be able to judge better than the learner who is best able to help him find and learn what he wants to learn, and because our learners have no choice about their teachers we now have no way of getting this very much needed information.

Since the jail function is not a humane function and works against the humane task of helping learning and growth, since we cannot at the same time and in the same place be in the jail business and in the learning business, we must get ourselves out of the jail business.

It seems unlikely that in the near future any state legislature will strike the compulsory school attendance laws off the books. But they could be broadened and stretched in a great many ways. We could reduce the number of days per year of required school attendance. We could, as we should for other reasons, keep schools open all year round, and let students get their days of school attendance whenever they want. If a student wants to get most of his schooling in the summer, because he has things he wants to do in the winter, let him do that—or vice versa. Let us say that a student has a school attendance ticket that he must get punched 180 days or so a year. Why not let him pick the days? Why should all students have to be in school on the same days? For that matter, if a student can get his ticket punched for five hours of classes, study, or activities, why should he not be able to go to double sessions, get two punches a day, and so get his schooling out of the way in 90 days and have the rest of the year for what is important to him? We could have schools in the evening, so that students could do other things during the day—work, apprentice—and get their school credit during the evening. We could give school credit for a much wider variety of activities, including work. If a college student can get academic credit for doing various kinds of work, why not a high school student? And for that matter, there seems no reason other than administrative convenience why a student should have to do all his school work, get his ticket punched, all in the same school. Why not let him get some of his schooling in one school, some in another? There are of course problems of state aid. I think ways could be found to work this out, if we wanted to. At any rate, a student should be able to go to any school he wanted within his home state, the schools getting aid according to the number of students attending. This would be an incentive—to a school to attract students. Some of the above suggestions would be quite easy to put into practice, some hard. But they do suggest ways in which we could begin to get ourselves out of the jail business, if we wanted.

The jail business is not the only wrong business we are in. The schools have another important mission, task, function. Edgar Friedenberg has often called it "social role selection." Other people have used other names for it. A once widely distributed memo from the Selective Service System called it "channeling." We might also call it grading and labeling. If we want to be blunt, we might call it meat stamping. Whatever we call it, it is the business of turning people into commodities, and deciding who goes where in our society and who gets what—who gets the best-paying jobs and the most interesting careers, who gets middle-paying jobs, who gets low-paying jobs, who gets no jobs at all. Every society has one mechanism or another for deciding such questions. I am not objecting here to the existence of such mechanisms. I do object, and very strongly, to their being in schools. Until quite recently they were not. As Paul Goodman has often pointed out, at the turn of the century only about six percent of the young people in this country finished high school and less than one percent went to college. Most people, including many who were in many ways prominent and successful, were what we would call dropouts. People may often have had to decide which of a number of applicants they would employ or promote, but they did not decide on the basis of diplomas and school transcripts, because there were none. People's school records did not follow them all through life. But now these choices, decisions are made very largely on the basis of information supplied by schools.

For many reasons, this is bad. Many people who have by now talked and written against schoolism and credentialism in our society—Ivan Illich, Paul Goodman, Everett Reimer, David Hapgood, Ivar Berg—have many times pointed out that this channeling is not a task that schools do or can do well. Almost nothing in experience supports the widely held idea that by looking at what a person has done in school we can tell what he will be able to do outside of school. People understood this once better than they do now. To be good at school meant only that you were good *in school,* a scholar, i.e., a "schooler." It suggested that you might do well to spend the rest of your life in schools or places like school. Today people seem to assume that being good in school, being able to remember what the teacher or the book says, being able to guess what the teacher wants and to give it to him, means that in life you will be good at almost everything. Some might object that it takes more than these trivial skills to succeed at the higher levels of schooling. Perhaps, sometimes, it does. But those who are not good at teacher pleasing at the lower levels of schooling never make it to the higher levels.

But there is a more important reason why, even if schools could find out which young people were more able than others, more likely to do well at this work or that later in life, they ought not to do so. If we turn schools into a kind of cream separator, if we give to schools the business of finding and training a future elite, if in short we turn education into a race, with winners and losers, as in all races we are going to have many more losers than winners. The trouble with this is that when we start calling someone a loser and treating him like a loser, he begins to think of himself as a loser and to act like a loser. When this happens, his chance of doing much more learning and growing becomes very slight. On the contrary, he is likely to put more and more of his energy into protecting himself against a world that seems too much for him.

Some people say, "It's competition that gets you good results, that brings out the best in people. Look at the mile—do you think without competition we would have people running the mile in under four minutes?" The example is perfectly chosen, though for the opposite reason than such people think. An educator in movement and dance once pointed out to me that everything in our traditional system of athletics is a *weeding out,* a cutting away of people until there is only one left. This describes perfectly the athletic program of most schools. We start off at first-grade level with 1,500 runners, players, participants. Not one child out of a hundred, at age six, would rather watch a game than take part in it. By the end of high school we may have at most 100 participants. The other 1,400 are sitting up there in the stands, watching them—maybe cheering now and then. Our so-called competitive athletic programs are perfect for turning participants into watchers, doers into consumers, runners into sitters.

Some years ago friends told me a story about public school athletics in their town. Their director of athletics was a rare genius in finding ways to encourage all children to take part in sports. Nobody was left out. Everybody was helped to find things he could do. Streets were closed during recess and lunch hour to make more room. Everyone was running, jumping, climbing, dancing, walking, bicycling. But—the varsity football, basketball, and track teams were not piling up winning records. Adults began to complain to the school superintendent and school board. Voices began to be heard saying that if the football team didn't start winning a few more games the next budgets and school bond issues might not be passed. Soon the director of athletics was fired. His successor, a typical enough would-be tough guy and Little Napoleon type, soon put an end to all the school sports programs—or let them die of neglect. All the energy and money of the athletic department went into those varsity teams. Soon they were beginning to rack up winning seasons—he was at least competent in that— and the great majority of the students retreated quietly into their accustomed places on the sidelines and in the stands.

I feel strongly that the professionalizing and commercializing of school sports, to make careers for adult coaches and to tickle the vanity of adult spectators ("Our basketball team went to the state finals three times in the last five years.") is one of the worst and most unforgivable things that the schools have done. The remedy is simple and clear enough. If we want to have amateur sports instead of professional, what we have to do, and all we have to do, is do away with paid coaches and paid admissions. This is the way and the only way that we can take sports away from the coaches, promoters, and spectators, and give them back to the players.

The channeling function, the task of separating the winners from losers may be a needed and proper function somewhere, but it is improper and inhumane in the schools. The things we do to select a few winners defeat whatever things we do to encourage the growth of all. We cannot do both of these kinds of work at the same time, in the same place. We cannot in any true sense be in the education business and at the same time in the grading and labeling business. We cannot expect large numbers of children to trust us if they know, as before long most of them do, that an important part of our job is compiling records on them which will be used to judge them for much of the rest of their life. In British detective stories the detective making his arrest used to say (and may still say) to the suspect, "Anything you say may be used against you." Our schools might well say to children, "Anything you do, or anything we say about what you do, may someday be used against you." It is grotesque and outrageous for an institution doing such work, and making no serious effort to stop doing it, to keep trying to pass itself off as the chief defender of children.

Another important mission of the schools is indoctrination, getting the children to think whatever the adults, or at least politically powerful adults, think, or want the children to think. Some of this indoctrination is straightforward and direct. Our society, like every other, demands that its schools teach children what is called "patriotism." This means teaching them to think that whatever country they live in is the best country in the world; that its ways of thought and life are better than anyone else's and that in past or present quarrels with other countries it has always been and can only be in the right. It is the patriotism of Admiral Decatur, who, they tell us (not quite accurately) first spoke the famous words, "My country, right or wrong." It is hardly ever that of Carl

Schurz, a German immigrant boy who later became mayor of New York, and who wisely replied, "My country, right or wrong; if right, to be kept right; if wrong, to be put right." Least of all do they teach G. K. Chesterton's grumpy reply, "My mother, drunk or sober," which in its odd way speaks a truth that might be useful and consoling to many disillusioned and alienated people—your country *is* your country, liking or not liking it has nothing to do with it. In time of war or near war, of course, schools teach children to hate and fear whatever country their government sees as rival or enemy, as British children were for years brought up to hate Napoleon, or French children to hate and fear Germans. Our society also wants to pass on to children certain beliefs about sex, morality, corporate enterprise and the profit system, etc. To this end it censors and approves textbooks, makes lists of approved or forbidden books and materials, purges books from school libraries, fires teachers for talking about dangerous ideas, demands or forbids programs on sex education or whatever. All simple and direct enough. We may not like what is happening, but at least it is fairly clear who is putting on the pressure, and why.

But there are other kinds of indoctrination, more subtle, more subliminal, less conscious or deliberate and far more powerful and destructive. Schools work hard to transmit to children certain other beliefs and attitudes, perhaps without even being aware what they are, or that they are doing it. Indeed, they might often sincerely deny that they do it. Some of these attitudes might be called consumer attitudes. In a small city, where large numbers of people are jobless and poor, some parents concerned with school affairs were taken by the school authorities to see a newly constructed school in one of the poorer sections of town. They were proudly shown, among other things, a room called the "grooming room." One whole wall of this room was lined with stainless steel sinks, and above them mirrors lighted with bulbs all around, as in an actor's dressing room. Much other space was given to full-length mirrors that a student could rotate so as to see herself from every angle. Later they were shown the Home Economics room, again crammed with the newest and most expensive stoves, ovens, refrigerator-freezers, washer-dryers, and sewing machines—the kind of equipment that, quite literally, not two percent of the people in that whole town could afford to buy. What is being taught here? The course may be called Home Economics, but obviously these young people are not being taught anything about the economics of running a home, far less how to run economically the kind of home that most of them will soon be running. On the contrary, they are being carefully trained in Consumerism, to think that they need, must have, cannot possibly get along without whatever latest gadget is being dangled before them in newspaper and magazine ads and on the TV screen. By now a great deal has been written and is being written about how to be a wise, skeptical, thrifty, and critical consumer. But this is not getting into the schools, least of all the schools of poor kids.

In an even deeper sense the children are being trained in a kind of alienation that Erich Fromm years ago called the marketing orientation. In an excellent article in the October, 1971 issue of the *Teacher Paper* (a magazine I recommend—see Appendix), Miriam Wasserman, teacher and author of "The School Fix NYC USA," describes this training very well. She writes, in part:

> . . . Schools want to train children in some essential academic skills, mainly linguistic and mathematical. They also want to train them to be alienated workers, i.e. to perform tasks at the behest of another, under the supervision of another, and largely for extrinsic rewards. So the child's learning, which is more or less unalienated and self-impelled before he begins to attend school, is taken away from him by the teacher when he becomes a pupil. The child's resistance to this process of alienation is identified by him, as well as by everyone else, as a resistance to acquiring academic skills. And so, indeed, it does interfere with the learning of relatively simple skills—tragically in the case of many individual children and many whole groups of children who do not accept alienation training gracefully.

She quotes from a memo that a New York City high school principal sent to his students, saying in part, "Study means doing well the things that may not interest you. . . . You don't deserve any special credit for doing assignments that interest you. . . .

Good grades equal a good education. The higher your grades, the more you've learned and the more you know. . . ." She continues:

> The problem . . . is how to seduce or coerce children into the classroom into abandoning their own "play culture" in favor of the grownups' "work culture." The usual means employed is to manipulate, corrupt, degrade, and destroy the "play culture." To the extent that the school succeeds in this, it tends to interfere with academic learning.
>
> The narrow, competitive, age-graded society of the classroom is, in large part, artificially created. It is in conflict with the social arrangements of the spontaneous children's groups of many subcultures, where a variety of cooperative as well as competitive relationships prevail, often among groups encompassing a considerable range of ages . . . there still survive (in our society) self-determined groups of children ranging sometimes from those barely past toddling to those verging on their teens. These children learn to accommodate their activities, including their disputes, to the various needs of the group and to limit competition in such a way as more or less to keep the group intact. . . . In the classroom this group sense is seriously damaged and perverted [My note—Jules Henry pointed out that whatever any child wins in the conventional classroom, he wins at someone else's, perhaps everyone else's expense.], and the naked ego must create its own defenses (of which hating oneself, hating the teacher, and slavishly seeking to please the teacher are among the most common) . . . school learning is pretty well sealed off from the children's other activities—home, street, church, and so on. Those responsible for the children's learning often fail not only to share but even to understand the vitality of the children's out-of-school existence. [My note—Fader's *The Naked Children* gives a vivid demonstration of this.]

In his first years, before he gets to school, the child lives his life, as he should, all in one piece. His work, his play, and his learning are not separated from each other. What is even more important, they are not separated from him. He *is* his work. He *is* his play. He *is* what he knows and does and learns. But in school (sometimes before school, if he has hard-pushing parents—the process can start very early) the child is taught to think that his work, his play, and his learning are separate from each other, and all separate from him, and that all of these, including his very self, are commodities, to be exchanged for grades, praise, approval, success, to be measured, evaluated, bought and sold. As Fader points out, the child who early reads well for his own pleasure soon gets adult approval and rewards for his reading; he then learns to read for the rewards instead of the pleasure; and when he has milked his reading ability for all the rewards he can get out of it—degrees, jobs, etc.—he stops reading. This is true of many teachers. It was certainly true of me; as a child I loved reading, in my schooling I always got A in English, but for the last six years or so of my schooling I never read an unassigned book, and did not begin to read again for pleasure until many years after I left school. As one college student put it, we are trained to sell our learning for grades so that later we will sell our work for money. Worse, we learn to think not only that work is what we do for money, out of fear, envy, or greed, but also that work is what we would never do *except* for money, that there could be no other reason to work, that anyone who talks about meaningful work must be the wildest kind of romantic dreamer and crackpot. We learn to take it as natural, right, and inevitable that our work should be boring, meaningless, hateful.

Finally the schools, as they separate and label children, a few winners and a great many losers, must convince them, first, that there must always be a few winners and many losers, that no other human arrangement is possible, and secondly that whether winner or loser they deserve whatever comes to them. Only thus can we be sure that the winners will defend the system without guilt and the losers accept it without rancor. G. B. Shaw once said, "Be sure to get what you like, or else you will have to like what you get." The successful students are trained to think that being superior they have a right to get as much as they can of whatever they like, a right to more of life's goodies, a right to order other people around. The losers are trained to like what they get. To them the schools say, in all the ways in which they deal with them, "Do not expect in your later life to be treated with consideration or respect, as if you had any dignity. You have none, you will not be, and you do not deserve to be. Accept what you are given, and do what you are told."

We might sum up and make concrete much of this by saying that the business of the schools is to make Robert MacNamaras at one end and Lt. William Calleys at the other. They are, each in his own way, perfect products of schooling; the one, unshakably convinced that his cleverness and secret knowledge give him a right to exercise unlimited and godlike powers over other men; the other, ready at an instant to do without question or qualm everything, *anything* anyone in a position of authority tells him to do. We may be sure that there are not many universities that would not be glad to have MacNamara as their president if he wanted the job, and just as sure that there are not many high schools in which, if Lieutenant Calley went there to speak, he would not receive a hero's welcome.

Now the schools, as if they had not trouble enough, are being given a new mission. A recent column in the *Boston Globe,* by Deckle McLean, states it clearly. The headline and story read, in part:

EDUCATION BEARS THE BURDEN OF
ELIMINATING RACISM

The United States has imposed on its public schools the burden of overcoming its race history. Why it should be this way is not at all clear.

One might say it follows from an American tendency to make education the institution of reform.

To this we might ask, what reforms? No matter; the idea that the schools are incubators for reform, the seedbed of a better world, is firmly believed by many schoolmen and defenders of schooling. With one breath, they defend oppressive school practices by saying that they are needed "to get children ready for reality." With the next they say, just as seriously, seeing no contradiction,

"Where but in the schools can children learn about, and so come to want, a world better than the world we have outside?" In short, schools should be for kids what church is for some adults—a place where a vision of something better is held up before us, so that we may then go out and try to get it. Perhaps at one time and for some children schools may have done this work. They can't do it now. Children have too many other ways of knowing what the world is really like. They learn, and quite early in their schooling, that their teachers often seem to know less about the world than they do, that the world they are told about in school looks less and less like the world they learn about and see outside. The outside world is the one they believe.

The *Globe* column continues:

> . . . But one might also suggest that it resulted from a failure of nerve, that public education was selected because it was guaranteed to be the slowest and least decisive way of addressing the racism.
>
> One thing is certain: public education wasn't the only possibility. Housing could be the central focus, as could employment; and both of these appear more likely targets. Racially balanced housing, for example, would also yield balanced schools.
>
> The fact is, then, that a choice was made: that education should carry the burden. . . . Mixed schools are the means the society has selected to alter its history.

Choice? Selected? Who has chosen and selected? Have we indeed decided to alter our history? When, where, and how did we decide? There is clearly widespread public opposition to any such decision. Where is there any evidence of strong public support? What backer of forced racial integration in schools would stake his political career on a referendum on the subject? Is it not more likely that we are trying to salve our consciences by asking our children to do what we can't do and don't want to do? And is there not at least a possibility that what really worries us is less racial segregation than the growing drive by black and other minority group people to gain control of their children's schools and so to make them places where their children are *not* second-class citizens?

We must, of course, make an important distinction here. *The New York Times* of December 5, 1971 reports, in part:

> The Department of Health, Education and Welfare accused officials here (in Boston) of maintaining a dual, segregated system at the intermediate—or junior high school—level, in violation of Federal law. That action marked the first such public charge against a major, urban school system outside the South under the 1964 Civil Rights Act, which forbids segregation in federally funded programs . . .

> The information made available to the H.E.W. from these investigations included:
> Cases of busing nonwhite children past predominantly white-schools with empty seats to other, more distant schools that are predominantly nonwhite.
> The totally white enrollment in a high school that, under district lines drawn by the School Committee, should have several hundred nonwhite students from an intermediate "feeder" system.
> Elementary school district lines that create schools within several hundred feet of one another that are totally segregated.

On this matter, *Newsweek* of December 13, 1971 reports, in part:

> A system of "middle" schools (grades six through eight) has been established in predominantly black areas; in white areas, however, the traditional junior highs (grades seven through nine) remain. The consequence has been that the high schools covering grades nine through twelve are predominantly black, while those covering grades ten through twelve are mainly white. . . .
> In fact, as state officials see it, segregation in Boston is a consequence not of ineptitude but of a lengthy and concerted pattern of deliberate discrimination. They charge that the Boston school system has given white children, but not black ones, choices of schools to attend, has drawn up enrollment patterns

in such a way that pupils go from segregated junior highs to segregated high schools and has bused black children as far as 5
miles to heavily black schools while nearby white schools operate
at less than capacity.

Such use of government power to create, maintain, and extend race segregation in schools is clearly improper and illegal, not
to say stupid, destructive, and wrong. Both federal and state governments would be neglecting their plain duty if they did not use
all their fiscal and judicial power to prevent and overturn such acts.
Nobody's schooling should be determined by the color of his skin.

But this is not what Mr. McLean is talking about. Of an
amendment to the racial imbalance law in Massachusetts, Mr.
McLean says:

> . . . It proceeds from the prevailing error of thinking the purpose
> of racial balance is high quality school education. It is not.
>
> The purpose is to provoke a racial balance in all corners of so-
> ciety. It is a political and social purpose, not a strictly educational
> one. The source of the error is probably the original 1954 deseg-
> regation decision of the U.S. Supreme Court. Though a great
> decision in drawing the line on an oppressive practice, it can be
> regarded a bad decision in its equivocation.
>
> Rather than speak with direct moral force by simply con-
> demning segregation as an offense to its understanding of the
> Constitution, the Court pussyfooted through unnecessary soci-
> ological proof that separate facilities impaired black children's
> ability to learn. . . .
>
> . . . That a school can be test measured as offering superior
> education says nothing about whether it is carrying its appointed
> burden of *providing multi-racial experience.* [Italics mine.]

Appointed burden? Appointed by whom? Not by the Supreme
Court, who went to some pains to say that they did not mean what
Mr. McLean thinks they meant or ought to have meant. But the
point I want to make here is a quite different one. With Mr.
McLean, I feel strongly, and have for some time, that our national
racism is a dangerous disease of which we must as quickly as possible cure ourselves. If government action, in or out of schools,

promised to speed this cure, I would be all for it. The question is, will this particular government action, *in schools as they are,* cure the disease? Or will it make it worse? The key words are *"providing multi-racial experience."* But what kind of experience? Good or bad? It makes all the difference. When racial groups meet in a good experience, their shared pleasure, satisfaction, and joy will bring them closer together. But if the experience is bad, it will almost certainly drive them further apart. If we were looking for a way to increase race contempt and race hatred among young people, we could hardly find anything better for the purpose than what they experience in most of our schools, particularly high schools, and above all the big city high schools where most of this racial balancing is going to take place. No need to go into details. Book after book has told us, truthfully, eloquently, painfully, what life is like for most children in most schools. Perhaps the most vivid picture of all of life in a typical American school, vivid because a picture, can be seen in Frederick Wiseman's by now famous documentary film *High School.* Anyone who thinks that we are going to do away with racism by mixing black and white children in our schools as they are should see this film. Remember, too, this is a"good" school, not a run-down, demoralized inner-city school, but middle class and successful. The people in the school approved the film—though later they withdrew their approval and tried to suppress the film when it began to draw bad publicity. Even now many school people seeing the film can find nothing wrong with the school, and can't understand why the film stirred up such outraged antischool feeling.

What is most striking and terrible about this school as we see it, and typical of most schools, even more than boredom and mindlessness, is the unrelenting and merciless attack it makes on the dignity and self-respect of the students. In countless ways they are taught to believe that they are worthless, that they have no rights and deserve none, that even to imagine that they might have some rights, some individuality, some dignity, is itself a kind of crime. The end of the film, in which a teary-eyed teacher reads in assembly, as a tribute to the school, a letter from a former student, a soldier in Vietnam who says that he is only a body, shows how well the students learn this lesson.

We might be ready to continue to overlook or accept that most of our schools deny and destroy the dignity of the young people in them. This is nothing new. But if we are serious—I'm far from sure that we are—about using the schools as a means of curing ourselves of racism, the matter of dignity becomes crucial. For racism is above all about dignity. Racial prejudice or contempt is a particularly cruel attack on another person's dignity. It attacks him where he has no way to defend himself, attacks something about him that he did not cause and cannot change. Moreover, racial contempt is rooted in a person's lack of any sense of his own dignity. It is above all scapegoatism. It is a way in which someone who feels that he has very little worth tries to feel better by believing that others have none. It is a way to turn against others the contempt and hatred one feels for oneself. Whatever increases people's sense of their own dignity, competence, and worth, is almost sure to reduce racism, to reduce their need to feel superior to others, to increase their willingness to extend to others the respect they feel for themselves. By the same token, whatever attacks and diminishes these is almost sure to make racism worse. And this is what conventional schools, by their nature, their structure, and their purposes, necessarily do.

Later in his column, Mr. McLean said that anyone who opposes the busing decisions, or the attempt to attack racism by integrating the schools, is saying in effect that only racism is workable. This is not necessarily so, and is not what I am saying. But, if we mean to give schools the humane task of increasing understanding, tolerance, respect, and even friendship between now hostile racial groups—an exceedingly difficult task at best—we will have to relieve the schools of the many other improper and inhumane tasks they are burdened with.

I have said before that we cannot at the same time be in the channeling business, the grading and labeling business, the winner-loser business, and at the same time work effectively for human growth. We certainly can not be in the winner-loser business and work effectively for racial understanding, respect, and good feeling. When we divide people into winners and losers, we create bad feeling. For the losers, the winners feel contempt. I was horrified to hear a thirteen-year-old friend of mine, who a few years ago was very troubled by the fact that poor kids in his class were treated very unfairly, not long ago dismiss these same kids as "not interested in learning." For the winners, the losers feel resentment, bit-terness, and even hatred—and this all the more if they feel that the winners did not win fair. This is true even when the students are all of one race and background and have no other reasons to despise or dislike each other.

Not long ago, I spent much of a day discussing education in a series of seminars in a suburban high school. Usually, when I speak to a small group in high school, it is all one class, and usually in the college track. On this day students could come to the seminars from many classes. The result was that in several seminars we had students from all tracks—advanced placement, college, general, business, and vocational. These feelings, of contempt on the one hand and bitter resentment on the other, came to the surface in a way I have seldom seen—usually because these groups rarely come into contact. I was talking, as I do, about learning without tests, grades, marks, etc. Many of the more articulate young people, whom I guessed were among the "good" students, objected to this. They liked a system in which they were getting rewards, which they felt they deserved because they were smarter and worked harder. They said, "If you didn't have homework, tests, and grades, nobody would do any work, everyone would just hang around and do nothing." I said, "Do you mean this is what you would do? Do you mean that there is nothing that interests you enough so that you would spend time on it without bribes or threats?" No, they didn't mean that, they had things that inter-ested them. But most of the *other* students wouldn't do anything. It was clear enough who they meant—the lower-track students at the same table. These in turn did not miss the message. One after another they said, in different ways and with great intensity, that the "good" students thought they were so much better just be-cause they got better marks in school, that they didn't know any-thing about many parts of life outside the school, that school was-n't everything and that many important things couldn't be learned there. What was sad was that even as they denied the schools' and the good students' low evaluation of themselves, they showed in their faces and voices how much they accepted it. And so great had the gulf become between the students that both groups talked, not to the other, but to me, as if the other students were not there. But these were all middle-class whites, from a homogeneous community. Had they been a more mixed group, from different races, their feelings would almost surely have been harsher and stronger.

By contrast, I think of a volleyball game I saw just the other day in Washington Square Park in New York City. The players were a very mixed group, young men in their early twenties, black, Puerto Rican dark-skinned and light, white, some hippie types and some fairly straight. They played loosely but intently, and very well, making difficult saves, setting up plays at the net, spiking the ball away—a ball so tattered that it would long since have been banished from any school sports closet. The atmosphere was serious but easy. Both sides were playing hard, to win. But there was a current of friendly talk and kidding, not enough to slow the game but enough to spice it up. One tall young white came in for extra attention because he was wearing a pair of brand new sneakers. Whatever he did, whether very good or very inept, the sneakers were usually held responsible. Other young men waited their turn to play. A crowd of older people watched. The air was alive with warmth, good feeling, pleasure. For a while, the brotherhood of man was not just a pious phrase or a vain hope, but a living reality. But how rarely do we see, could we see, such a scene in school. Even in sports we would not be likely to see it, what with coaches barking away, and prayers for victory in the locker room. In professional sport, though outright discrimination has been banned for years, long and close association does not seem to have lowered racial barriers very much; from all I read, black athletes tend to hang out with black, white with white.

A *New York Times* story about Maury High School in Norfolk, Virginia, integrated for ten years and more, says:

> All over Maury, blacks and whites are finding that racial inhibitions diminish when communities of interest develop. In sports, in the band, on the cheerleading squad and in the Naval Reserve Officer Training Corps suspicion appears to be lessening and natural friendship building.
>
> . . . The third stage (of relations between the races), which Maury is now said to be entering, is one of decreasing self-consciousness about race. This was evident the other night as the Maury football bus passed Church Street, the historic main

street of Norfolk's Negro community. Black students began a jolly, self-mocking chant, and white students immediately joined in with no apparent reticence.

"Where do all the niggers go? Church Street, Church Street!"

Well, I don't know about that scene, what was being expressed, and felt, and by whom. If the team had just won a game, and was feeling pretty good, the scene might have been as good natured and innocent as it sounds. But that chant, in that place, and the whites joining in, might have many meanings other than pure racial ease and good feeling.

The article speaks of Maury's integrated cheerleading squad, and the trouble the blacks had to go to get some black cheerleaders. There, it seems to have worked out. But I was not long ago in a midwestern city where for two days the city schools were closed down, because of disturbances and riots, growing from a demand by black students for a black Homecoming Queen. A black community leader said that the schools ought to give up the whole Homecoming Queen foolishness. He is right—this kind of competitive social-ritual event is more likely to stir up bad feeling than good, by reminding the blacks in an immediate and painful way of the culture from which they are excluded. But it seems unlikely that anyone will listen to him, or that, in that town at least, the relations between the races will improve. Perhaps somewhere racially integrated schools are turning out adults who are not only free of racism themselves, but also enough opposed to it to work to root it out of society. The evidence that this is happening seems slight. It will stay slight until our schools become very different from what they are.

Dostoevsky once wrote:

Whoever has experienced the power, the complete ability to humiliate another human being with the most extreme humiliation, willy-nilly loses power over his own sensations. Tyranny is a habit, it has a capacity for development, it develops finally into a disease. I insist that the habit can dull and coarsen the very best man to the level of a beast. Blood and power are intoxicating. . . . The man and the citizen dies within the tyrant forever; to return to human dignity, to repentance, to regeneration, becomes almost impossible.

The tyranny that schools and school people exercise over the young is milder than the tyranny about which Dostoevsky was speaking. Schools do not have the power of life and death over children. But they do have the power to cause them mental and physical pain, to threaten, frighten, and humiliate them, and to destroy their future lives. This power has been enough to corrupt deeply many schools and school people, to turn into a cruel and petty tyrant many a teacher who did not start out to be one and may even now not want to be one. If there were no other reasons to rid themselves of this power, this would be enough: only by doing so can the schools save their own souls.

Recommended Readings, Films and Other Sources of Information about Education and Society

Books and Articles

Education and Society

Holt, John *Freedom and Beyond,* E. P. Dutton, 1972.

——— *What Do I Do Monday?,* Dutton, 1970; Boynton/Cook Publishers, 1995.

——— *The Underachieving School,* Pitman, 1969; paper, Delta.

——— *How Children Learn,* Pitman; paper 1967, Pitman and Dell; Addison-Wesley, 1995.

——— *How Children Fail,* Pitman; paper 1964, Delta and Dell; Addison-Wesley, 1995.

——— "To The Rescue," a review of *The Lives of Children* by George Dennison, *N.Y. Review of Books,* 10/69.

——— "Why We Need New Schooling," *Look* Mag., 1/70.

——— "Big Bird, Meet Dick and Jane," a critique on Sesame St., *Atlantic,* 5/71.

——— "I Oppose Testing, Marking, and Grading," from *What Do I Do Monday?,* Today's Ed., *NEA Journal* 3/71.

——— "The Little Red Prison," from *Freedom and Beyond, Harper's* Magazine, 1972.

Axline, Virginia *Dibs: In Search of Self,* paper, Ballantine, 1971.

——— *Play Therapy,* Ballantine, 1969.

Bennett, Hal *No More Public Schools* (a manual on how to get your child out and what to do then) c/o The Bookworks, 1409 5th, Berkeley, Calif. 94710.

Berg, Ivar *Education and Jobs: The Great Training Robbery,* Praeger, 1970, also in paper.

Berg, Leila *Look At Kids,* Penguin Education, Great Britain, 1972.

Campbell, David *A Practical Guide to the Open Classroom,* paper, $1. The Book Ctr., 4000 5th Ave., Pittsburgh, Pa. 15213.

Cole, Lawrence *Street Kids,* Grossman Publishers, 1970.

Coles, Robert *Uprooted Children,* Univ. of Pittsburgh, 1970.

———— *Children of Crisis,* paper, Delta.

Dennison, George *The Lives of Children,* Random House, 1969.

Dillon, J. T. *Personal Teaching,* Merrill Publishers, 1971.

Fader, Daniel *The Naked Children,* Macmillan, 1971; Boynton/ Cook Publishers, 1996.

Fader, Daniel and E. McNeill *Hooked on Books,* paper, Berkeley Press, 1968.

———— *Farallones Scrapbook* (on rebuilding and changing spaces), c/o The Book People, 2940 7th, Berkeley, Calif. 94710.

Featherstone, Joseph *Schools Where Children Learn,* Liveright, 1971.

Friedenberg, Edgar *The Vanishing Adolescent,* paper, Dell, 1959.

———— *Coming of Age in America,* paper, Vintage, 1963.

Gaines, Richard *The Best Education Money Can Buy,* Simon & Schuster, Fall 1972.

Gattegno, Caleb *Toward a Visual Culture,* Outerbridge and Dienstfrey, 1969.

———— *What We Owe Children,* Outerbridge and Dienstfrey, 1970.

Goodman, Paul *Compulsory Miseducation,* paper, Vintage, 1962.

———— *Growing Up Absurd,* paper, Vintage, 1956.

Gordon, Julia My *Country School Diary,* paper, Dell, 1970.

Hapgood, David *Diplomaism,* Donald Brown Publishers, 1971.

Hansen, Soren and Jensen, Jesper *The Little Red School Book,* Pocket Div. of Simon and Schuster, 1971.

Hawkins, Frances *The Logic of Action, From a Teacher's Notebook,* Elem. Science Advisory Center, Univ. of Colorado.

Herndon, James *How to Survive in Your Native Land,* Simon and Schuster, 1970; paper, Bantam, 1971.

—— *The Way It Spozed to Be,* Simon & Schuster, 1968; paper, Bantam.

Illich, Ivan *Deschooling Society,* Harper & Row, 1970; also paper.

—— *Celebration of Awareness: A Call for Institutional Revolution,* Doubleday, 1970; also in paper.

Jerome, Judson *Culture Out of Anarchy,* Herder and Herder, 1970.

Joseph, Stephen (ed.) *The Me Nobody Knows,* paper, Avon, 1969.

Koch, Kenneth *Wishes, Lies and Dreams,* Chelsea House Pub., 1970.

Kohl, Herbert and Hinton, James *The Open Classroom,* Vintage, 1970.

—— *Thirty-Six Children,* New American Library; paper, Signet, 1968.

—— *Golden Boy as Anthony Cool,* A Photoessay on Naming and Graffiti, Dial Press, 1972.

Kozol, Jonathan *Death at an Early Age,* Houghton Mifflin, 1968; paper, Penguin, 1968.

Lillard, Paula *Montessori: A Modern Approach,* Schocken, 1971.

Macrorie, Ken *Writing To Be Read,* Hayden, 1971.

—— *Uptaught,* Hayden Book Co., 1970; Boynton/Cook Publishers, 1996.

Mayerhoff, Milton *On Caring,* paper, Perennial, Harper and Row, 1971.

Murrow, Liza Casey *Children Come First,* American Heritage Press, 1971.

O'Gorman, Ned *The Storefront,* Harper and Row, 1970.

Postman, Neil and C. Weingartner *Teaching as a Subversive Activity,* Delacorte Press, 1969.

Rasberry, Salli and Greenway, Robert *Rasberry Exercises: How to Start a School and Make a Book,* Freestone, 1970, c/o Bookworks, 2010 7th, Berkeley, Calif. 94710.

Rathbone, Charles and Barth, Roland *Open Education: Selected Readings,* paper, Citation, 1970.

———— *Open Education: The Informal Classroom,* Citation Press, Scholastic Book Services, 50 W. 44th, N.Y., N.Y. 10/71.

Reimer, Everett *"School Is Dead,* Doubleday, 1971.

Richardson, Elwyn *In the Early World,* Pantheon Books, 1970.

Schoolboys of Barbiana *Letter to a Teacher,* Random House, 1970.

Silberman, Charles *Crisis in the Classroom,* Random House, 1970; paper, Vintage, 1971.

Skutch, Margaret *To Start a School,* Little-Brown Pub., 1972.

von Hilsheimer, George *How to Live with Your Special Child,* Acropolis Books, 1970.

Wasserman, Miriam *The School Fix: N.Y.C., USA,* Outerbridge & Dienstfrey, 1971; paper.

Weber, Lillian *The English Infant School and Informal Education,* Prentice-Hall, 1971.

Related Social Problems

Ahern, James *Police in Trouble: Our Frightening Crisis in Law Enforcement,* Hawthorne Books, 1972.

Jacobs, Jane *The Economy of Cities,* paper, Vintage, 1970.

———— *The Death and Life of Great American Cities,* paper, Vintage, 1963.

Novak, Michael *The Experience of Nothingness,* Harper and Row, 1970.

Rottman, Barry, and Paquet (3 eds.) *Winning Hearts and Minds, War Poems by Vietnam Veterans,* paper, 1st Casualty Press, 208 Dean St., Brooklyn, N.Y., $1.95.

Slater, Philip *The Pursuit of Loneliness,* Beacon Press, 1970; also paper.

Taylor, Edmond *Richer by Asia,* Houghton-Mifflin, 1964.

Human Psychology and Development

Cobbs, Price, and Grier, William *Black Rage,* Basic Books; paper, Bantam, 1968.

Fromm, Erich *Man for Himself,* paper, Fawcett World, 1968.

———— *The Art of Loving,* paper, Harper & Row, 1956.

—— *Escape from Freedom,* paper, Avon, 1971.

—— *The Sane Society,* paper, Fawcett World, 1955.

Green, Hannah, *I Never Promised You a Rose Garden,* Signet, 1964.

Laing, R. D. *The Politics of Experience,* paper, Ballantine, 1967.

—— *The Divided Self,* Penguin, 1965.

—— *Self and Others,* Pantheon Books, 1970; also paper.

—— *The Politics of the Family,* Pantheon, 1971.

—— and A. Esterson *Sanity, Madness, and the Family,* Pelican Books; paper, 1965.

Maslow, Abraham *Motivation and Personality,* Harper & Row, 1954.

—— *Toward a Psychology of Being,* Insight (van Nostrand) paper.

—— *The Farther Reaches of Human Nature,* Viking Press, 1971.

May, Rollo *Man's Search for Himself,* paper, Signet, 1967.

—— *Love and Will,* W. W. Norton, 1969.

O'Brien, Barbara *Operators and Things,* paper, Ace, 1958.

Rogers, Carl *On Becoming a Person,* Houghton-Mifflin, 1961.

van den Berg, J. H. *The Changing Nature of Man,* Norton, 1961; paper, Delta, 1964.

NOTE: English books may be ordered from Blackwell's, Broad Street, Oxford, England. Good resource for children's literature. Request their education catalog.

Films

Jerry Bloedow *Sometimes I Even Like Me,* one hour on the Lewis-Wadhams School, c/o J. Bloedow.

Henry Felt *Battling Brook Primary School,* (four days in September). *Medbourne Primary School,* (four days in May).

Al Fiering *Children As People,* 16mm, b/w, 35 min. On Fayweather St. School, narrated by John Holt. Polymorph Films.

Caleb Gattegno *Math At Your Fingers. Words In Color. Pop-Up Films* (to *teach* children or illiterate people to *read* in their own tongue, *not* for those who can already read), one-minute reading spots, 16mm; set/12 8mm cassettes. 18 different sets available in English (for English speakers) and Spanish (for Spanish speakers). See them on Saturday mornings, nationwide NBC-TV. Plans for 45 sets. Gattegno Language Schools.

Ghetto kids *The Jungle,* Churchill Films.

Alan Leitman *They Can Do It,* 16mm, b/w, 35 min.

National Film Board of Canada *Summerhill,* 30 min. *Warrendale.* Films come from New York.

Lillian Weber *Infants School,* 30 min.

Fred Wiseman *High School,* 16mm, 35mm. *Law And Order,* 16mm, 35mm. *The Cool World,* 16mm, 35mm. *Hospital, Basic Training, Essene.* Zipporah Films.

Other Sources of Information

Many of the groups and publications listed in the 1992 edition of this book no longer exist, but we include them here for historical interest. We have updated addresses whenever possible and have added several new organizations.

Advisory For Open Education, now defunct.

Boston After Dark now published by *The Phoenix,* see below.

Changing Schools, 534 Detroit St., Denver, CO 80206-4314. Publication on educational alternatives and alternative schools.

CIDOC (Center for Intercultural Documentation), now defunct. Center founded by Ivan Illich. Illich's books are still available.

CSCS City Schools Curriculum Service, now defunct. Educational publishers.

Colloquy Magazine, now defunct.

Curtis-Smith, Inc., no longer in operation. Educational consultants in environmental design.

EDCO, 20 Kent Street, Brookline, MA 02146. Educational project, Title 111, concerned with metropolitan collaboration;

brings together the public school systems of Arlington, Brookline, Boston, Cambridge, Concord, Lexington, Newton, and the diocesan and independent schools serving those areas.

E.D.C. (Educational Development Corp.), 55 Chapel Street, Newton, MA 02160. Much information about all aspects of education, film center, brochure of available films. (617) 969–7100.

Education Warehouse, now defunct.

Educational Solutions, Inc., 99 University Place, 6th Fl., N.Y., N.Y. 10003-4555 (212) 674-2988. Specialized seminars in reading, math, foreign languages. Individual consultancies, educational films. Also Gattegno Lang. Schools.

Harvard Center for Law & Education, "Alternative Schools: a practical manual." (no longer publishes this).

Illich, Ivan "Outwitting the Developed Countries," *N.Y. Review of Books* '69.

——— "The False Ideology of Schooling," *Saturday Review* 10/70.

——— "Education Without School: How It Can Be Done," *N.Y. Review of Books,* 1/71.

Manas, now defunct.

N.E. Free Press Movement printing, now defunct.

New Nation Seed Fund, now defunct.

New Republic, 1244 19th St., N.W., Washington, D.C. 20036.

New Schools: A National Directory of Alternative Schools. For current directory of Alternative Schools, see National Coalition of Alternative Community Schools, p. 249.

New York Review of Books, 250 West 57th St., New York, N.Y. 10019.

New Schools Exchange, now defunct. The National Coalition of Alternative Community Schools is an equivalent organization. See p. 249.

Observations from the Treadmill, Mort Yanow, ed., now defunct.

Outside the Net, now defunct.

The Phoenix, 126 Brookline Ave., Boston, MA 02215. Local newspaper, covers all happening in and around Boston and Cambridge.

Dan Pinck, Dan Pinck Associates, Hawksmoor Press, 26 Dwight St., Boston, MA 02118. School staff development; system reorganizing, all levels, from school to community.

Project Follow Through, now defunct.

Rathbone, Charles, and Barth, Roland "The Open Classroom: Underlying Premises," Urban Review 10/71.

——— "Bibliography of Open Education." c/o Advisory For Open Ed. $1.25.

Saturday Review, now defunct.

Summerhill Collective and the Summerhill Society, now defunct, but the Friends of Summerhill Trust is at 42 Lancaster Road, Rugby, Warwicks, CV21 2QW, England.

The Teacher Center, now defunct. A radical Boston teachers group.

Teacher Drop-Out Center, now defunct.

The Teacher Paper, now defunct.

Teachers and Writers Collaborative Newsletter, 5 Union Square West, New York, N.Y. 10003.

This Magazine Is About Schools, now called *This Magazine,* Red Maple Foundation, 16 Skey Lane, Toronto, Ontario, M6J 3S4, Canada.

The Village Voice, 36 Cooper Square, N.Y., N.Y. 10003. Nat Hentoff's column, weekly.

Vocations for Social Change, now defunct.

Washington Monthly, 1161 Conn. Ave., N.W., Washington, D.C. 20009.

Other Sources of Information New to This Edition

Alliance for Parental Involvement in Education, P.O. Box 59, East Chatham, NY, 12060; (518) 392-6900.

Alternative Education Resource Organization, 417 Roslyn Rd., Roslyn Heights, NY 11577; (516) 621-2195.

Committee to End Violence Against the Next Generation (EVAN-G), 977 Keeler Ave., Berkeley, CA 94708. This committee is against corporal punishment.

Growing Without Schooling, Holt Associates, 2269 Massachusetts Ave., Cambridge, MA 02140; (617) 864-3100. A bi-monthly magazine founded by John Holt, also a catalog of books.

National Association for the Legal Support of Alternative Schools, P.O. Box 2823, Santa Fe, NM 87501; (505) 471-6928.

National Center for Fair and Open Testing (FairTest), 342 Broadway Cambridge, MA 02139; (617) 864-4810.

National Coalition of Alternative Community Schools, P.O. Box 15036, Santa Fe, NM 87506; (505) 474-4312. The coalition publishes a directory of schools and a newsletter called *Skole.*

Rethinking Schools, 1001 East Keefe Ave., Milwaukee, WI 53212.

Sudbury Valley School Press, 2 Winch St., Framingham, MA 01701.

Teaching Tolerance, Southern Poverty Law Center, 400 Washington Avenue, Montgomery AL 35195.

ABOUT THE AUTHOR

John Holt (1923–85), writer, teacher, lecturer, and amateur musician, wrote ten books, including *How Children Fail, How Children Learn, What Do I Do Monday?,* and *Teach Your Own.* His work has been translated into fourteen languages. *How Children Fail* has sold over a million copies in its many editions. For years a leading figure in school reform, John Holt became increasingly interested in how children learn outside of school. The magazine he founded, *Growing Without Schooling,* continues to reflect his philosophy.

251